Teachers at the Front
1914–1919

To the British and Dominion teachers who fought and died in the Great War of 1914 to 1919.

As they made in common an offering of their lives, they each received praise that will not grow old and the noblest of tombs, not in the place where they lie, but rather where, on every occasion calling for word or deed, their fame is left behind them in everlasting remembrance.

Pericles' Oration, Thucydides II. 43

Teachers at the Front
1914–1919

Barry Blades

PEN & SWORD
HISTORY

First published in Great Britain in 2021 by
Pen & Sword History
An imprint of
Pen & Sword Books Ltd
Yorkshire – Philadelphia

ISBN 978 1 47384 885 6

Typeset by Mac Style
Printed and bound in the UK by TJ Books Ltd,
Padstow, Cornwall.

Pen & Sword Books Limited incorporates the imprints of Atlas,
Archaeology, Aviation, Discovery, Family History, Fiction, History,
Maritime, Military, Military Classics, Politics, Select, Transport,
True Crime, Air World, Frontline Publishing, Leo Cooper, Remember
When, Seaforth Publishing, The Praetorian Press, Wharncliffe
Local History, Wharncliffe Transport, Wharncliffe True Crime
and White Owl.

For a complete list of Pen & Sword titles please contact

PEN & SWORD BOOKS LIMITED
47 Church Street, Barnsley, South Yorkshire, S70 2AS, England
E-mail: enquiries@pen-and-sword.co.uk
Website: www.pen-and-sword.co.uk

Or

PEN AND SWORD BOOKS
1950 Lawrence Rd, Havertown, PA 19083, USA
E-mail: Uspen-and-sword@casematepublishers.com
Website: www.penandswordbooks.com

Contents

Maps

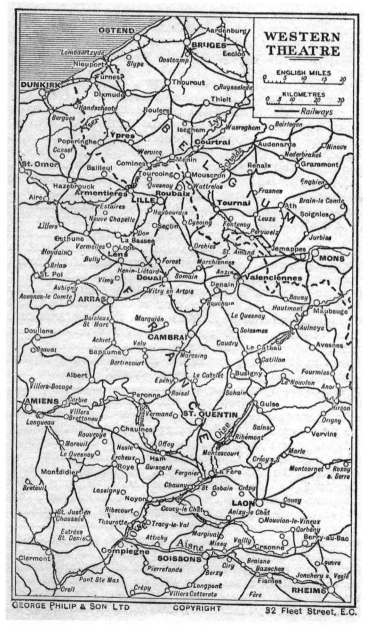

1. The Western Front. (Knight, W.S.M. *The History of the Great European War: its Causes and Effects*, p.155)

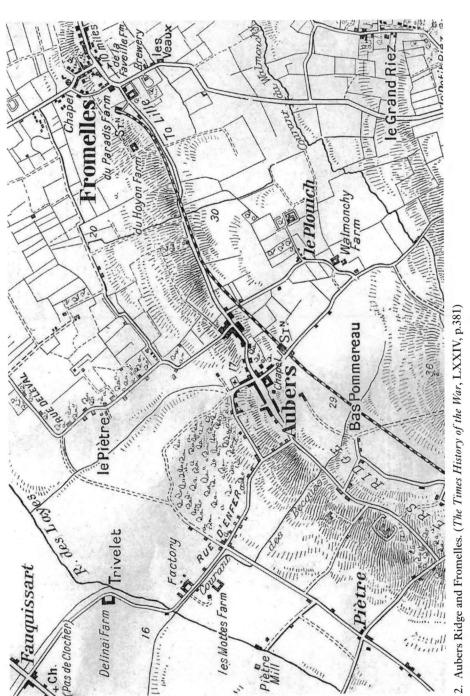

2. Aubers Ridge and Fromelles. (*The Times History of the War*, LXXIV, p.381)

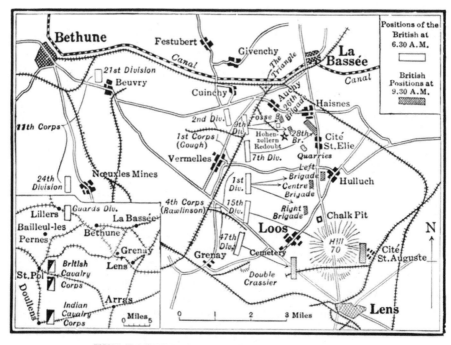

THE BATTLE OF LOOS; AUTUMN OF 1915

3. Loos and Lens. (*Public domain*)

4. High Wood. (*Trench Map. Longueval. 57C SW3*)

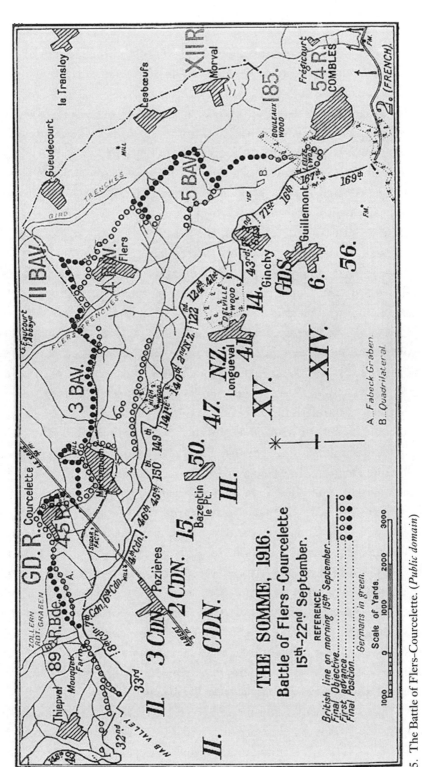

5. The Battle of Flers-Courcelette. (*Public domain*)

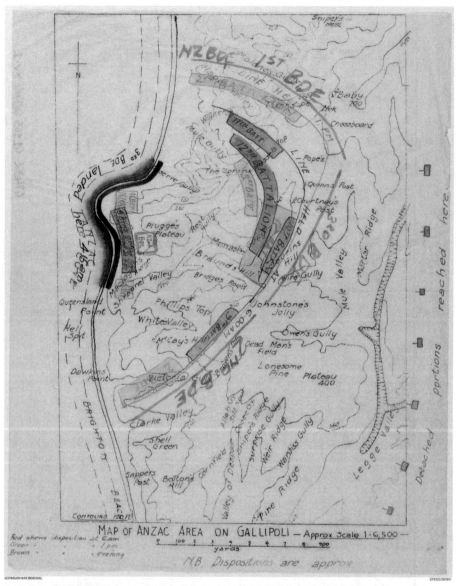

6. Anzac Gallipoli. (*Courtesy of the Australian War Museum*)

MAP OF THE HEIGHTS EAST OF YPRES.

7. Third Ypres. (*The Great War*, 182, p.508)

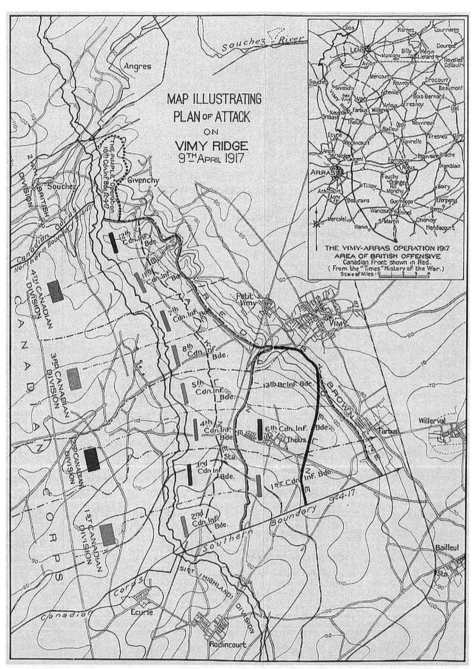

8. Vimy Ridge. (*Canadian Department of National Defence. Courtesy of Library and Archives Canada*)

Prologue

The Assembly

In the heady days of August 1914, the Reverend Charles Smith stood before the ranks of schoolboys gathered together in the daily morning assembly at Latymer Upper School (LUS). The audience listened attentively as their Head Master briefed them on the latest developments in the great European conflict and invoked the spirit of war. The school's Roll of Honour was proclaimed, and the subscription to the nation's war effort by hundreds of Latymerians was noted with evident pride. News of enlistments, promotions and honours awarded to the school's Old Boys duly followed.

As the war continued beyond its first Christmas, however, the tone of the morning briefings in this English secondary school changed from enthusiasm to sadness. Four years of war severely tested Revd Smith's early optimism. His pride in those Latymerians who had responded to their country's call was tempered by the growing casualty lists, and it was his painful duty to inform the school of the names of former pupils who had joined the ranks of 'The Fallen'.

The Armistice of November 1918 brought the fighting to an end and, in the months which followed, the task facing local communities everywhere was to find forms of remembrance which would both honour the dead and make sense of their sacrifice. Another, less strident, form of pride emerged as leaders of institutions great and small galvanized their followers and established war memorials. In May 1919, Revd Smith used the pages of the school magazine – the *Latymerian* – to mount an appeal to the wider school community to raise funds for a memorial in the School Hall to the 222 fallen Old Boys he had known and taught. Recognizing the potency of a single named individual as an exemplar of all that the school stood for, he cited the heroic military actions of former pupil Albert Baswitz (see plate 1). A letter received from a British Army officer who had fought alongside Captain Baswitz during the Battle of the Somme in 1916 described the 'fair-haired officer' as the epitome of 'a glorious and inspiriting type of manhood'. The letter went on to describe a man of uncommon bravery and ingenuity:

> He was known and beloved throughout the whole Brigade. Many times, he had performed feats of daring no others would attempt. Knowing German, he had often obtained German uniform and equipment, light-heartedly donned them and set out from the trenches. He stopped German patrols at the imminent risk of his being shot as a spy and gained from them most valuable information in the guise of a German officer. Sometimes he even lured their patrols into our own lines, where they were taken prisoners. Similarly disguised, he had coolly dropped into the German trenches, walked through them and made sketches of all the important features for the advantage of our troops. For his splendid services he had been awarded the MC. He was idolised by all who knew him, and always had a cheery greeting for one and all, any of whom would gladly have risked his life to save the boy a pang. He would never set a man to do a job he would not do himself. He was generous of heart, cheery of spirit, utterly fearless.[1]

Few, if any, of the boys attending LUS in 1919 would have personally known the brave former pupil whose example they were now expected to emulate in a post-war world. Avid readers of the school magazine might have recalled an earlier reference to him, one of the many obituaries featured in the wartime editions. In stark contrast to his wartime exploits, Albert Baswitz's school career had been relatively unexceptional. He appears to have been a diligent pupil but was not one of the brilliant young men who shone at all activities. There is no evidence that he represented the school on the playing field or was the lauded recipient of the most prestigious glittering prizes the school had to offer. Unlike the majority of entrants to LUS, he spent only four years at the school. Whilst most parents paid fees for their boys to attend LUS, Albert enjoyed his brief stay in secondary education at the local ratepayers' expense. His unusual surname indicated his family's migrant origins and religious affiliation. As such, he was hardly typical of boys who attended such schools in the Edwardian era.

Albert left LUS in 1911 intent upon a career in teaching. The assassination at Sarajevo, and all that followed in the cheering and flag-waving summer and autumn months of 1914, interrupted his formal training. Like millions of other young Britons he responded to the call to arms, donned his khaki uniform and made his way to the battlefront. Amongst the patriotic ranks were thousands of schoolmasters and trainee teachers, including many of Albert's fellow students and friends from the London Day Training College. War fever was contagious. In the far reaches of empire, young colonials also pledged their allegiance and prepared to serve their King and his empire. Recently established teacher training colleges in the Dominions bade farewell to hundreds of students and alumni as they made their way to the military training grounds and then embarked for the 'old country' in her hour of need. Most college principals watched from a distance as members of their community were promoted and honoured, fell in foreign lands or returned home with the scars of war; some followed their young protégés to the killing fields and died alongside them.

Teachers at the Front, 1914–1919 tells the story of these teacher-soldiers. It recalls the decisions made by men who were united by their training, occupation and imperial connections but were divided by social and geographical contexts, personal beliefs and considered actions. It travels with them as they land in France or on the beaches of Gallipoli, and as they attack across no man's land in Flanders or struggle through the dust and mud of the Somme and Passchendaele. Many did not survive the carnage of what became known as the Great War. For those who did – wartime officers and men who had been proud to call themselves Tommies, Diggers, Enzeds and Canucks – returning home presented further challenges and adjustments. Individuals take centre stage; their early lives, teaching careers and military histories are set within the greater context of the time and place in which they lived and the disruption caused by war. This is the story of Alfred Baswitz, William Loring and Ben Bateman from London; of Sydney Forbes, Adolph Knäble and Fred Albrecht from Perth in Western Australia; of Frank Wilson, Bert Milnes and Ormond Burton from Auckland in New Zealand; and of Gordon Scott, Percy Barber and George Cline from Toronto in Canada. 'The greatness and smallness' of each of their stories is worthy of remembrance.[2]

Chapter 1

To Be a Teacher

*The refuse of all other callings, discarded footmen, ruined pedlars, men
who cannot work a sum in the rule of three, men who do not know whether
the earth is a sphere or a cube, or do not know whether Jerusalem is in
Asia or America. And to such men, men to whom none of us would entrust
the key of his cellar, we have entrusted the mind of the rising generation,
and with it the freedom, the happiness, the glory of our country.*

From Thomas Babington Macaulay's
speech to the House of Commons, 1847.

Albert Baswitz began his secondary schooling in 1906. In that
same year, the political establishment had been shaken by a
General Election which brought the Liberal Party to power and
marked the birth of the Labour Party as a force to be reckoned with at
Westminster. A period of reforming legislation followed, transforming
the balance of power between Lords and Commons, introducing
arrangements for social welfare and increasing access to post-elementary
forms of education. Thousands of families began to take advantage of
new benefits and opportunities for social advancement.

Such considerations were probably not at the forefront of Albert
Baswitz's mind as he walked from his home in Fulham and passed
through the gates of LUS in nearby Hammersmith for the first time.
The transition from elementary to secondary schooling can be daunting
for even the most confident and able child. For 12-year-old Albert it may
have been particularly difficult. He was a 'new boy' in more senses than
one, a relative newcomer to London as well as to this particular part of
the capital. One of the new 'scholarship boys', he had gained admission
on his own ability, rather than on the ability of his parents to afford the
fees which had traditionally enabled educational institutions to select

their clientele; he had a strange surname which few could pronounce correctly; his father was officially a 'foreign subject'; his mother had died the previous year.

The Baswitz family had been in England for less than fifty years. Albert's mother had been born in Germany, in Halle, Saxony. Catherine – known to all as Kate – was born in 1861, the daughter of Monius and Elvire Gottheil. In 1871 the National Census recorded the presence of 40-year-old Monius Gottheil and his growing family in the West Riding of Yorkshire. Monius quickly established himself in his adopted country. Described variously as a 'fent [cloth remnant] dealer' and 'stuff merchant', Albert's maternal grandfather had joined a community of other migrants who had made the city of Bradford one of the pre-eminent centres of British woollen textile manufacture. Since the 1820s, the industrial revolution in the northern counties had attracted thousands of other workers and entrepreneurs from Germany. Many of the hundred or so German families in Bradford were also Jewish. The contribution of the Behrens, Mosers and Rothensteins, amongst others, to the mercantile and civic development of the Victorian city was enormous. Monius Gottheil played his part too. His business interests flourished, and by 1881the Gottheils had taken up residence – complete with a domestic servant – in Bradford's Hanover Square. The family's allegiance to their religious faith remained strong. Monius Gottheil was a founding member of the Bradford Reform Synagogue of British and Foreign Jews. Being German or Jewish did not, however, preclude formal affiliation to the new country. In 1865 the *Jewish Chronicle* had observed that the newcomers 'do not want to pass for Jews although every child in Bradford knows them to be Jews'. In 1880, Albert's grandfather became a naturalized British citizen.

Albert's father had also been born in Germany, in the Brandenburg town of Frankfurt an der Oder in 1857. Hermann Alfred Baschwitz (later Baswitz) worked as an insurance underwriter. In the early 1880s he migrated to England as an associate of one of the German trading houses looking to benefit from the warehouse trade in Bradford and other commercial centres. In October 1884 Hermann Baswitz married into the Gottheil family. He maintained an office near Ludgate Square in London, operating as Hermann A. Baswitz & Co., Manufacturers'

Agents. The births of his daughters Ida and Rose were also registered in the capital, at offices in Stoke Newington and Hackney. By 1891 Hermann and Kate Baswitz were living in the Shipley area of Bradford, sufficiently established to be able to employ a live-in cook and nursemaid to cater for their growing family. The birth of another daughter, May, was followed by that of Albert in August 1892.

It was shortly after this that the fortunes of the Baswitz family began to falter. In March 1894, the *Bradford Daily Telegraph* reported on a court case in which Hermann Baswitz – connected to the Baden Marine Insurance Company, and with a bankruptcy to his name already – was in dispute with a former business partner over company debts and liabilities amounting to thousands of pounds. With his good name and reputation seriously compromised, Hermann Baswitz subsequently moved his young family away from Bradford to make a new home in London. By the turn of the twentieth century the capital of the British Empire had become a magnet for German migrants of all classes and religious faiths. Nearly half of the 50,000 Germans living in England and Wales at that time were in London. They and their compatriots in other British cities comprised merchants and skilled craftsmen, such as piano and cabinet makers, tailors and furriers. Enterprising German shopkeepers supplied their neighbours with pork products and bread; German hairdressers plied their trade; German musical bands were a common and popular sight in streets and parks. Until the early 1890s, the German expatriate community was the largest of its kind. Many, like the Baswitzes, were Jewish.

However, most of the new Jewish migrants to London were not from Germany but were families fleeing famine and persecution in Central and Eastern Europe, and from Russia in particular. Most of the newcomers settled in and around Spitalfields in the East End, an area familiar to earlier arrivals from Germany. During the first half of the nineteenth century many of the wealthier Jewish families had moved from there to the leafier districts of Finsbury, Islington and Highbury. From the 1860s there was a similar migration westward to Battersea, Shepherds Bush and Ealing. The geographical, economic and social distance between 'old' and 'new' Jewish migrants was evident to contemporaries. The former included a few very wealthy and influential families such as the

Goldsmids (later Goldsmiths), Rothschilds, Montefiores and Sassoons, to whom the bastions of the establishment such as parliament and the judiciary were beginning to open their doors. Many others followed the example of the Gottheils in Bradford and entered the world of the Victorian bourgeoisie or skilled artisan class. In stark contrast, many of the new arrivals to the East End experienced a world of overcrowding, sweated labour and poverty.

The 1901 National Census recorded the Baswitz family as residents of Meanley Street in East Ham, some eight miles north-east of Spitalfields, but by 1902 they had moved to Fulham in the capital's western suburbs. They lived in North End Road (see plate 2), named after the hamlet which lay between the original village of Fulham itself and Hammersmith to the west. Evidence for Albert's earliest years of schooling is difficult to find. From 1902 to 1906, however, he was a pupil at Gloucester Grove East School, situated in the now affluent and fashionable area of South Kensington. Opened by the School Board of London in 1881, the school was designed to accommodate six hundred of the area's poorer children. Albert's elementary schooling was determined by the Board of Education's Revised Code of 1862 and provided little more than a rudimentary training in the 'three Rs' of 'Reading, Riting and Reckoning'.[1] Nevertheless, for some of the brightest and most diligent pupils, elementary education was not an end in itself. Scholarships financed by the London County Council (LCC) enabled a select few to do something which today is regarded as a natural progression for all children, whatever their academic ability, social class or economic status: to move onwards and upwards into secondary education. Albert's admission to LUS in 1906 was an opportunity for him, and by association his family, to secure a foothold in middle-class society, find employment in the professions and experience a cultural milieu denied to most of the population. Hermann and Kate Baswitz had chosen not to send their son to one of the many Jewish schools which had been established in London during the previous century. Institutions such as the Jewish Free School (JFS), situated in the very heart of the East End near Petticoat Lane and Brick Road, intentionally provided a form of schooling which would help children and their families to integrate, rather than fully assimilate, into English society. Pupils were taught to become 'a good Jew and a good

Englishman'.[2] Schools like LUS were far more likely to emphasize the latter, rather than the former, sense of identity.

It is highly unlikely that such demographic and educational considerations were at the forefront of Albert Baswitz's mind as he made his way to LUS each day. The boy who had been born in Bradford, the son of migrants whose first language at home was probably still German, found himself walking through the streets of the capital of the biggest empire the world had ever known. Then as now, London was a city of great contrasts and disparities. Fifty years previously, Henry Mayhew had noted that its inhabitants contained 'a class of people whose misery, ignorance, and vice, amidst all the immense wealth and great knowledge of the first city in the world, is, to say the very least a national disgrace to us'.[3] On the eve of the Great War, Rupert Brooke referred disparagingly to the greasy pavements and streets full of lean, vicious and dirty people and 'pitiable scum', whilst his fellow poet Edward Thomas observed a dispiriting 'sea of slate and dull brick' in Battersea, just south of the river from where the Baswitz family lived. The development of the North End of Fulham had been subject to the pressures of population growth and the vicissitudes of progress. Where once there had been a country road lined with handsome houses interspersed with market gardens and orchards, by the late nineteenth century there was a busy thoroughfare with many smaller houses and shops catering for the growing number of residents. Nearby Fulham Fields, one of many such areas which had once been considered somewhat remote by those living in the city centre, also succumbed to building development as the population of London continued to boom. When Charles Booth conducted his survey of the area he found an economically diverse community. Families with 'good ordinary earnings' lived in 'comfortable' housing alongside the 'middle class and well-to-do', while nearby Grove Avenue contained jerry-built houses inhabited by poor tenants and 'the lowest class of prostitute'.[4]

Albert's London, however, was far richer than the city described by social researchers and celebrated poets. The sights and sounds and smells of the North End Road combined to paint a vibrant and colourful scene. True, the busy road and adjoining streets which Albert crossed on his way to school were messy and pungent, the natural and inevitable consequence of reliance upon horse-drawn buses, hansom cabs and delivery drays. Crossing the cobbled streets involved avoiding the manure and dodging the bakers' carts and butchers' boys on bicycles. Smoke and dust from innumerable coal fires corrupted the air. Noisy and crowded, the scene was nevertheless one of purposeful activity and enterprise. Albert would have passed the fish shop owned by Mr Philips, Hogate's eel and pie shop and the premises of Mobbs the butcher, where customers were served by assistants wearing striped aprons and straw hats. Benson's sweet shop sold liquorice pipes and bootlaces, and lemonade and still cider by the jug. Costers sold fruit in season, with oranges and pomegranates imported from Spain a special treat during the winter months. The cries of the rag-and-bone men, lavender girls, knife-grinders, chair-menders and tinkers mingled with the noise of children playing the fashionable street games of the period: skipping, marbles, tops and kites. The Penny Bazaar sold other small toys, all made of tin and all made in Germany. Public houses such as The Seven Stars, The Three Kings and The Jolly Brewer provided refreshment and hospitality for drinking men and women and attracted members of the Salvation Army selling their *War Cry*. On street corners, the newspaper vendors shouted out the latest headlines: Blériot flying across the English Channel in 1909; the Suffragette 'Black Friday' outrages outside Parliament in 1910; the execution of the wife-murderer Dr Crippen in 1910. From his home near the junction with Fulham Broadway, Albert's daily walk to school covered nearly the whole length of North End Road. Passing the Headquarters and Rifle Ground of the South Middlesex Volunteers, he reached the Junction with Lillie Road, where the Cannon brewery stood opposite one of LCC's elementary schools. From there he would have cut through the new housing developments in the parishes of St Andrew and St John, before walking westward along the equally busy and bustling Hammersmith Road. Approaching LUS on King Street, he passed other institutions of entertainment and instruction: music halls, Nonconformist chapels, the Temperance Hall, and the historic, and far more prestigious and expensive, St Paul's School.

Today, LUS is a very successful co-educational independent school, with a long tradition of awarding scholarships to enable pupils from all social classes to access the education provided there. As with many British schools, it has existed in various incarnations. Nearly three hundred years before Albert Baswitz joined its ranks, Edward Latymer had made provision in his will of 1624 for the education of 'eight poore boies' in Hammersmith, to be dressed in 'doublets and breeches' and to wear the founder's cognisance (a cross of red cloth on their sleeves) to mark them out as charity boys.[5] Latymer Foundation School opened three years later, one of hundreds of such institutions established in the seventeenth and eighteenth centuries. Poverty, however, is a relative concept; its use as a basis for determining charitable support, in this case school admission criteria, is problematic. By the nineteenth century the 'poor' boys and girls admitted to charity schools were more likely to have been selected from the 'respectable' lower classes than from the most destitute families. The 1850 Admissions Register for the Latymer Foundation School includes the sons of parents variously describing their occupation as gardener, carpenter, labourer, maltman, bargeman, coachman, tailor, wheelwright, greengrocer, baker, shoemaker, laundress, charwoman and housekeeper. Similar parental occupations were recorded in 1875 but, reflective of changing patterns of employment in Victorian England, the sons of railway, police, gas and postal workers also entered the school. Further change to the social composition of the school resulted from the Charity Commissioners' 'New Scheme' of 1878, part of a national rationalization of foundation schools. The world had changed, and 'the dead hand of the founder' no longer served the educational needs of many growing communities.[6] Guided by a pragmatic blend of altruism and response to market forces, the new arrangements resulted in the original Latymer Foundation School on Hammersmith Road operating henceforth as an elementary school for boys; a new and separate 'Upper School' was to provide secondary education to a broader clientele. LUS formally opened in January 1895 in its new buildings on King Street. Boys aged eight to sixteen were now admitted on payment by their parents of school fees set at £5 per term. Poor but able boys could still attend: the provision of Foundation Scholarships for up to ten per cent of pupils enabled the school to demonstrate a degree of adherence to the founder's original intentions. New entrants were drawn predominantly from the middle classes. The 106 pupils in the first cohort included the sons of clerks, confectioners, wine and spirit merchants, accountants, architects, solicitors, bank managers, surgeons, dentists, art dealers – and insurance brokers. That such a school was needed in this part of London was clearly demonstrated by its growth over the following decade. In 1906, Albert Baswitz was one of over five hundred boys on the school roll.

Close links with the local education authorities ensured a steady stream of scholarship boys, especially after the 1903 (London) Education Act which gave LCC responsibility for the overall administration of the increasing number of elementary and secondary schools in the city. Nationally, the number of boys – and girls – gaining Junior County Scholarships by competitive examination increased tenfold in the period 1895 to 1906, from just over 2,000 to over 23,000.[7] Some 25 per cent of pupils in secondary schools were exempt from payment of fees. Most, like Albert, had previously attended elementary schools. This did not necessarily mean they were poor, however. Elementary schools administered by the London School Board often took great pride in securing scholarships. Fleet Road School in North London, for example, was so successful that it was dubbed the 'Eton of the Board Schools' and attracted children from more affluent and even professional families. Scholarships were intended to provide an 'educational ladder' from elementary to secondary education for the working classes. The reality was somewhat different. Charles Booth noted in 1902 that most scholarship boys 'come from the richer homes, for by the age of 11 the influence of the home atmosphere has had time to handicap severely the boys from rougher homes.'[8]

Albert Baswitz, the 12-year-old son of an insurance clerk and recipient of a bursary from LCC, began his secondary schooling in April 1906. He initially joined Class IIIB at LUS and appears to have made good progress in all subjects. Albert was particularly interested in mathematics and science, areas in which the school had gained a reputation for academic excellence. In July 1908, Albert gained Junior Level Honours in the Cambridge Local Examinations. His attainment of Senior Level Honours Class IIb a year later ensured that he had the necessary matriculation requirements for entry to the University of London. At the school prize-giving in December 1909, an event reported in some detail in the *West London Observer*, Albert was awarded his Certificate for Excellence in Arithmetic and Practical Chemistry. Secondary schooling in the Edwardian era was not confined to the pursuit of academic success, however. LUS provided a wider education, one which mirrored that experienced by fee-paying pupils in the great public schools of England. Based upon notions of 'character building', 'muscular Christianity' and 'manliness', the ethos of many new secondary schools was deliberately underpinned by a range of athletic, martial and cultural activities. Under Revd Smith, Head Master of LUS since its opening in 1895, sport of various kinds flourished. Association football was introduced, and representative teams played regular fixtures against St Olave's, Aske's, Emanuel and other local public schools. Cricket was encouraged, and games were played against Revd Smith's alma mater, St Mark's College in nearby Chelsea. A swimming club was established, and a Sports Day was held annually. Gymnastics (see plate 3) was introduced in 1904, followed by boxing in 1907. A school Cadet Corps, under the supervision of Colour Sergeant Fraley, met for the first time in 1905, albeit without uniforms and equipped with dummy rifles. When General Sir John French, the future Chief of Staff of the British Army, officially opened the Rifle Club in 1908, he reminded the assembled boys that their primary duty was to prepare themselves to take their share in defending the British Empire.

There is no hard evidence that Albert Baswitz took part in any of these sporting and military activities. Nevertheless, like all pupils and teachers at the school, he would have been exposed to the intense and all-pervading culture of achievement on the playing field and prowess on the parade ground. Watching sport was equally important. Each year, the whole school viewed the Oxford and Cambridge University boat race from a specially erected grandstand in the school grounds. Observing Empire Day was another annual ritual for both the school and its local community. The *West London Observer* recorded the 'Empire Day Celebrations' attended by Albert and the rest of his fellow pupils on 28 March 1909. The whole school assembled in the School Hall at 11.30 a.m. to hear Revd Smith explaining the meaning of Empire Day. This was followed by a rendition of Rudyard Kipling's *Recessional* and *Rule Britannia*. Sir John Cockburn, the guest speaker and former Premier of South Australia, then urged the boys to be 'animated by the spirit of loyalty to the Empire'. There was more rousing singing of *Bonny Dundee* and *Men of Harlech*, and a soloist sang *Land of Hope and Glory*. The Head Master then read aloud a telegram from Sir Henry Bull, a Latymer

Governor and local Member of Parliament, containing the simple message: 'God Bless you children, future guardians of the Empire.' The boys then marched to the front of the hall, where they saluted the Union Jack. As a finale, Revd Smith called for three cheers for the King.

We might well imagine the young Albert Baswitz standing, listening, watching, saluting and reflecting thoughtfully at such events. Gaining an understanding of this young man's attitude towards individual occasions, let alone his experience of schooling or wider public issues generally, is far more difficult. That he was interested in some of the issues of the day is evident from reports in the *Latymerian* of the proceedings of the school Debating Society. At its second meeting, in December 1908, there was an impromptu series of debates in which motions were written on slips of paper by all the members and then drawn from a box. The motion that 'A Classical Education is superior to a Scientific one', an assumption held by many in the educational community at the time, was proposed and opposed by fellow pupils Burton and Osborne respectively. Baswitz, noted the magazine report, seconded Osborne. The speeches were apparently very brief but then 'warmed up a great deal and the discussion soon became very animated', before the motion was defeated by fourteen votes to nine. Later motions on topical issues such as free trade and socialism reflected the wider concerns of a society undergoing rapid change. The motions 'That sports which involve the killing of animals are immoral' and 'That women should be given the vote' were avidly debated by the boys; the former was carried decisively, the latter narrowly defeated.

By 1910 Albert had completed the first stage of his secondary schooling. At this point, at the age of sixteen, many of his fellow pupils moved into employment, their time spent at LUS itself a valid qualification. Others stayed on at school with a view to scaling other educational ladders. As Sir Henry Bull observed at the time, 'In the Latymer Foundation they had the means whereby boys could climb up to the Universities and make their way in the world.'[9] Entering the school's Higher Sixth Form enabled pupils to study for the first-year Intermediate Degree examinations of the University of London, or prepare for vocational qualifications awarded by the London Chamber of Commerce. For the most able there was the prospect of admission to the Universities of Cambridge or Oxford. The choices made by these young men were determined by considerations of individual aptitude, career aspirations and the levels of financial support available to them. Opportunities existed, but they came at a cost. For many wealthy families, payment of university fees and maintenance allowances was merely a continuation of previous spending on preparatory and secondary education at their chosen public school. For the most brilliant students, a place at a Cambridge or Oxford college might be part-financed by a Latymer Foundation School Leaving Scholarship and, for some, a bursary from the college in question. For other families, the opportunity costs of progression to the universities were prohibitive. There was, however, another route to higher education which was becoming increasingly attractive to secondary school-leavers from working and lower middle-class backgrounds: preparation for a career in teaching. In 1910 Albert climbed a further rung on the educational ladder when he was awarded another scholarship, a Student Teacher Bursary from LCC, tenable at LUS.

Teachers in the fee-paying public schools rarely received any formal training; personal educational experience in a similar institution and the possession of a university degree or clerical status was usually considered sufficient qualification for appointment. Schooling the masses in nineteenth century England was a different matter altogether, and teachers cast in a different mould were required. The monitorial system, whereby young assistants helped adult teachers to instruct large numbers of working-class children in basic literacy and numeracy, had been introduced by the established church and Nonconformist religious societies in the 1820s. This 'great teaching machine' model may have been deemed to be technically efficient by its philanthropic proponents, but it was educationally ineffective. From 1846, bright children from the lower classes were selected to teach other children of the same class. Indentured as pupil teachers at the age of thirteen, they served a five-year apprenticeship. They worked towards the award of the Teacher's Certificate, supervised by headteachers in officially approved elementary schools. Many pupil teachers, however, served as uncertificated assistants in a closed world of working-class educational provision. The school-based model did ensure that pupil teachers gained practical experience from an early age, but such on-the-job training was often narrow, of poor quality, lacking in academic foundation and inadequately remunerated. The growing demand for elementary and secondary school places was recognized by the 1870 and 1902 Education Acts respectively. In rapidly expanding urban areas more people needed more schools, and more schools meant more teachers. Reforms of the pupil teacher system raised the required age and physical and educational qualifications and introduced Pupil-Teacher Centres. The introduction of Student Teachers in 1907 reinforced the notion of teaching as a learned and worthy profession, as opposed to the former persistent and widespread perception of it as a relatively menial craft or trade. Student Teachers had to have experienced three years of secondary schooling and to have already gained the qualifications necessary, such as London Matriculation, for entry to higher education. Albert's Student Teacher Bursary enabled him to spend a further year in secondary education, combining academic study with practical classroom experience and instruction and guidance from qualified and experienced teaching staff. It was expected that Albert and his fellow Student Teachers would subsequently proceed to a teacher training college.

Good teachers need good role models, both in their initial training and then throughout their careers. Albert was fortunate in having several mentors of the highest quality. The first was his own headmaster at LUS. Charles Smith was the embodiment of what might be achieved by a bright child from the working and middling classes of society climbing the educational ladder. Born in 1854 into a family of traders in Hammersmith, Charles had attended Latymer Foundation School as a young boy. Five years spent as a pupil teacher at the nearby St Paul's National School was followed by a scholarship to St Mark's College for more formal teacher training. Promotion took Charles from London to Cambridge, where he combined headship of an elementary school with studies at the city's ancient university, where he was awarded a First. He was then ordained into the Anglican priesthood in Ely Cathedral and returned to St Mark's, aged thirty-one, as Vice-Principal. A decade later, he was back at his old school in Hammersmith. The first head master of LUS wore clerical dress and was known to the staff as 'CJ' and to his irreverent pupils as 'Tubby'.[10] This remarkable man, who combined humour and rigour in both his personal and professional life, exerted a powerful influence on all who came into contact with him. He surrounded himself with colleagues of similar ability and disposition. Granville Grace and George Francis, who taught Albert science and maths respectively, were regarded so highly by their fellow professionals that both the national Board of Education and LCC sent visiting teachers and officials from home and overseas to observe their lessons. During his final year at LUS, Albert also spent time at the nearby Lillie Road Board School. This was a much larger school than any he had previously experienced. Built by LCC in 1893, with accommodation for some 1,600 infant and junior boys and girls, it was nearly three times the size of both Gloucester Grove East School and LUS. As a Student Teacher there, Albert became familiar with the routines of classroom organization, lesson preparation, assessment of work and, especially important for a new teacher, pupil management and discipline. It was at Lillie Road that he first found his teaching voice and professional manner. Taking inspiration from his previous role models, incorporating guidance from teachers in his practising school, and learning by reflecting on classroom triumphs and disasters, Albert embarked upon his new career.

In 1911 another scholarship enabled Albert to attend teacher training college. He had several to choose from in London. The oldest, and at that time still one of the foremost, was Borough Road College (BRC). At first known as Borough Road Normal School, it had been established in Southwark in 1818 by Joseph Lancaster of the Nonconformist British and Foreign Schools Society. Originally little more than a hostel for selected monitors, it had developed as a centre for preparing pupil teachers for certification and employment in elementary schools. By 1890 BRC had moved from its squalid inner-city surroundings just south of the Thames to rural Isleworth, having expanded rapidly in the wake of the capital's increasing need for properly trained teachers in the Board schools. BRC combined academic rigour with practical application of teaching theory and methodology. At the same time, its new site, with gymnasium and extensive playing fields, enabled it to emphasise the importance of sport – including compulsory games for all students – and physical fitness. The reputation of BRC was such that its alumni filled positions of responsibility in schools and colleges throughout Britain and as far away as New Zealand. BRC was a possibility for Albert, but there were alternatives nearer to home. By then the family had moved within Fulham to a newly developed area immediately adjacent to the South Middlesex Volunteers' Rifle Ground. The 1911 National Census recorded the presence of the 18-year-old Student Teacher living at home with his father and siblings Ida and Julius in Tamworth Street. The nearest training college was that attended by his mentor Charles Smith. St Mark's College on the King's Road in Chelsea had been founded in 1841 by the National Society. Not surprisingly, given its proximity and institutional connections, several boys from LUS had previously gone on to St Mark's, notably Philip Kingsford in 1910, a great athlete at school and college who represented England at the Stockholm Olympic Games of 1912. Across the river from Fulham were two further possibilities: St John's College in Battersea, founded on the same principles and in the same decade as St Mark's and, further to the south-east, Goldsmiths' College in New Cross, which had opened in 1905. In 1911, however, it was the London Day Training College (LDTC) which was the preferred destination for Student Teachers from LUS. For ambitious young men intent upon a career in teaching, the appeal was obvious. Day training colleges, with the close involvement of universities, enabled trainees to continue to live at home and to combine vocational training with degree studies. A university education, in this case at the University of London, was also now accessible to the 'new boys' from the lower, if not the lowest, social classes.

When LDTC opened in 1902, it was one of twenty such institutions nationally. The *London Daily News* of 7 October 1902 reported its opening under the headline 'Important Step Forward'. The LCC, responsible for the administration of over 2,000 schools containing a total of 1,000,000 children, had recognized the need for a steady supply of well-qualified and well-trained teachers to fill the 20,000 teaching posts in the capital.[11] Part of its annual expenditure of £4,000,000 was now devoted to training new entrants. The LCC retained financial control of LDTC and established a College Council to oversee its educational management. One of its first and most important roles was to secure the appointment of an eminent educationalist as leader of the new institution, and Sir John Adams, previously Professor of Education at the University of Glasgow, fulfilled the necessary criteria. John Adams was well versed in the merits of different forms of teacher training. His own schooling and career progression mirrored that of Charles Smith: from elementary school to pupil teacher, to training college and then on to degree studies at university. Professor Adams' appointment was symbolically important, too, combining as it did his leadership role at LDTC with that of Professor of the Theory, History and Practice of Education at the University of London. From its original foundation in 1828 as 'the godless institution in Gower Street',[12] the University of London was a pioneer and pace-setter which broke the monopoly in higher education held for centuries by the Universities of Cambridge and Oxford. It quickly formed associations with schools of medicine and other colleges, both in London and further afield, by permitting approved partners to offer University of London degrees to their students. Unlike the ancient universities, with their traditional and narrow syllabus and insistence upon social and religious exclusivity, the University of London promoted the study of the sciences, engineering, economics and foreign languages. Its Charter of 1858 held out the prospect of a university education to all who met the university's educational entry requirements and could pay the necessary fees. Geography was no barrier; degrees were awarded to students in the Dominions. Part-time study was possible; those in employment were able to study after work and to fund their own higher education. Dubbed 'the peoples university',[13] the University of London also ensured that higher education was no longer a male preserve; the first women students graduated in 1880.

Albert Baswitz gained a place at LDTC after being interviewed by Principal Adams. The latter spent most of his time liaising with the college's key stakeholders, namely LCC and the University of London, especially so after LDTC became a college of the University in 1908. The day-to-day training of students and oversight of personal development was devolved to the next tier of management at LDTC. The reputation of the grandly titled Master of Method, Percy Nunn, may have been another reason why so many young men like Albert Baswitz chose LDTC over its rivals. Dr Nunn was one of the greatest teachers of his generation and, like Charles Smith at LUS before him, was to have an immense influence on Albert and his fellow trainees. Christened Thomas, but known to all by his second name, Percy Nunn had been born in 1870, the year Forster's Education Act transformed the provision of schooling in England. Percy came from a family of teachers. His father was the second-generation proprietor of a small private school in Weston-Super-Mare. The young Percy attended the school, taught there and then inherited it, before selling up and moving to London to gain teaching experience in grammar schools and obtain degrees from the University of London. He joined LDTC the year after it opened (see plate 4) and quickly established a reputation as a brilliant and inspirational teacher, a pioneer in educational theory and a very capable administrator. By the time Albert joined LDTC, Dr Nunn was Vice-Principal and a key role model for each new intake of aspiring teachers. It was generally agreed amongst his students and fellow academics that Percy Nunn could teach calculus to a class of whelks.

One of Dr Nunn's clerical tasks was to maintain the college's Admission's Register. Far from being a bureaucratic chore, the meticulous handwritten entries appear to have been a labour of love. Details of each new trainee's previous schooling, scholarship awards and entry qualifications are followed by reports on course attendance and achievements. Summaries of lessons observed in the practice schools include telling comments about personal characteristics and teaching styles. Details of passes and failures in university courses were collated from material forwarded to him by his colleagues at King's College (KCL) and University College (UCL). Later additions to the record include details of first teaching appointments and subsequent promotions and relocations. In 1911, Dr Nunn's fourth entry for the new cohort of trainees was that of 'Baswitz, Albert'. The new trainee was one of fifty-eight young men admitted to LDTC that year. All but three were aged between eighteen and twenty. Most had been Student Teachers in London secondary schools such as St Olave's, Whitechapel Foundation, Hackney Downs and LUS. Amongst Albert's fellow students were familiar names and faces. Nine other young men from LUS had also gained admission to LDTC that year. They included Richard Garland, Herbert Handley and Edward Mount (see plate 5), the sons of a railway guard, omnibus driver and butcher respectively. They, too, had attended elementary schools before gaining scholarships to secondary and now higher education. Ben Bateman, the son of a policeman, had gained Class I Honours and Distinction in the Cambridge Local Examinations, was the undoubted star on the football field at LUS and directly followed Albert Baswitz in Dr Nunn's Register.

By the time the tenth cohort of trainees began their courses, LDTC had firmly established itself as a leading centre for teacher training. The college offered experienced and well-respected teaching staff, links to the university and a state-of-the-art training environment. In 1907, new buildings funded by LCC replaced the original temporary accommodation at the London School of Economics and elsewhere. At the opening ceremony on the new Southampton Row site, Lord Rosebery, former Liberal Prime Minister and now Chancellor of the University of London, outlined the rationale underpinning the expansion of provision for teacher training. Referring in quasi-military terms to the 'educational conscription' of the lower classes that had taken place since 1870, he then stressed the importance of the vast host of teachers who 'required the same training that staff colleges gave to officers of an army'.[14] A rigorous training regime in specialized facilities was essential, he added.

The new buildings at LDTC contained the necessary classrooms, laboratories, lecture theatre and library. In addition, trainees had access to a nature study room, a display museum and the all-important gymnasium. The creation of the right learning environment was important, but establishing an institutional culture was crucial. Before the move to a permanent site, Professor Adams had stated that the college already existed, even without its own buildings. The college was its students and teachers: 'it has a real identity, a real corporate life, a reputation to be made by its students and teachers and an *esprit de corps* to be cultivated by them.'[15] The new buildings, complete with student common rooms and a communal refreshment area, further promoted the notion of collective endeavour in a worthy professional and national cause.

Albert and his fellow trainees embarked upon a three-year course. This gave them time to practise their craft in the classroom and to study the theory behind it. In parallel to this, they also became subject specialists by undertaking undergraduate studies at one of the colleges of the University of London. The combination of a teaching qualification and a degree meant that successful trainees would be qualified to teach in secondary as well as elementary schools. The workload, however, was intense. Albert attended the Master of Method's lectures and demonstrations at Southampton Row, then put theory into practice in nearby schools such as St John the Evangelist Church of England School and LCC's Cromer Street School. These Practice Schools had been identified by Dr Nunn and his female counterpart Miss Margaret Punnett as exemplar institutions led by committed headteachers and specially selected staff. Albert's progress as a teacher was carefully monitored and assessed. His teaching ability was summed up succinctly and very positively by Dr Nunn in the Admissions Register:

> Mr. Baswitz
> An industrious and painstaking student with a high sense of duty. As a teacher he has worked hard and consistently improved both in the arrangement of his lessons and in class-management. He is at his best in teaching mathematics and science, but he teaches all subjects with equal conscientiousness, is able to interest his pupils and shows tact and observation in dealing with their individual needs. Altogether he promises with further experience to develop into a useful and trustworthy class-master taking a real and kindly interest in the boys entrusted to him.[16]

Albert's training to become a teacher of mathematics and science was reinforced by his degree studies at King's College, London. In the 1911 LDTC cohort, male trainees were allocated to either KCL or UCL. Some of his friends from LUS also attended KCL, including Richard Garland, Herbert Handley and Edward Mount. Women trainees were allocated to Bedford College and Birkbeck College. In his first year at KCL Albert made very good progress in his chosen subjects of Pure Mathematics, Applied Mathematics, Chemistry and Physics. In the end of year examinations he was placed in 'Class I. Very Good' in all subjects, except for Physics (Practical), in which he achieved a Class II. These results were sufficient for him to be awarded an Intermediate Bachelor of Science degree.

Colleges and universities offered more than simply vocational preparation and academic learning. Clubs and societies helped to foster the corporate life and common identity that men like John Adams and Percy Nunn valued so highly. LDTC's magazine, the *Londinian*, recorded the many social, theatrical and sporting activities which took place during Albert's time at college. A Christmas Social was held at the end of his first term and attracted 116 trainees from across the different year groups. Organized by the editor of the *Londinian*, Leonard Despicht, it was also attended by Dr Nunn and Miss Punnett, partly out of support for the venture but also to ensure the necessary and expected degree of decorum from their young charges. Male and female trainees had their own separate common rooms in which to socialize and to take breaks from their hectic schedules and heavy workload. Comments in the magazine about too much noise and the regular use of ping-pong balls as missiles in this social area are a reminder of how young the male trainees were. The Hon. Sec. of the Men's Common Room, Leonard Hussey, was one of the undoubted stars of the social scene, organizing Common Room Smokers at which he 'gladdened our hearts, as he always does, with his inimitable banjo solos and musical monologues'.[17] Lionel Bentke and Alfred Knowles were also prominent amongst their fellows, organizing productions by the Musical Union and Dramatic Society of Gilbert and Sullivan's *Yeoman of the Guard* and Sheridan's *The Rivals* respectively.

Sporting activities flourished; soccer, badminton, swimming, hockey and tennis clubs were all well supported. The women's hockey club played against East London College, whilst the men's football team played competitive fixtures against St Bart's Hospital, KCL, St Mark's, St John's and Goldsmiths' colleges. Ben Bateman, by now playing for the England Amateur Football Team and Southern League side Crystal Palace, as well as the college team, dominated the match reports in the *Londinian*, just as he had done in the pages of the *Latymerian*. Another fellow pupil from LUS was also making a name for himself. In the final year before the war, Edward Mount was elected President of LDTC's College Union. He was also a prominent member of the Debating Society. The college magazine reported that the motion 'That the disadvantages of war are greater than the advantages of war' was carried by one vote, despite an 'energetic speech from E. A. Mount opposing the motion'.[18] The *Londinian* contains no direct reference to Albert Baswitz and his extra-curricular activities. There are, however, numerous references to an organization that many of the young men from LDTC had joined. The University of London Officer Training Corps (ULOTC) attracted hundreds of would-be soldiers in the final years of peace before 1914. Albert Baswitz was both teacher and soldier.

Chapter 2

To Be a Soldier Too

Oh, Coll. is no place for me, for me,
Since I've joined the O.T.C.
And a soldier I am
Who can swear and can 'cram'
With the pick of the British Army.

Extract from *The O.T.C* by 'Terrier',
Londinian, Summer Term 1914.

In late September 1901 a small military column halted near Moedwil
Farm by the Selons River in South Africa. Commanded by Colonel
Robert Kekewich, the British force comprised infantrymen from
the Derbyshire Regiment, gunners from the Royal Field Artillery and
squadrons of cavalry from the 1st Scottish Horse and Imperial Yeomanry.
Having quickly established their makeshift defensive encampment,
they awaited the arrival of the enemy units known to be operating in
this part of the Transvaal. A Boer force over a thousand men under
Commandant-General Koos De La Rey duly arrived during the early
hours of 30 September and quickly surrounded the British bivouacs. In
the fighting which ensued, soldiers, cooks, orderlies and batmen put up
a determined resistance and, after two hours and a blizzard of bullets
from both sides, succeeded in driving off the Boers. This engagement in
the Second Boer War was costly to both sides, but unlike in the war to
come, with its characteristic trenches, barbed wire and machine guns, it
was the defensive force which paid the higher price. The British suffered
over two hundred casualties, including more than sixty killed in action or
mortally wounded.

Amongst the depleted ranks of the Scottish Horse was Corporal
William Loring (see plate 7). He had volunteered to help his country

in its struggle against the insurgents in the Orange Free State and Transvaal, enlisting in January 1900, not long after the 'Black Week' of British military reversals. His attestation paper for service in the ranks of the Imperial Yeomanry gave his age as thirty-four, his trade or calling as 'Barrister and Civil Servant' and his address as 'Rooms, 2 Hare Court Chambers, Temple, London'. He signed on for 'Short Service', namely one year with the Colours, 'unless the war in South Africa lasts longer than one year'. He was duly discharged the following December, having served his allotted time. On his journey home, however, Corporal Loring disembarked in Madeira, only to be told that the conflict with the Boers had resumed, and he set out immediately to rejoin his old unit. In the action at Moedwil the Scottish Horse lost three of its officers and seventeen other ranks. A further fifty-three were wounded, including Loring, who received severe wounds to his right arm and thigh. For his bravery during the skirmish with the Boers he was mentioned in dispatches and awarded the Distinguished Conduct Medal and the Queen's Medal. He was also commissioned into the Scottish Horse.

William Loring was born in 1865, the fourth of son Revd Edmund Loring, the Vicar of Cobham in Surrey, and his wife Charlotte. William attended Fauconberg School in Beccles before becoming a King's Scholar at Eton College. Another scholarship took him to King's College at the University of Cambridge, where he was awarded a First in Classics, the Chancellor's Medal and a College Fellowship. With social and educational qualifications such as these, William's career options were numerous and varied. He spent four years at the British School of Archaeology in Athens and conducted excavations at Megalopolis in southern Greece. He then returned to Britain, qualified as a barrister and joined the Civil Service in 1894. Appointed as an Examiner at the Board of Education in Whitehall, he later became Private Secretary to both Sir John Gorst, Vice-President of the Committee on Education, and Sir William Anson, Parliamentary Secretary to the Board of Education. The 1902 Education Act, which established local education authorities and encouraged the expansion of secondary schooling, afforded new opportunities to this capable and very ambitious administrator. In 1902 Loring was appointed Director of Education for the West Riding of Yorkshire County Council. Three years later, he became the founding Warden of Goldsmiths'

College in London. The man who had been a brilliant student, academic, archaeologist, barrister, administrator, soldier and commissioned officer – but never a schoolmaster himself – thus became a teacher of teachers.

Goldsmiths' College admitted its first students in September 1905. Its origins and mission bore some resemblance to those of the LDTC. The tripartite interests of the Board of Education, LCC and the University of London in securing more trained teachers for the capital led to its foundation on the site of the Goldsmiths' Company's Technical and Recreative Institute in New Cross. It was non-denominational and admitted female and male trainees. The workload was onerous, with lectures from 9.45 a.m. to 5.00 p.m. without pause, but social and sporting activities provided some respite from academic work. As at the LDTC, the young men and women at Goldsmiths' organized musical, literary, dramatic and debating societies, published a college magazine (the *Goldsmithian*) and joined the various athletics clubs.

There the similarities with LDTC end. Within a year of opening, Goldsmiths' College was the largest teacher training institution in England. Its annual intake of 250 students was drawn from London, Croydon, Kent, Surrey, and Middlesex, with each county or borough council allocated a set number of reserved places. The two-year course emphasised general education rather than practical training; for the most part, Goldsmithians were learners rather than practitioners, pupils rather than trainees. Albert Baswitz and his friends had been attracted to the LDTC by the prospect of specialist subject learning to degree level, combined with intensive periods of teaching practice. Goldsmiths' College, on the other hand, insisted upon compulsory general subjects for all: English Literature and Language, Elementary Mathematics, Elementary Science, English History, Geography, Music and Nature Study. Woodwork was compulsory for the men, Domestic Training, including Needlework, for the women. All students studied Physical Training, which included 'Exercises Suitable for Elementary Schools'. The teacher-training element of the course consisted of lessons in the Theory and History of Education, School and General Hygiene, and Blackboard Drawing. Only six weeks were devoted to school-based teaching practice.

The differences in emphasis and provision reflected the prior experience of the respective clienteles at LDTC and Goldsmiths'. The vast majority of those admitted to the former had been educated in secondary schools. The courses at Goldsmiths' College were designed for those whose own schooling, and teaching experience as pupil teachers, had taken place in elementary schools. Vice-Principal Caroline Graveson, one of Warden Loring's foundation appointments, observed how narrow in outlook many of her charges were. Most of them already believed themselves to be experienced young teachers; they were 'vigorous, outspoken and varied in type, and at once more mature and more ignorant than the present Sixth Form product.'[1] Miss Catty, a lecturer on the academic courses, recognized the challenges and opportunities faced by the college's teaching staff: 'We felt most acutely that we were explorers, or rather older inhabitants, introducing young, and indeed often brilliant and enthusiastic settlers to a new country.'[2] By 1914, however, the subjects on offer included 'Advanced' courses, in recognition of the ever-increasing number of trainees who had experienced a secondary school education in the wake of the 1902 Education Act. Success was nevertheless still measured by the award of a teaching qualification, the Board's Certificate of Education, but without a degree.

Most of the staff appointed by Warden Loring were themselves the products of secondary schooling and a university education. Together they created a culture of corporate endeavour which drew inspiration and example from the nation's ancient and elite educational institutions, albeit in a form diluted to meet the needs of teachers destined for employment in elementary schools. William Loring himself personified high academic and professional standards, although he was noted by some for his 'authoritarian and unsociable temperament'.[3] Like his counterpart John Adams at LDTC, he believed in the development of a 'College Spirit' based upon a deep sense of moral and civic purpose and strong loyalties to the institution. At Goldsmiths' College a disciplined environment encouraged subscription to the ideal and helped to add at least a modicum of polish to some of the less sophisticated members of the student community. Attendance at morning assembly, complete with Christian hymns and uplifting addresses, was compulsory for all staff and students whatever their religious beliefs. So too was the midday meal, at which the Warden and his colleagues sat at High Table wearing their academic gowns. Prefects were appointed to keep good order. Gender segregation operated everywhere: in classrooms, corridors, assembly and, of course, in lodgings and residential hostels. Prowess on the sports field was vigorously promoted. Wednesday afternoons were kept free for the men to play football, rugby and cricket against other teacher training and university colleges; women students participated in gymnastics, eurythmics and dance.

William Loring was directly responsible for the establishment of the Goldsmiths' College Cadet Corps and was for a decade its Commanding Officer. He had seen action and could teach others something of the realities of soldiering. The Corps was initially affiliated to a battalion of Royal West Kent (Queen's Own) Regiment. After the Haldane reforms, the Corps transferred to the new 20th (County of London) Battalion, The London Regiment, a Territorial unit. Staff appointments strengthened the Corps. Captain Fitzgerald and Lieutenant Bell were Goldsmiths' lecturers and part-time Territorial Army officers. Such men of action, as well as men of learning, served as role models. The Corps deliberately promoted virtues which were essential in the armed forces and deemed necessary for the schooling of the masses: loyalty, service, discipline, obedience. Drill, marching and a miniature rifle range introduced young men to some of the more technical aspects of soldiering. So too did the Annual Camp, where they mixed with cadets from other corps and were paid a shilling a day plus messing allowances and expenses for wear and tear on boots. Membership of the Corps promoted camaraderie and group identity. Cadet E. H. Hallows later recalled how 'red tunics, blue trousers, white belt and white bayonet frog were de rigueur' for the Goldsmiths' contingent of the 20th Londons.[4]

Other teacher training colleges in London also had direct links with military units. St John's College in Battersea and St Mark's College in Chelsea made up A and B Companies respectively of the 10th (Duke of Cambridge's Own) Battalion, Middlesex Regiment. They and their fellow trainees in the Corps at Goldsmiths' College were part of a long tradition of students joining 'irregular' forces containing part-time and part-trained amateur soldiers which supported the professional regiments of the British Army. Undergraduates from the University of Oxford had joined volunteer bands raised in 1642 during the English Civil War. Aberdeen University students responded to the Jacobite rising of 1745 by rallying to the Hanoverian cause, and later served in volunteer home defence units in readiness to counter any invasion from France. Rifle Volunteers from the University of Cambridge sent men to fight against the Boers. One might consider such examples to be no more than evidence of youthful enthusiasm and undergraduate high spirits, but this would be to underestimate the appeal of soldiering to many different groups in British society. The amateur military tradition was a fundamental British safeguard against internal disorder and invasion by external enemies. It also reflected a historic national distrust of standing armies and the consequent importance of raising local militias. In Victorian and Edwardian Britain not only students but many of their teachers were, or had been, soldiers, subscribing to the popular notion of 'a nation in arms' at times of external threat.[5]

There were plenty of opportunities for part-time soldiering. The introduction of cadet corps in the public schools gave many future members of the teaching profession their first taste of the military, initially as schoolboy cadets and later as corps officers when appointed to a school's teaching staff. The introduction of Officer Training Corps (OTC), established in schools and universities after 1908, prepared young men for commissions and leadership of other young men. Beyond the world of schooling, the 'Volunteers' (including various incarnations of the Militia, Yeomanry, Reserve and later Territorials) provided a pool of men to be called upon in times of national emergency and offered further opportunities for teachers to become soldiers. Men from across the educational spectrum became part-time soldiers – and sailors – in peacetime by joining such units. Before serving in the Scottish Horse in the Boer War, William Loring, alumnus of Eton College and the University of Cambridge, had been a member of the Lothian and Berwickshire Yeomanry. John Paulson, a teacher in one of the new secondary schools, held a commission in the Special Reserve and was recalled to his battalion when the British Expeditionary Force (BEF) mobilized in August 1914. Archibald Buckle, a teacher in one of London's elementary schools and a member of the Royal Naval Volunteer Reserve, similarly reported for duty when Britain declared war on Germany.[6]

* * *

Goldsmiths' College Cadet Corps prepared men for military service as private soldiers and non-commissioned officers, collectively and commonly referred to as 'other ranks'. Across the river at the LDTC, men like Albert Baswitz were preparing to lead them. By becoming an undergraduate at KCL Albert was able to join the University of London OTC (ULOTC), one of many such contingents brought into being by Haldane's Territorial and Reserve Forces Act of 1907. In England, the universities of Cambridge, Oxford, Nottingham and Sheffield established some of the first and largest of the OTCs. In Scotland, the universities of Glasgow, Edinburgh, Aberdeen and St Andrews also made provision for officer training, as did the universities of Belfast and Dublin in Ireland and their counterparts at Aberystwyth and Bangor in Wales. By 1910 there were 19 Senior Division OTCs based in universities and 152 Junior Division OTCs established in the public schools. All were affiliated to the Territorial Army. Uniformed recruits took part in parades, lectures, camps, field days and musketry training, experiences designed to be far more than simply occasions for playing soldiers. The OTC inducted young men into a new world of military jargon, organization and practice. It also developed leadership skills which would one day be called upon in battle. Training to be an officer of the crown also gave vent to cadets' masculinity, facilitated their access to new social and professional networks and created opportunities for them to become gentlemen.

In March 1908, the Rt Hon. R. B. Haldane MP, Secretary of State for War, had addressed a meeting of students in the Great Hall of the University of London. The first Military Education Committee was then appointed by the University Senate, and a formal offer to furnish a contingent of the OTC was forwarded to the War Office by the end of December that same year. Duly sanctioned in January 1909, the new ULOTC held its first general parade in May, and 18 officers and 389 cadets stood assembled in front of the university buildings in South Kensington.[7] They soon saw peacetime action, mounting guards of honour on separate occasions that year for Viscount Haldane, the Duke of Connaught and King Edward VII. Specialist Medical and Engineer Units were created to augment the main body of OTC infantrymen. Within a year, the numbers of ULOTC officers and cadets had nearly doubled, to 24 and 783 respectively. By the time Albert Baswitz joined the corps in the autumn term of 1911, Artillery and Army Service Corps Units had also been established. More guards of honour and parades followed, part of a process whereby Britain's new citizen soldiers were formally introduced en masse to the great military men of their generation: Lord Kitchener, Lord Roberts and General Sir John French, the latter already familiar to the former pupils of LUS now in training. After the coronation of King George V, some 16,000 OTC cadets, including 400 from ULOTC, took part in a Review by the King at Windsor. The new monarch subsequently assured Haldane that:

> This patriotic effort on the part of the Universities, the Public Schools and other seats of learning to take their share of the responsibilities of national service, and to do their best to train our future leaders, will be followed with much interest by His Majesty.[8]

Over a quarter of the trainee teachers who started their courses at LDTC in the autumn of 1911 joined the ULOTC. Of the ten young men from LUS in that year's cohort, five signed up for the Corps: Albert Baswitz, Richard Garland, Herbert Handley, Edward Mount and Vernon Watts. The new cadets, under the watchful eye of fellow trainees Despicht and Hussey, both by then Company Sergeants in the ULOTC, made full use of the Corps' new Headquarters, which opened just three months after their enlistment. Underneath the Great Hall of the University, Albert and his fellow recruits were introduced to the complexities of drill and practised their musketry on the miniature rifle range. They mixed with students from other London colleges and met serving soldiers too. Experts, many of them senior officers from Regular Army battalions, gave them the benefit of their wisdom and experience on topics such as 'Night Operations', 'Approach Marches' and 'The Aeroplane in War'. Brigadier-Generals Henderson, Wilson and Gough also made a point of visiting the Corps, their lectures to the part-timers a reflection of how important the new Territorial Force was to the country's defence. Major General Sir William 'Wully' Robertson, an ex-ranker and product of one of the nation's elementary schools, gave one of the final lectures entitled 'The Demands of Modern War' – before the Great War challenged all previous notions of expertise in military matters. Concerts, smokers, theatrical performances and the annual dinner facilitated new friendships and promoted camaraderie and corporate affiliation.

In June 1914 the ULOTC held its Sixth Annual Inspection in Hyde Park. Nearly 700 cadets and their officers assembled in the centre of the capital. This conspicuous display of military preparedness came after a decade of debate in which the 'military caste' in British educational institutions had won the day.[9] Earlier debates and divisions of opinion about the credibility and expense of schoolboy and student soldiering, both within the institutions themselves and in society more generally, were subsumed by the necessity to prepare for war. The cult of athleticism and of 'playing the game' on the school field still had its propagandists and followers, but it was no longer the major vehicle employed for the development of character, leadership skills or corporate spirit. Other forms of instruction, personal development and team building now took place beyond the time constraints of the school day or academic year. Much of the development of the nation-in-arms took place in public. Since the Boer War, the British Army had used field exercises and manoeuvres to prepare its Regular battalions, and especially its senior officers, for any future conflict. Squadrons of cavalry and lines of infantry moving through the English shires had increased the visibility of Britain's land-based forces. The mobilization of the new Territorial units for their Annual Camp in the summer months had much the same effect in accustoming the general public to the presence and importance of the military. For many schoolboy and student cadets, one of the highlights of the year was the annual OTC Camp, and in the summer months of 1914 pupils and teachers alike headed off to military bases for a period of intensive training.

The ULOTC had previously encamped with other Senior Division units at Aldershot, Camberley, Bulford and Shorncliffe, names now synonymous with the history of military training. On Sunday, 26 July 1914, the bulk of the London contingent set up camp at Ludgershall on Salisbury Plain (see plate 6). As in previous years, the Artillery, Engineer, Medical and ASC Units joined specialist training camps located in the same area. The camp was scheduled to last for two full weeks. To be considered 'efficient', and for his OTC contingent to receive the necessary capitation grant from the War Office, each Senior Division cadet had to spend at least eight days under canvas each year, in addition to the prescribed minimum of fifteen parades and a demonstrable proficiency in musketry. The Annual Camp was the most important single event of the year and, in the university contingents, virtually everyone on roll attended. Full uniform was insisted upon, discipline was strict and training in the field taken seriously. Officers from the Regular Army, including one attached to each Corps by the War Office to act as Adjutant throughout the year, supervised the part-timers.

The British declaration of war against Germany on Tuesday, 4 August 1914 was the signal for many members of the OTC to become full-time soldiers. We can only speculate on the reaction of individuals to the news that war had finally broken out. Whilst there had been numerous invasion scares to excite the popular imagination, as well as localized conflicts in the Balkans and plenty of posturing by the German Kaiser Wilhelm II, the prospect of a major European war was not the only preoccupation of the general populace in Britain. Prime Minister Asquith had used the mandate from three successive election victories to pursue progressive and highly controversial social and political reforms, including the introduction of old age pensions and the limitation of the constitutional powers of the House of Lords. In the early months of 1914, however, his Liberal government was destabilized by the issue of Irish Home Rule and the real possibility of armed revolt by Sir Edward Carson and his Ulster Unionist followers. Suffragette agitation had also escalated. In March, Velasquez's 'Rokeby Venus' in London's National Gallery was vandalized by 'Slasher Mary', the militant suffragette Mary Raleigh Richardson. Further acts of violence followed, as other supporters of 'Votes for Women' set fire to railway stations, seaside piers and sports pavilions. In May, Emmeline Pankhurst, the leader of the Women's Social and Political Union, was arrested outside Buckingham Palace. A growing sense of societal disquiet and unrest was exacerbated by the nearly ten million days lost to strike action and subsequent newspaper reports of socialist and syndicalist militancy and subversion.

The worsening diplomatic relationship with Germany thus played out against this backdrop of historic Anglo-Irish tensions and the increasingly vocal demands of social and economic pressure groups. Strong commercial links existed between Britain and Germany, as the

Baswitz, Gottheil and thousands of other migrant families had found to their advantage. British and German university students studied in Leipzig and Oxford respectively. The works of Beethoven and Shakespeare were the subjects of mutual admiration. In the last months of peace, an exhibition of 'Modern German Art' was held in London and works of German opera and ballet were performed at the Theatre Royal. Conversely, for a decade the popular press had tapped into a deep and genuine concern about the unpredictable Kaiser and his country's growing population, competitive industry and ambitious and expansive foreign and naval policy. The British government's response to such fears was to bolster their alliances with other powers through a series of formal Ententes, implement Haldane's army reforms and increase the level of funding given to the Royal Navy as demanded by Winston Churchill, the First Lord of the Admiralty.

These measures made war more likely, but not inevitable. As David Lloyd George later observed, in 1914 'all the nations of Europe tumbled into war.' The assassination of the Hapsburg Archduke Franz Ferdinand in Sarajevo on 28 June 1914 precipitated a war in the Balkans which subsequently triggered a more general conflagration between European powers bound by alliance obligations. In the final days of July and first days of August 1914, when the part-time soldiers of the ULOTC and Goldsmiths' College Cadet Corps were in their respective camps and erstwhile allies mobilized to meet the very real threat from Germany, Britain stood apart. The British government, parliament, press and public opinion were divided on whether the country should go to war, even after German troops violated Belgian neutrality. Behind the scenes, however, the July Crisis had prompted the War Office to begin the first stages of mobilizing the nation's armed forces. The first recall of key Army personnel and reservists began at midnight on Thursday, 30 July, before the German declaration of war against Russia on the following Saturday. The mobilization of naval reservists also began two days before Britain officially entered the conflict. For the thousands of part-time citizen-soldiers watching these developments unfold in such a dramatic fashion from the relative safety and comfort of their annual training camp, the time had come to stop playing war games and to experience the realities of modern warfare.

In the first weeks of the war, thousands of men with OTC Senior Division training and experience – validated by their Certificate A qualification – presented themselves to university boards. The names of those deemed suitably qualified were forwarded to the War Office, and the King's Commission was then granted without further formality. Men like Albert Baswitz were exactly what the Army needed: 'From the point of view of dash and endurance it would be difficult to find a more suitable candidate for a commission than a 'Varsity man in his third year.'[10]Albert and his fellow students chose to enlist rather than return to college to take their final examinations, which were scheduled for October. At the LDTC, Dr Nunn began the process of adding further detail to the Admissions Register. The new entry for Albert Baswitz, in the section headed 'Subsequent Career', stated simply: '2nd Lt. 22nd Batt. C. of L. 1914–.' Albert was one of over a hundred LDTC trainees who had joined the ULOTC before the war.[11] His officer cadet training had qualified him to become a subaltern in the County of London Regiment, one of the first Territorial units to see action in the Great War. By the end of 1914 Dr Nunn had added details of the nascent military careers of seventy-eight of his former students to the Admissions Register. Of these, forty-one were commissioned officers and sixteen were non-commissioned officers.[12] The rest were privates on enlistment, including three former officer cadets who chose to join prestigious 'class' units such as the Honourable Artillery Company and the Public Schools Battalion rather than take commissions in Territorial or County regiments. From Albert Baswitz's 1911 cohort, eighteen of the fifty-eight male trainees responded to the first call to arms.[13] Among them were friends and schoolfellows from LUS. Second Lieutenant Herbert Handley joined the 23rd Londons. Second Lieutenant Richard Garland and Private Ben Bateman both enlisted in the 2nd (Royal Fusiliers) City of London Regiment, their military rank determined by their respective pre-war predilections for playing soldiers in the OTC and playing football at a high level.

In universities and schools throughout the country, principals and headteachers responded to the call to arms in August 1914 by collating details of students and pupils, past and present, who had enlisted in the service of the King and his Empire. Institutional pride at the transformation of their alumni from civilians to armed combatants led to the production of

Rolls of Honour. The level of subscription to the military caste would not have surprised contemporary observers in the way that it might surprise us today. Many young men were already affiliated to the armed forces, albeit in a reserve capacity. Their childhoods had been militarized by books, magazines, games and pageants which glorified war. Their teachers, too, had extolled the virtues of discipline, loyalty and service. In the autumn term of 1914, in teacher training colleges throughout Britain, Percy Nunn's counterparts were similarly engaged in documenting the latest news of enlistments, commissions and postings to battalions. There was one notable exception, however. Warden William Loring at Goldsmiths' College was far too busy to be updating student records. Just two days after the declaration of war, Captain Loring had returned to his old battalion and was supervising the mobilization of the Scottish Horse in Blackheath. This urgent task did not, however, stop him from promoting the war. Shortly after his re-enlistment, the Warden sent a letter to the male students at the college encouraging them to follow his example once more:

> If this war continues, there will be opportunity of enlistment, with the full approval of the Board of Education, even for students who are committed to a course, perhaps a shortened course of pedagogic training. I venture to hope that many will avail themselves of the opportunity. And to those who do so I can wish nothing better than that the fortune of war may send them where their services will be drawn upon to the uttermost, and faith receive its keenest edge. This will, I believe, be good for the country, good for themselves, and good to the profession to which they belong.

Warden Loring's letter was subsequently published in the December edition of the *Goldsmithian*, by which point many of his former charges had already joined the colours. The Cadet Corps' Annual Camp at Shorncliffe was followed, on the outbreak of war, by the immediate mobilization of two companies of 'Smiths' attached to the 20th Battalion of the County of London Regiment. The first 'List of Smiths on Military Service' recorded 172 former students, of whom 143 had joined the 20th Londons. Of these, only three were commissioned officers. A further thirty-seven were non-commissioned officers. The same edition of the college magazine contained an editorial piece which epitomized the growing sense of a world turned upside down by war:

> Smiths! We are at the end of the first term of yet another year – possibly the most momentous in our Island story. We are anticipating the vacation which should usher in a season of peace and Goodwill. Alas! Ours ears are deafened by the booming of cannon, the clash of steel, and the lamentation of war-stricken nations.[14]

The clarion calls of war were also heard in the Dominions. In Perth, Western Australia, Principal William Rooney documented the rush to the colours by the young men of Claremont Teachers College. Herbert Milnes, an English alumnus of BRC who later followed his protégés to the battlefront, did the same at Auckland Training College in New Zealand. Proud Canadian patriots from William Pakenham's Faculty of Education at the University of Toronto followed suit. Great Britain, the 'Old Lion', called to her cubs, and the call was answered by legions of teachers and trainees in the remote outposts of empire.

Chapter 3

Tommies

They went with songs to the battle, they were young,
Straight of limb, true of eye, steady and aglow.
They were staunch to the end against odds uncounted,
They fell with their faces to the foe.

From *The Fallen* by Laurence Binyon.

In early August 1914, Albert Baswitz crossed the Thames and headed for Bermondsey. The Jamaica Road Drill Hall, the training base and administrative home of the 22nd (County of London) Battalion, The London Regiment (The Queen's) was busy mobilizing for war. The 22nd Londons were a new military unit, a small component of the Territorial Force which came into being on 1 April 1908. It was one of twenty-eight designated battalions of the London Regiment, each of which had a distinct identity derived variously from the geographical, ethnic, occupational or social background of its recruits. The 20th Londons (Blackheath and Woolwich) drew most of its recruits, including the cadets from Goldsmiths' College, from two London boroughs. The 14th Londons and 18th Londons attracted men of Scottish and Irish descent respectively. When the 8th London (Post Office Rifles) (POR) went to war in 1914, the great bulk of its fighting strength was made up of privates and NCOs who had previously worked in the postal service as letter-carriers, sorters, drivers, porters and telegraphists. In stark contrast to these so-called 'other ranks', the officers were drawn from elite educational institutions and the professions but did not necessarily have previous employment experience in the Post Office. Alan Maude, a serving officer in the 8th Londons who subsequently documented the battalion's wartime service history, noted that the company and junior officers of the POR included the following: two Fellows of Oxford and

Cambridge colleges, the secretary of a great London bank, several men from the Home Civil Service who had got Firsts at Oxford, four barristers, three solicitors, several businessmen, seven or eight boys straight from university, and a schoolmaster. The Officers' Mess included eight Old Etonians.[1]

Other battalions also attracted part-time soldiers from the professional and middle classes. Men for whom rank was not the sole determining factor chose to serve as privates and NCOs in the 'very smart' units – the 28th London (Artists Rifles) for example – rather than take commissions in the 'rather less smart' ones. According to popular opinion at least, the latter included the 11th Londons (Finsbury Rifles), known alternatively and far less glamorously as the 'Pentonville Pissers'.[2] It is not clear why Albert Baswitz chose to serve in the 22nd Londons. Other alternatives were available to this able, conscientious and ambitious young man. The 'very smart' 13th Londons (Kensingtons) were based not far from his home in Fulham, although the battalion had deliberately cultivated a reputation for being extremely conservative when awarding commissions. Albert may have made a deliberate decision to take his ULOTC training and status to a battalion where the opportunities for development and advancement were greater. Personal connections may also have been a deciding factor. Many volunteers enlisted with friends and work colleagues; the 'Pals' battalions of the Great War were the most obvious manifestation of this phenomenon. Unlike the mass subscription of Goldsmithians to the 20th Londons, evidence from LDTC records paints a different picture. The eighty LDTC men in the armed forces in 1914 were serving in twenty-eight different regiments; fifteen former trainees were in the London Regiment, but they were assigned to eleven different battalions. Albert Baswitz was the only alumnus from LDTC serving in the 22nd Londons when they first went off to war.[3]

Second Lieutenant Baswitz was gazetted on 28 August 1914, having been granted a Temporary Commission for the duration of the war only. Like many young men and women of his generation, he had lived through momentous times. Born during the reign of the Queen Empress, he would have been fully aware of the links with Germany which had so recently been severed in the most dramatic fashion. The young Baswitz was just nine years old when Queen Victoria, head of the royal house of Hanover and Saxe Coburg Gotha, had died in the arms of her grandson Wilhelm. The German Kaiser had dutifully attended her funeral in London on that bitterly cold day in February 1901 but had since become the epitome of foreign militarism and naked aggression against smaller and weaker states. There had been attempts at Anglo-German rapprochement during the reign of King Edward VII, but much rested upon the personal relationship between the vulgar and extravagant King on the one hand and the petulant and erratic Kaiser on the other. On the death of the former in 1910, the latter once more took the opportunity to attend a very public royal funeral procession through the streets of London. The subsequent accession of King George V provided more opportunities for royal cousins to dress up in the uniforms of each other's elite military units, but dynastic ties ultimately gave way to broader diplomatic endeavours to secure alternative sources of mutual security. British-born and educated, but of German parentage and heritage, Mr Baswitz the trainee teacher must surely have reflected upon the growing tensions between Britain and Germany. The possibility of Baswitz and Gottheil cousins fighting in the German armed forces may well have been a topic of discussion within his extended family in London and Bradford. By enlisting in the British Army on the outbreak of war, Second Lieutenant Baswitz had clearly indicated his allegiance to the family's adopted home, just as the adoption of British citizenship by his maternal grandfather and father had done. His very evident sense of duty now extended to the defence of the institutions to which he had committed himself as a boy and young man.

Family, friends and former scholastic institutions travelled with him, in spirit at least, as he took his first steps along with millions of other young men as a combatant in the great European conflict. Percy Nunn had noted Albert's suspension of his studies in September, at the start of the 1914 autumn term. In October his old school used the pages of the *Latymerian* to record news of his enlistment. In its December edition his commission was noted with pride. The *Jewish Chronicle* also followed his military career with interest. The newspaper's third listing of 'Officers', published in early October, contained details of 'BASWITZ, 2nd Lieut. Albert, 22nd Batt. County of Lond. Regt'. In a separate listing of 'Non-Commissioned Officers and Men' was his younger brother, Private Julius

Baswitz, who had joined the Royal Army Medical Corps. Under the heading 'Our Honour Record of all Jews who are Serving', the purpose of the roll of honour was made explicit:

> The *Jewish Chronicle* is compiling a list of all Jews in the Empire who are serving in all arms during the War. At the end of the War, when the list is completed, the whole of the names will be printed in a separate form on fine art paper, and a bound copy will be submitted to THE KING for His Majesty's gracious acceptance.

At a time when the term 'Jew' was used by some as a byword for the German enemy, the editor the *Jewish Chronicle*, Leopold Greenberg, wrote a letter to *The Times* pointing out that 'Jews are bound in loyalty to the country of which they are citizens.' An earlier leader had stated unequivocally that 'England has been all she could be to Jews; Jews will be all they can be to England.' Leaders of the Jewish community countered the blatantly anti-semitic smears and charges of disloyalty – even of cowardice and unmanliness – with genuine and unambiguous patriotic exhortations. Thousands of their readers, particularly from the professional middle classes, responded accordingly. As the *Jewish Chronicle* also acknowledged, however, enlistment in His Majesty's forces could still be problematic. On the same day that the service of the Baswitz brothers was noted, another *Jewish Chronicle* headline proclaimed, 'Jewish Recruits Refused in London'. Fear of the 'foreigner' – and potential spy – in their midst led first to public unease and later to civil unrest. Those German shopkeepers who had been welcomed and widely valued now came under intense suspicion as potential purveyors of vital military information to the enemy. Germanophobia even led to questions being raised about the royal family, with its Germanic name and some of its junior members serving in the Germany Army.

Kaiser Wilhelm's erratic behaviour in the years before the war resulted in corresponding and violent swings of opinion towards Germany. His attacks on Jews and Jewish influence merely confused matters further. Now that war had been declared, 'alien' became a catch-all term for all who were not irrefutably 'British'. The Aliens Restriction Act, passed by the House of Commons on 5 August, just one day after war was declared, required the registration of all aliens within less than a fortnight. A witch-hunt ensued, whipped up by the weekly newspaper *John Bull* and other voices of outrage in the popular media. In both London and the provinces, the first weeks of the war witnessed the internment of some 2,000 aliens considered to be dangerous suspects,[4] frenzied attacks by mobs on pork butchers' premises and serious anti-German riots. As the war dragged on, news of genuine spies, reports of atrocities in Belgium and details of enemy attacks on non-combatants by land and sea increasingly made the headlines. Being of alien origin, however defined, became far more problematic. At LDTC, some of Albert's contemporaries experienced the backlash of public opinion at the very point of offering to serve their adopted country. Adolph Brodman was prevented, perhaps understandably, from joining the British Army as he was an Austrian by birth. Keva Muscovitch, born in France to a Russian father, was also declared ineligible to serve in His Majesty's forces, in this case despite his connections to Britain's Entente allies. Aaron Harris was similarly debarred from military service on the grounds that he was born in Russia. Any suggestion that religious rather than national affiliation was the real reason for such rejections is somewhat confounded by the relative ease with which other LDTC trainees with names of German or Jewish origin managed to enlist. Leonard Despicht and Morris Cohen, for example, both secured commissions in 1914. For British-born Second Lieutenant Albert Baswitz, whose father had previously and propitiously changed his official status from 'Foreign Subject' to 'British Resident', the eligibility tests were clearly not an issue. Previous attendance at prestigious educational institutions and, especially, successful participation in Haldane's OTC scheme would certainly have enhanced his credentials and overridden any reservations about his suitability to command men in the British Army.

The 22nd Londons were originally part of the 2nd London Division; other London Regiment battalions formed part of the 1st London Division. Both had been created in 1908, two of the fourteen infantry divisions of the peacetime Territorial Force. Each contained three four-battalion infantry brigades, plus artillery batteries, medical services, engineers and transport services. Originally part of the 6th London Brigade, the 22nd Londons – together with the 21st, 23rd and 24th

Londons – were mobilized almost immediately after they had arrived for their annual camp on Salisbury Plain. By mid-August Divisional Headquarters had been established at St Albans in Hertfordshire, and the 22nd Londons had marched with the rest of the 6th Brigade to their base in nearby Watford. Having obtained and part-financed his own uniform, boots, Sam Browne belt, Webley service revolver and other equipment, Second Lieutenant Baswitz spent the next four months training with his battalion. The emphasis was on individual and small unit training, working as members of a platoon, then company, then battalion. Musketry proficiency was central to this. Larger scale brigade and divisional training came later, in February 1915. Those first few months of monotonous but necessary preparation for war included frequent route marches (the lot of infantrymen through the ages) and trench-digging (a relatively novel technique of warfare and one they would later become accustomed to). The men remained cheerful, despite delays in the provision of essential clothing, equipment and shelter. They were billeted in requisitioned schools, parish rooms and other public buildings. Local householders demonstrated their support for the war effort by allowing as many as eight men at a time to sleep on their floors. For some of the new servicemen the only accommodation available consisted of overcrowded barns and sheds, often open to the elements. The wet weather during the first winter of the war added to the Londoners' discomfort but did little to dent their resolve. Food was plentiful, but the men soon became fed up with a regular diet of meat stew, cheese and plum and apple jam served up by inexperienced army cooks. This led to a (strictly forbidden) interchange of supplies with enterprising locals.

* * *

In early March 1915 the 22nd Londons and their sister battalions were ready for war. They were not the first Territorials to see action, however. Some, including the London Scottish and the Kensingtons, had been sent overseas in brigades of the Regular Army as early as 15 September 1914. With stalemate on the Western Front, and the original units of the BEF battered and severely depleted, the time had come to commit the bulk of the Territorial Force to the fray. The Territorials would hold the line until Lord Kitchener's New Armies had been trained and were ready to take the field. The North Midland Division led the way, followed by the 2nd London Division. Second Lieutenant Baswitz was one of 26 commissioned officers and 994 other ranks under the command of Major General Charles St Leger Barter who embarked for France from Southampton on 14 March 1915.[5] Thousands of British service personnel had made the very same journey since the beginning of the war, and millions more would do so over the next few years.

The young officer and his men crossed the Channel and arrived at the port of Le Havre in the early hours of the following day. At 0800 hours they disembarked and made their way to an area that would soon become all too familiar to them. Divisional HQ was established at Marles-les-Mines, in the mining district of Bethune. The troops were billeted in nearby villages, including Allouagne and Labeuvrière. After a full week spent settling in to their strange foreign environment, they were inspected by none other than Sir John French, the British Commander-in-Chief. A familiar figure to many of the young subalterns who had been members of the ULOTC, and especially to those who had also been members of the LUS Rifle Club, the Londoners paraded before him. In his address to the assembled troops French complimented them upon their smart appearance and welcomed them to the Army in France. More training followed, the essential precursor to any commitment of new troops to the front line. The first weeks in France were taken up with more drill, more musketry training and the inevitable but necessary route marching. New ways of fighting meant an introduction to the training trenches at Ham-en-Artois, and plenty of bayonet practice. Selected parties of officers and NCOs took it in turns to move up to the front line trenches held by other battalions, including the 4th Brigade of Guards. Their first experience of enemy shelling and its inevitable casualties, at Richebourg St Vaast in early April, was essential preparation for the moment when they, too, would be expected to take over their part of the British line.

After just six weeks in France, the 22nd Londons and the rest of the 6th Brigade moved up to Rue-de-L'Épinette and the trenches at Indian Village, so called because it had recently been vacated by units of the Indian Army which had been fighting in France since the previous September. The Londoners were now in the Festubert sector, and from

25 April they worked tirelessly to secure their new home against enemy attacks: fortifying parapets, checking their barbed wire, and sending night-time patrols into no man's land. After the Germans had launched a surprise attack using poison gas at the Second Battle of Ypres, the men were issued with primitive gas masks. These were

> composed of a brown knitted cap-comforter, folded into a pad to cover nose and mouth, and furnished with four long white tapes. This we were ordered to tie on our faces after damping the pad with a solution of carbonate of soda, if we happened to have such a thing about us, but if not then with another liquid which contains a certain amount of ammonia, and is obtainable even in the trenches.[6]

Holding the line in the trenches soon gave way to attack and counter-attack by both sides. In May, French forces began a major offensive in the Artois region, and they called upon their British allies to launch a series of supporting operations. Despite some 11,000 British casualties in the disastrous attack at Aubers on 9 May 1915 (see Map 2),[7] the attacks continued. Six days later, the 2nd London Division was called into action in the Battle of Festubert. Holding the Givenchy to Festubert line against the 91st Prussian Guard Reserve, they faced exploding mines, heavy shelling and enemy sniping. On 22 May the Londoners experienced a particularly intensive assault by enemy troops around the trenches named by British battalions which had held them previously: Scottish Trench, Grouse Butts, New Cut and Sidbury Mound. This action was their true baptism of fire, and the 6th Brigade suffered particularly heavy losses. The 22nd Londons used their machine guns to halt the enemy attackers, but their defensive action nevertheless resulted in numerous casualties. Six of Second Lieutenant Baswitz's fellow officers were killed in action, seven were wounded and a further two were 'incapacitated by shock'.[8] For three days burial parties worked at Windy Corny interring the bodies of their fallen comrades. The young subaltern had survived his first major engagement, but Second Lieutenant Herbert Handley of the 23rd Londons was not so fortunate. Albert and Herbert had known each other since their schooldays at LUS, they had trained to become teachers and soldiers together at the LDTC and ULOTC and were officers together

in the 6th Brigade in Flanders. Herbert Handley was killed in action at
Givenchy on 25 May.

After being inspected and congratulated for their part in the Battle of
Festubert by Lieutenant General Sir Charles Monro, the 22nd Londons
returned to their billets at Beuvry. There they bathed and rested, but still
found time to attend gas demonstrations. Moving to new billets at La
Bourse in early June, the troops continued their training, accustoming
themselves to the other new weapons developed for use in trench warfare.
And it is at this point that the fog of war lifts and the part played by
one individual emerges from the collective endeavour. The first direct
reference to Second Lieutenant Baswitz's contribution to the British
campaign on the Western Front is to be found in the Unit War Diary
of the 22nd London Battalion. It appears that he had become an early
specialist in the art of 'bombing': the use of hand grenades to clear enemy
trenches and silence their machine gunners. In August the war diary
begins referring to him as the Battalion Bombing Officer and records his
work in training the battalion bombers and leading them as they stood
by to repel potential enemy attacks. They had spent the months of June
and July 1915 in the trenches at Maroc and Grenay, not far from the
small mining town of Loos (see Map 3). They were so close to the enemy
lines that they could hear unsettling noises at night as the Germans
moved equipment, dug more defensive positions and, most worrying
of all, began tunnelling towards them under no man's land. The legend
of the fair-haired British officer disguised as a German, as related by
Revd Smith to the boys at LUS in the post-war assembly, may well have
originated during this period. In response to the Germans' nocturnal
activity, the newly promoted Lieutenant Baswitz led information-
gathering patrols. At first, and often in conjunction with officers from the
Royal Engineers (RE), the patrols were ordered to check the condition
of the barbed wire in front of the British lines, a key element of defence
which was routinely targeted by enemy artillery. Increasingly, however,
Lieutenant Baswitz and his small group of men would crawl on under
cover of darkness through the battered terrain towards the German wire.
There is no verification at this point in the war of the claim that disguises
were employed, that enemy trenches were entered or that patrols were
captured and taken back for interrogation, but nevertheless the official

record notes that, at 0030 hours on 1 August, 'a patrol of men under Lt Baswitz succeeded in approaching within 60 yards of a (German) working party.'[9]

It is a widespread misconception that British 'Tommies' spent the whole of the war in the trenches. After a few weeks, or even just a few days, of direct confrontation with the enemy, front line battalions were relieved by fresh units and marched back to their rest camps and billets in villages behind the fighting and reserve trenches. More training, inspections, medical examinations and inoculations then prepared the troops for their next assignment on the battle front. The morale of recent combatants was considered, too, for example by granting leave – Lieutenant Baswitz returned from seven days' leave on 15 August – and organizing events such as the Divisional Sports meeting in the area close to the familiar and welcoming billets of Allouagne. Rest and recuperation soon gave way to another tour of duty, however. On 4 September the whole division, by now re-designated the 47th Division, returned to their previous line at Maroc and Grenay. As they looked out from their defensive positions they could see the town of Loos to their left, clearly identifiable by a landmark in this coal-mining district which the Londoners had nicknamed 'Tower Bridge', with its distinctive pithead gear and pylons. To their right was the town of Lens. Directly ahead of them was the fortified redoubt of Hill 70. For the next three weeks the London battalions, now part of the newly renamed 140th, 141st and 142nd Brigades, competed with the enemy opposite to strengthen their positions even further. They dug nearly 1,500 yards of new front line, constructed large equipment and ration dumps and laid miles of telegraph and telephone cable.[10] This was to be an extremely busy but relatively quiet period for all concerned, with just the occasional bout of shelling from both sides to disrupt the work parties. A violent thunderstorm on 23 September 'which made the guns sound foolish in comparison'[11] filled the trenches with a foot of water and made the preparations for the widely anticipated offensive even more difficult.

Britain and her allies had now been at war for over a year. Little had been resolved; indeed, the conflict had intensified and spread to other theatres of war. In the autumn of 1915 the Germans still occupied large swathes of French and Belgian territory. Trench warfare intensified the stalemate. The British assault on the Dardanelles, intended to force the Ottoman Empire out of the war, had simply strengthened the resolve of the Central Powers and their supporters. Mounting casualties for the French forces in Artois and military reversals for the Russians at Brest-Litovsk put pressure on the Entente's political and military leaders to demonstrate that the enemy could, and would, be beaten and driven back. The preparations in Flanders were intended to break the deadlock, get the war moving again and at the same time serve as a demonstration of tangible British commitment to her flagging allies. The ensuing Battle of Loos was more than simply a gesture of solidarity. It was preceded by four days of bombardment by the British heavy guns. The artillery was supported by aeroplanes of the Royal Flying Corps (RFC), up all day 'working with the guns' as observers to aid accuracy.[12] In such a complex logistical operation, getting the infantry into position was far from easy. On the eve of the battle the British troops struggled to move up to the line through congested traffic in the rear and muddy communication trenches to the front; one battalion took nine hours to get from its billets to the attack assembly position. The Territorials were no longer the only British citizen-soldiers fighting in France, however. The first three divisions of Kitchener's New Armies, composed of enlisted men from the Scottish Lowlands and Highlands and the English shires and industrial towns, had arrived in France four months earlier and were now committed to General Haig's First Army in the Lens sector. Despite Kitchener's early distrust of volunteer soldiers such as the Territorials, the men of 47th Division dug in near the village of Maroc were entrusted with a task vital to the successful outcome of the forthcoming battle. The Regulars of the original BEF were by now a dwindling force; the pre-war 'Saturday night soldiers' were now seasoned troops.[13] The pivot for the forthcoming British attack by IV Corps was the point held by the 21st and 22nd Londons, situated on the extreme right of the three-mile-long divisional line (see Map 3). Directly opposite, but some 1,200 yards distant from them across a valley scarred by industrial activity, were two huge colliery spoil heaps known as the Double Crassier. These formidable obstacles had to be taken; enfilading fire from them would seriously jeopardize any advance towards the town of Loos, the capture of which was the key British objective for the first wave of attacks. The double line of enemy trenches occupied by men from the Sixth German Army were deep, well-maintained and fronted by strong and wide belts of barbed wire.

At zero hour (0550) on 25 September 1915, the British used poison gas for the first time in battle. The RE Special Brigade released their chlorine gas, code-named Accessory Number 1, some of which was blown back towards the British lines, causing confusion and casualties. Some forty minutes later, troops from the 141st and 140th Brigades moved forward through the yellow haze of gas and smoke. At the pivot point on the right flank of the attacking units, Lieutenant Baswitz and the rest of the men of the 142nd Brigade were ordered to stand firm, guard the flank of the attacking units and employ a deception tactic (known as a 'Chinese attack') to draw enemy fire away from their sister battalions. A 'gallant army of dummy figures', worked by strings controlled by men from the 21st and 22nd Londons, 'made progressive appearances in the smoke-cloud, and did their duty',[14] whilst the other men cheered and raised their bayonets over the parapet.

The Battle of Loos (see plate 8) was the largest and most ambitious offensive operation by the British Army in the war so far. The 47th Division captured the Double Crassier, an achievement the London press hailed as 'The Slag Heap Victory'.[15] The *Illustrated London News* of 30 October 1915 praised the 'awe-inspiring charge' made by the London Territorials and referred to a report in a German newspaper that the 'Englishmen in thick lines and storming columns ... rose suddenly from the earth, wearing smoke-masks over their faces, and look[ed] not like soldiers, but like devils.' To the immediate left of the Londoners in the British line was a New Army formation, the 15th (Scottish) Division, which advanced through Loos and began the ascent of Hill 70. The hoped-for breakthrough did not materialize, however. The inability of British artillery to provide the infantry with further support in the face of enemy defensive bombardments, and the difficulty in getting reserve battalions into attacking positions, brought the advance to a halt. In reality, and this was part of a pattern repeated countless times during the Great War, the attacking force had simply moved its line forward and the defenders had moved back and established new lines. Retaining newly gained territory could not be taken for granted, nor could the prospect of advancing further. The failure to capture and hold Hill 70 on the first day proved to be costly. On 27 September the Welsh Guards and 4th Grenadier Guards passed through the divisional lines to attack Hill 70 but were forced to dig in on the slopes by enemy machine gun fire from the crest of the hill. They were relieved two days later by other Guards battalions, assisted by the 142nd Brigade. With the two opposing forces in such proximity, the engagement became a bomber's battle. Once again, the exceptional actions of one of the officers involved was deemed worthy of official note in the divisional record, and may well be the basis of the 'fair-haired officer' legend referred to previously:

> Lieutenant Baswitz, bombing officer of the 22nd Battalion, with some bombers, explored some dugouts in no man's land on Hill 70, and brought back six Guardsmen and two Germans, who had been there in forced alliance, the Englishmen for three days and the Germans for four days.[16]

French forces eventually relieved the British troops in the sector. The first day of the Battle of Loos had resulted in nearly 20,000 British casualties, including 6,350 killed in action. Many of them were senior officers. For Kitchener's New Army Battalions in particular, their first experience of war came at a very heavy price. The Territorials suffered too: casualties in the 47th Division amounted to 60 officers and 1,352 other ranks.[17] Many of the Londoners killed in action were buried in the British Cemetery at Maroc. Those, including Lieutenant Baswitz, who survived the battle spent the following weeks in the trenches, resisting several counter-attacks and sustaining further casualties but successfully holding the line. The Germans held their lines, too, and continued to do so despite repeated attacks by British and Dominion troops in the Lens sector over the next two years of war.

Lieutenant Baswitz spent the rest of 1915 away from his battalion. He and a sergeant from the 22nd Londons became instructors at the Divisional Bomb School at Noeux-les-Mines, teaching other soldiers how to make best use of grenades. The stalemate of trench warfare had demonstrated the vital importance of no man's land: it was not simply an empty demilitarized zone separating the two warring parties, but an area to be dominated and owned. The British High Command was particularly keen to ensure that the space was contested in the most aggressive fashion possible. Listening posts were established, and working parties were sent out to extend the lines and instal increasing amounts of barbed wire. Raiding parties were especially encouraged and were designed to weaken the enemy's morale and give him sleepless nights. The fighting patrol, under the cover of darkness, was the favoured method; the 'bomb' the usual and most effective weapon of choice and, in skilled hands, a useful form of short-range artillery. After trials of different forms of bomb – General Headquarters ordered that this slang term be replaced by the word 'grenade' – the Mills bomb [*sic*] was made and used in large quantities, and largely replaced the rifle as the primary offensive weapon in the confines of the trenches. Previous forms of hand-thrown explosives 'were all pretty bad'.[18] The first Mark 1 stick grenades were both unreliable and dangerous. Shortages of supply led to the production of home-made 'jam-tin' bombs filled with explosive gun cotton and shrapnel ball projectiles. 'Battye Bombs' and 'No. 15s' also presented safety and reliability issues. The Mills bomb was made of cast iron, weighed 1¼lbs and was filled with ammonal or amatol; crucially, it featured a four-second delay on the ignition system.

In his training sessions at Noeux-les-Mines Lieutenant Baswitz drew upon his previous teaching knowledge and military skills, combining elements of both to instruct other officers and men in his specialist field: how to conduct a bombing raid. He had some experience of organizing and teaching large groups of schoolboys in the classroom; now he was engaged in something similar, albeit in a very different and far deadlier context. He was now an instructor, drawing upon his own battlefield experience to impart vital information and develop expertise in others. Mills bombs were carried in boxes of twelve, with separate detonators, and armed only minutes before the patrol was due to go over the top. Careful selection of personnel would have been emphasized: bombing required men with steady nerves and steady hands, especially when removing the base plate and priming the grenade. Four or five riflemen and two or three 'bagmen' would also be needed to support the bombers, the former to deal with any response from the enemy, the latter to block sections of a captured trench with sandbags when necessary. The trainee bombers practised the key components of a raid, honed their skills and worked as a team. Climbing their parapet in silence, then creeping through gaps in their own barbed wire, they were to move steadily towards their objective, flattening themselves hard on the ground in response to enemy flares or machine gun fire. They would need to get close enough to the enemy line, cutting their defensive wire if necessary, to be able to throw two to four Mills bombs into the targeted trench. If possible, the raiders would jump into the trench and use more grenades to clear it of defending troops. The riflemen would assist; the bayonet men dealt with any resistance.

Whilst Lieutenant Baswitz was busy instructing personnel from other battalions, his own unit had spent the three months since the Battle of Loos alternating between spells at the front and training behind the lines. He rejoined them on 26 December at their billets in Vermelles which, in comparison with their regular accommodation at Allouagne, were disgustingly dirty. He had missed spending Christmas Day with his fellow officers and men but, by all accounts, the big day had been something of a disappointment. To avoid any repetition of the scenes of fraternization with the enemy witnessed during the first Christmas of the war, the big guns had continued to fire. Winter conditions were hardly conducive to festive activities. Some of the trenches held by the 47th Division 'resembled the cave dwellings of primitive man', and 'liquid, penetrating mud flowed over the top of knee-boots.'[19] There were few signs of peace and goodwill shown by either side over the holiday period. The front line British trenches remained on high alert, especially after men from the Royal Welsh Fusiliers attached to the 47th Division detected the telltale noises of German subterranean activity. On 30 December five enemy mines were detonated in the Loos area. The massive explosion at the Hairpin trench, where Lieutenant Baswitz and his bombers were stationed, was followed by heavy shelling. 22nd Battalion's casualty rate was particular high in this engagement: twelve men were killed in action, sixty-eight were wounded, thirty-six were reported missing and numerous others were considerably shaken by the impact of the high explosives.[20] Lieutenant Baswitz was not amongst the casualties; he and his men were 'holding on well and keeping cheerful' despite everything the Germans had thrown at them.[21]

The first months of 1916 saw little change in what was now becoming the standard service routine for most British troops on the Western Front. Periods of duty in the front line trenches alternated with time behind the lines in divisional reserve. The 47th Division remained in the Loos sector throughout January, February and March. The 22nd Battalion continued to experience heavy shelling in the trenches at Maroc, and on 27 January prevented the Germans from storming their positions, 'This, presumably to celebrate the Kaiser's birthday'.[22] The bombers continued their nocturnal tours of no man's land, and the Unit War Diary continued to record the exploits of their leader:

13 January. Maroc. 10.00 p.m. Lt Baswitz went out on patrol. Very good report about enemy wire and work.

14 January. Lt Baswitz went on patrol. Nearly ran into enemy patrol and also got fired on. Too light for very near observation, but useful information tendered about enemy work in advance of their line.

These prosaic and understandably limited descriptions once more fail to confirm fully the stories told later by the young subaltern's admirers. They also fail to convey the very real dangers to which the bombing patrols were exposed. That Lieutenant Baswitz's actions were exceptional, however, is evident from the military honours he was awarded during this period. The *London Gazette* of 31 December 1915 reported that he had been Mentioned in Dispatches 'for gallant and distinguished service in the field.' Two weeks later, the *Gazette* announced that he had been awarded the Military Cross (MC).

After returning to their billets at Allouagne in February, the battalion continued to provide groups of men for working parties at the front but spent most of the time engaged in brigade training exercises. After a year of fighting in the Festubert and Loos sectors, the Londoners moved on 28 March to a different part of the British line, south of Lens at Souchez, near Vimy Ridge. The divisional history noted that the area contained 'pleasant rolling countryside, very pretty in springtime, and a welcome change after a winter in the black mining district'.[23] The trenches near the division's new billets situated around the village of 'Extra Cushy'

(Estrée-Cauchy) almost lived up to the soldier's slang name for the location. At first, both sides adopted a 'live-and-let-live' policy, which resulted in a relatively peaceful and uneventful stay in the front line. Once again, however, the Londoners had to contend with water-filled trenches, sporadic attacks by German *Minenwerfer* (mortars), and the knowledge that enemy tunnelling companies were advancing towards the British lines. Machine guns continued to spray their deadly projectiles across no man's land, attacks were followed by counter-attacks, casualties mounted and neither side made progress in a war in which defensive tactics consistently frustrated attempts at offence.

*   *   *

In the last week of May and throughout June 1916, Lieutenant Baswitz and the troops of the 47th Division joined with the rest of the British Army in France in preparing for the great offensive which was designed to break the stalemate on the Western Front. In their latest quarters behind the front at Divion, the 22nd Battalion welcomed reinforcements of officers and other ranks. New weaponry also arrived, including the latest Short Magazine Lee Enfield (SMLE) rifles. Steel helmets replaced the soft caps they had worn at Festubert and Loos, 'in spite of the unfavourable report on them by a senior officer on the ground that they were unbecoming.'[24] The battalion was not scheduled to take part in the initial actions of the 'push' on the Somme; instead, it would hold the line further north and engage the enemy there. On 1 July 1916 the Territorials from Bermondsey were back in familiar territory, taking turns with the Nelson Battalion of the Royal Naval Division in manning the trenches in the Lens sector near Liévin. Trench raids here and elsewhere by other British battalions kept the Germans busy, absorbed their resources and prevented them from moving their forces south to support the greater struggle taking place on the Somme. After weeks of ferocious assault on the German defensive positions, however, the Battle of the Somme had not achieved the anticipated breakthrough. Following another period of preparatory training, the 47th Division was informed that it would soon be committed to the fray. Lieutenant Baswitz had since been promoted to Temporary Captain and given command of 22nd Battalion's B Company.

On 1 August he and his men began their journey south to the latest and most fearsome killing fields of the war, part of one of the 'many fresh divisions ... brought up for the occasion'.[25] They marched at night, to avoid the worst of the hot summer weather.

The town of Albert was the marshalling yard for the British war effort on the Somme. It was here that newly arrived units found their billets, continued their organizational and logistical preparations, trained for up to nine hours a day and improved their fitness. The 22nd Battalion occupied a series of billets in villages situated just north of the main road from Albert to Amiens. They spent the whole of August near St Riquier, the BEF's Fourth Army training area. They worked in their sections and companies, then combined to operate as a battalion, before finally engaging in large-scale brigade and divisional assault practice. Whilst the newcomers trained, just a few miles away to the north-east of Albert other units maintained the momentum of the attack. Training involved practice attacks, exercises informed by the experience of those previously engaged in the fighting and by the latest battlefield obstacles to be encountered. Familiarization with the type of terrain each unit would encounter in their designated part of the battlefield was a key part of their induction. On 15 August the whole battalion practised advancing through a wood. On the next day a group of eighteen officers also undertook a night-time mock advance through the Forêt de Crécy. Here the Londoners were following in the footsteps of King Edward III and the Black Prince, who in 1346 led an expeditionary force of English knights and Welsh longbowmen to their first major victory against the French in the Hundred Years War.

In early September the whole division rehearsed tactics on a flagged course made to resemble the real ground over which they would be fighting. A group of five battalion officers then reconnoitred a section of the front line held at the time by troops from the 1st Division. Looking out across no man's land from trenches which they and their men would soon occupy, they observed their forthcoming objective and reflected upon their recent training. The Germans had established a formidable network of defensive positions in what had once been an area of unfenced green fields interspersed with areas of leafy woodland. The woods in this part of the Somme, namely Bazentin-le-Petit Wood, Delville Wood and High Wood (see Map 4), collectively formed a 'deadly triangle' which had to be cleared of enemy forces if the advance was to continue.[26] By the second week of September, and after several days of additional training and the necessary inoculations against paratyphoid fever (an endemic feature of trench warfare), the troops of the 22nd Battalion and their divisional comrades were ready to play the part assigned to them by General Henry Rawlinson, the commander of IV Corps. The Londoners were ordered to drive the enemy out of one of the heavily defended woods, assisted, so some of the senior commanders were informed confidentially, by a new secret weapon.

Battalion headquarters moved into Albert on 10 September. Captain Baswitz and B Company were in billets and bivouacs nearby. Before the war, this relatively small and straggling provincial town contained the customary residential areas, small businesses, a few factories and a recently built church. The latter was constructed as a shrine to the Virgin of Albert (see plate 9) which, the town's elders had once hoped, might one day come to rival Lourdes as a site of pilgrimage and miracle cures. On the summit of the church tower, secured by an iron rod, stood a gilded statue of the Madonna and child. Situated just north of the River Somme, on the main road running from Bapaume in the east to Amiens in the west – the great highway of war for German and British forces alike throughout the remaining years of the conflict – Albert had already been subjected to numerous enemy bombardments. Much of the town lay in ruins. The statue of the Virgin remained intact, but in 1916 it hung, with the precious child still in his mother's arms, at a precarious angle, face down towards the cobbled streets below. To the west of the town, the straight, tree-lined road from Amiens was a conveyor belt carrying men and the materiel of war. Troops awaiting orders to move up to the front witnessed an unending cavalcade of lorries and waggons transporting provisions and ammunition. Heavy guns lined the roads, before they too moved slowly eastwards and passed the detritus of war moving in the opposite direction.

The men of the 47th Division did not have to wait long in the holding pen. They were ordered forward on 11 September. The division's twelve battalions 'went in fit and strong, full of confidence to take their part in the great British offensive.'[27] Two main roads led from the centre of Albert to the front line: north to Bapaume (see plate 10) and east to Peronne.

The triangle of land between these three strategic settlements held the killing fields of the Somme for the British and Dominion forces in the summer of 1916. Minor roads and tracks led off the main highways. The poet John Masefield noted a year later that 'those roads then were indeed paths of glory leading to the grave.'[28] They led to villages, farms, small copses and large woods, or what remained of them, whose given names were to be imprinted on the minds of men and their communities for generations to come. The once pretty and tranquil villages of Pozières, Fricourt, Bazentin, Contalmaison and Mametz had been swallowed up and broken by the great attack, and their fields were now the informal graveyards of countless British and German soldiers. Where buildings had once stood were now 'the offices and stores of war: HQ dugouts, telephonists, dumps of bombs, machine gun ammunition, barbed wire, jars, tins, cases.'[29] Transport vehicles covered the gently rolling hillsides, squadrons of cavalry awaited their call to action, and the heavy field guns stood in Caterpillar Valley and the despoiled fields near Flat Iron Copse and the Bazentins. For weeks, gun batteries had roared both day and night. Lines of long-barrelled naval guns and howitzers of all calibres, some under camouflage netting to avoid detection by enemy aircraft, had transformed the once verdant landscape into a frightful sea of craters and torn trees. Leaving the Peronne Road, the 47th Division made its way forward through the area so recently contested and devastated. Slowly, and often in single file, the men of each brigade began to move along the communications trenches to take up their allocated marks. Two battalions of the 142nd Brigade, the 21st and 24th Londons, proceeded directly to the new front line. The 22nd and 23rd Battalions took up support positions in Mametz Wood. On the horizon several miles away, 'like a ghost in the distance',[30] stood High Wood, 'the rottenest place on the Somme'.[31]

The French inhabitants of the area knew this place as Bois de Fourcaux, its name derived from the preponderance of sweet chestnut trees which had traditionally provided wood for the making of pitchforks. By 1916 a cartographic misspelling had designated it 'Bois de Foureaux', or 'Raven Wood'.[32] British trench maps, those strange depictions of a land transformed by the impact of war, labelled it simply High Wood, in recognition of its elevated position in a relatively flat landscape. Situated on a ridge some 100ft high and covering some 75 acres, the diamond-shaped wood overlooked the surrounding land for some way around. Looking back to the south and east across the battlefield, one could see similar obstacles which had been taken, albeit at great cost, during the recent British advance: Mametz Wood, Delville Wood, Trones Wood and the Bazentin Woods. To the west, along the D107 road which High Wood fronted, lay the villages of Martinpuich, Pozières and Courcelette; to the east lay Longueval, Guillemont and Ginchy; to the north were Flers and Bapaume. Some of these settlements had been captured, but in others the enemy remained, stubbornly defiant. The town of Bapaume had been Haig's objective for the first day of the Somme offensive, but ten weeks later his forces were only halfway there and had stalled once more in the face of the most impressive and determined enemy resistance.

As Captain Baswitz and his men looked out from their trenches they saw a scene of utter devastation. The British troops, veterans of the bleak environs of Loos, had never seen anything like the 'mass of corruption' that was now High Wood.[33] Once thickly wooded, leafy and green, the area had been reduced to charred tree stumps by previous attempts to blast its defenders into submission and move the line forward. The decapitated trees were surrounded by bodies: many were dead, others were most definitely alive. The bloated battlefield corpses, and the bones and dismembered lumps of flesh which were scattered everywhere, attracted swarms of flies and rats. In this hellish charnel house, poisoned by the fumes of high explosives and the distinctive stench of death, the living enemy waited beneath the surface in their concrete and iron girder-reinforced positions for any further attempt by the British to take the wood. Hundreds of miles of barbed wire, numerous craters and a northward slope made any advance through it even more difficult. Direct attacks would result in numerous casualties. Previous attempts to take the woods had demonstrated how incredibly difficult the task was. Delville Wood, for example, had been captured on 28 July but was not finally cleared of defenders until 25 August. For the troops involved, the experience had been traumatic. A Tommy serving in a Regular battalion at both Mametz Wood and Delville Wood stated, 'Murder is not the word for it. These are places where hundreds of men have said their prayers who have never said them before.'[34]An alternative strategy might have been to move beyond the wood, leaving its isolated defenders to be mopped up later. Any attempt to outflank this particular group of Germans, however, would be countered by enemy artillery 'handing out heavy stuff' from their higher positions on Flers Ridge to the north.[35] The hillside to the right of High Wood was already a torn brown slope covered with English, Scottish and Indian dead. Advanced trenches dug by pioneers at night in the featureless wilderness surrounding the wood were simply destroyed by enemy shelling during the day.

The attack about to take place at High Wood in September 1916 should not have been necessary. On 1 July the wood had been behind the German second line of defensive trenches. By 14 July, when the Battle of Albert gave way to the Battle of Bazentin Ridge, it was on the front line. So intense was the attack that day upon their positions by British artillery and infantry divisions that at one point the Germans decided to abandon High Wood. Instead of pushing infantry forward into High Wood to secure it, however, the Commander of XV Corps, Lieutenant General Henry Horne, decided to deploy the 7th Dragoon Guards and 20th (Indian Army) Deccan Horse. The time had come for the cavalry to exploit the long-anticipated breakthrough. Moving up from near Mametz Wood, the mounted troops had cantered through Flat Iron Valley – then ironically known as 'Happy Valley' but subsequently renamed 'Death Valley' – and passed Crucifix Corner, before charging up the slopes to the east of the newly-vacated wood. Armed with lances and small arms, they were met by a volley of machine gun fire and suffered serious casualties. German infantry, meanwhile, had moved back into High Wood. Horne's fateful decision not to occupy the empty wood led to another two months of costly attacks. Ten British divisions rotated in and out of the line in front of High Wood, sacrifices to Haig's belief in steady offensive pressure. Here and elsewhere on the Somme, the offensive had developed into a series of scattered battles in which great armies struggled to take small objectives. Captain Basil Liddell Hart, a military historian who served on the Somme in July 1916, observed huge numbers of men 'nibbling away' for occasional and limited gains and 'petty prizes'.[36] Breakthrough remained the stated and hoped-for objective, but attrition – the destruction of enemy personnel and resources at a faster rate than he could replace them – characterized the 'grim pattern' of fighting on the ground.[37] Set-piece encounters, like the Battle of Flers-Courcelette in September 1916, were intended to be both attritional *and* achieve potential breakthroughs.

After nearly two years of war, Britain and her allies recognized the need for concerted action. The first six months of 1916 had been punctuated by a series of defeats and disasters. The evacuation of the final contingents of troops from Cape Helles on 9 January finally signalled the end of the disastrous Dardanelles campaign against the Ottoman Empire. On 21 February the German Fifth Army launched a massive attack on the French fortress city of Verdun. In April thousands of British and Dominion troops surrendered to the Turks at Kut in Mesopotamia. Closer to home, the Easter Rising in Dublin shook the very foundations of Great Britain as a united political entity. The Battle of Jutland at the end of May proved inconclusive and dented the pride and much-vaunted reputation of the Royal Navy. When Lord Kitchener was lost at sea in the sinking of HMS *Hampshire* off the coast of Orkney less than a week later on 5 June, the nation went into mourning. Amidst these cataclysmic events, the stalemate in the trenches in Flanders continued. The grand plan for September 1916 involved yet another assault on the Isonzo by the Italians, attacks in Transylvania by combined Russian and Romanian forces and a new offensive in Salonika to support the Serbs. The French Army would continue to defend Verdun and bleed the Germany Army dry. For the British, aware of the international imperative to show their continued commitment and resolve, the agreed priority remained a breakthrough on the Somme. Rawlinson and his Fourth Army commanders were ordered, once again, to capture Bapaume, and then to push on to Arras some 14 miles to the north. Major General Barter's 47th Division was responsible for one small but crucial part in the greater scheme: the taking of High Wood. The success of ambitious strategic aims ultimately depended upon the ability of several thousand London Territorials to turn the key which would open the German defences in Northern France. Captain Baswitz and the 22nd London Battalion stood ready to play their part in this next stage of the big push forward.

The British attack was scheduled for 0620 hours on 15 September. Preparation had been particularly thorough. The RFC had maintained air superiority, enabling almost constant observation from aircraft and balloons of Germany infantry movements and defensive preparations. Sappers from the Royal Engineers had built eight miles of tramlines to bring up the necessary supplies and equipment. The three-day artillery bombardment, which commenced on 12 September and involved 1,500 guns on a 5-mile front, was even greater than that which had preceded the first day of the Battle of the Somme on 1 July. The day before the guns began to pound the German defences, the men of the 47th Division had moved forward along the communication trenches, in silence and in a darkness punctuated occasionally by star shells bursting 'as white and bright as burning magnesium wire'.[38] They took up their positions in the centre of the 7-mile British line (see Map 5), held by twelve British divisions, which stretched from the Windmill at Pozières away to their left to Leuze Wood to their right. To either side of them were men from every tribe, occupation and social grouping that the country had to offer to the god of war: 'Geordies' and 'Cockneys', civil servants and window cleaners, aristocratic officers and their servants. In that same line were representatives by proxy of the country's leading political parties: Raymond Asquith, son of the Liberal Prime Minister, and Harold Macmillan, a future Conservative Prime Minister, were fellow officers in the 3rd Battalion, Grenadier Guards; Captain David Henderson (19th Londons) was the son of the leader of the Labour Party. In their central position in the British line the Londoners were flanked by an array of troops from Britain and its Dominions. There were men from five Scottish and twenty English county battalions. A division of Guards – Grenadiers, Coldstreams, Scots, Irish and Welsh – also stood in the line. Riflemen from the King's Royal Rifle Royal Corps and the Royal Fusiliers were there, too, as was the 56th (First London) Division, the 47th (Second London) Division's sister unit. 'Canucks' and 'Enzeds', troops from the Dominions of Canada and New Zealand respectively, were also in their allocated positions. Facing them were four Bavarian divisions and a Reserve division from the German First Army manning three defensive lines: Switch Trench, Flers Trench and Gird Trench. The fortified lines were separated by some 500 yards of ground which afforded little cover to an attacking force.

For the thousands of men ready to play their assigned roles, the greater strategic plan was obscured by the realities on the ground and their own individual thoughts and fears. Hundreds of men from the 22nd Londons spent much of 11 and 12 September digging assembly trenches. Under constant shell fire, they suffered their first eight casualties before the planned infantry attack even began.[39] Together with the rest of the 142nd Brigade, Captain Baswitz and his men had their first experience of their new front line on 14 September. Whilst they may have found some comfort in hearing the 'sighing and droning' of thousands of shells passing over them towards the enemy,[40] they quickly found that their own positions were not safe either. Throughout the night 'there was the ceaseless mutter of guns and the flickering in the sky ... flares shed their green radiance over the torn fields.'[41]

As a chill drizzle fell upon the troops waiting for zero hour the following morning, many, including Captain Baswitz, must surely have reflected upon their long journey to this place and what the next day would bring. It was over two years since Mr Baswitz the teacher had enlisted and nearly eighteen months since the young officer had begun his active service in France and Flanders. He had survived the Battles of Festubert and Loos and returned relatively unscathed from several dangerous bombing raids across no man's land. He had been promoted twice, mentioned in dispatches and awarded a Military Cross. Unlike many of the young officers who had to come to terms with the prospect of killing for the first time, Captain Baswitz had already experienced close-quarter combat and the mental imperative and physical challenge of 'kill or be killed'. As a company commander, he also had a responsibility to the men in his charge, many of whom he knew well. The 47th Division still contained within its ranks many of the original Territorials who had enlisted as part-timers before the war. New drafts of men had replaced the casualties of 1915 and early 1916, but they were quickly absorbed, and the 47th was still very much a London division in character and spirit. Captain Baswitz and his men were well trained, experienced and determined, but so too were the German divisions facing them. As one member of the division noted, the enemy had had plenty of time to prepare, and 'was ready for us'.[42]

At dawn on the morning of Friday, 15 September the confidence of the British troops was boosted by the issue of a warming tot of rum and the arrival of the much-anticipated secret weapon. The British guns continued to pound the enemy positions on the skyline beyond High Wood, but the proximity of the trenches in the wood itself meant that, unlike the position on either side of the wood, there would be no creeping barrage to clear the way for the advancing formations. Instead, that crucial task was to be assumed by the new landships – armoured tanks – which had crawled laboriously and noisily from near Mametz Wood to their starting lines during the night. At 0620 hours as planned, accompanied by a 'wide circle of flame and a great crash of sound' created by the heavy artillery,[43] the British line erupted, with shouts and yells of encouragement, into a headlong assault on the German positions. In the centre, the 140th and 141st Brigades spearheaded the 47th Division's advance into High Wood. The first wave of London Territorials included the 17th (Poplar and Stepney Rifles), 18th (London Irish) and 15th (Civil Service Rifles) Battalions. The response from the Germans was immediate and murderous, and the attackers were forced to fight for every foot of land. Machine gun fire across the narrow strip of land dividing attackers and defenders smashed into the men of the Civil Service Rifles, making casualties of most of their officers and NCOs. Survivors were driven back to starting lines by now occupied by the second wave of men and under heavy bombardment by German artillery. The 8th (Post Office Rifles) Battalion suffered a similar fate. At 0700 hours the second wave – 19th (St Pancras) and 20th (Blackheath and Woolwich) Battalions, the latter containing many who had served in the Goldsmiths' College Cadet Corps before the war – began their assault. The savage, often hand-to-hand fighting raged for five hours; to the men 'it seemed like five centuries.' The noise was incredible: 'machine guns rattled so loud they even drowned out the noise of the artillery.' The smell of death 'hit you between the eyes.' Crouching, then crawling, they advanced inches at a time. They witnessed 'good lads dropping on every hand' and, despite the noise, still heard the cries of the stretcher bearers.[44]

Captain Baswitz and the men of the 142nd Brigade, meanwhile, had waited in reserve near Mametz Wood. At dawn they, too, had tightened their equipment, gripped their rifles and received their last-minute orders. At zero hour the 142nd Brigade had moved forward along Flat Iron Valley to a position between the Bazentins known as Mill Street, a prominent landmark in full view of enemy gunners, and from there used communication trenches to provide material support to the other divisional brigades attacking High Wood some 600 yards ahead. The 21st, 23rd and 24th Londons were held back at first, ready to fill the gaps in the assaulting force and exploit any breakthrough. Captain Baswitz and the 22nd Londons spent virtually the whole day carrying up ammunition for the men of the 140th Brigade fighting in the eastern section of the wood.

The much-anticipated support from the four tanks which entered the wood proved to be of little direct value. Moving at only two miles per hour, the new bullet-proof machines had arrived late to their start positions for the attack and all were quickly put out of action. The tank advancing in front of the 19th Londons was an early casualty, receiving a direct hit from an enemy shell as the attack began. The tank in front of the 20th Londons suffered mechanical failure but continued firing its 6-pounder gun until the six-man crew was forced to abandon the vehicle and set fire to it. The breakthrough finally came when the attackers deployed another weapon which had been developed in response to the demands of trench warfare. 'God bless the guns!' shouted one of the sergeants,[45] as the 140th Brigade's Trench Mortar Battery unleashed a hurricane bombardment from their 3-inch Stokes Mortars at 1140 hours. This massive strike silenced some of the machine guns and forced many of the defending troops – mainly men of the 23rd Bavarian Infantry Regiment – out from cover. Some started to surrender, their nerves wrecked by the shellfire. An officer shouted 'Bayonets, lads!', and the Londoners attacked in earnest.[46] By 1300 hours the 140th Brigade had bombed their way forward, overrun the German strongholds and cleared their part of the wood. Following closely on their heels were the 142nd Brigade. Captain Baswitz and his men tackled the remaining by-passed enemy positions and consolidated the ground taken by their fellow Londoners.

A similar story was unfolding in other parts of the wood. There, too, the fighting was frenzied. A corporal in the Civil Service Rifles recalled:

I saw men in their madness bayonet each other without mercy, without thought ... I saw men torn to fragments by the near explosion of bombs, and – worse than any sight – I heard the agonised shrieks of men in mortal pain who were giving up their souls to their maker ... the cries of those poor, tortured and torn men I can never forget. They are with me always.[47]

British forces had finally taken High Wood, and it was the London Territorials of the 47th Division who had claimed the prize. Their part in the Battle of Flers-Courcelette was far from over, however. The capture of High Wood was simply the precursor to the planned seizure of the Starfish Line some 700 yards further on. In the brilliant autumn sunshine, and under intense fire from enemy artillery, other 47th Division battalions – the 6th Londons and 7th Londons – had reached that objective just two hours after the attack had begun and some four hours before High Wood had been finally cleared. Leutnant Hermann Kohl of the 17th Bavarian Infantry Regiment summed up some of the reasons why the British attack towards the Switch line was so successful, stating that 'a sea of iron crashed down' on the German positions during 'an unparalleled hurricane of fire' from the 'crushing machine' of the Royal Artillery. Tanks also made an impact (see plate 11): these 'unearthly monsters' were 'spewing death' in the 'seething cauldron of no man's land'.[48] Major General Ernest Swinton had intended that his new invention be 'capable of destroying machine guns, of crossing country and trenches, of breaking through entanglements, and of climbing earthworks', thus countering the deadly obstacles that had so effectively frustrated infantry units when attacking.[49] Tanks had failed conspicuously in High Wood, but in more open (albeit pockmarked) territory some had managed to provide vital support to advancing troops. The psychological impact of the new machines was also profound. Men on both sides 'gazed in dumb and awe-stricken amazement' at the sight and sound of tanks looming suddenly out of the mist, rumbling mightily and belching steam and smoke.[50] Ormond Burton of the New Zealand Division later recalled how effective tanks could be:

> Then at last came two caterpillars that had crawled over the ridge and lumbered slowly down the slope across a wilderness of shell-holes. A rain of bullets glanced harmlessly from their iron sides. They lurched up against the rusty masses of wire, their blunt snouts rising high and then crashing down from the height, smashed and flattened the obstacle and rolled on toward the enemy line. The Germans, helpless before these new dragons of war, ceased firing in terror. Some put their hands up; some ran.[51]

Attempts to reach the German second-line Flers Trench on 15 September, however, were repulsed. Later reinforcements helped to dig a new, but far from consolidated, front line at a position known as the Cough Drop. By nightfall the Londoners had made contact with the leading Enzeds to the right of them and prepared to make further assaults the following morning.

Captain Baswitz had survived the first day of this battle within a battle. He had experienced the horrors of High Wood, albeit in a supporting role initially, and witnessed the mixed fortunes of the British tanks. In the early hours of 16 September he stood ready to take a leading role in the next stage of the assault. At 0730 hours Captain Baswitz and B Company set out to support three companies of the 23rd Londons. Joining them at 0930 hours, the composite group attacked five minutes later. Their objective was to clear the trenches around the new advanced positions and to link the lines held by the 47th and 50th Divisions. The 22nd Battalion Unit War Diary entry recorded what happened next:

> They advanced in artillery formation until clear of High Wood when they came under fire. Casualties caused a break in the line but they pushed forward over the Starfish Line and German Strong Point M34 which at that time was not held. The objective appears to have been gained and passed and it is not known how far the attack punctuated.

Subsequent reports indicated that the attacking force had indeed passed the Cough Drop and had headed straight for the heavily defended Flers Line. An aircraft of the RFC 'reported that some of our men were in the Flers Line, even as far as Eaucourt L'Abbaye.'[52] Any territorial gains were short-lived, however, and what was left of B Company – just twenty-eight men – eventually returned to their lines. Captain Albert Baswitz was not among them.[53]

The Somme offensive of 1916 did not end with the capture of High Wood in the Battle of Flers-Courcelette. The British continued to advance as they had done previously, but each massive strike was quickly followed by a period of consolidation of the few miles of territory taken, and by determined German counter-attacks. There was no breakthrough in the months which followed, despite further large-scale assaults at Morval, Thiepval, Le Transloy and Ancre. On 18 November 1916, after 141 days of brutal fighting, the great offensive on the Somme officially came to an end. The capture of Bapaume – the original objective of the first day of the Battle of the Somme – had not been achieved. The exhausted British and German forces, increasingly hampered by the weather and inadequate supply lines, prepared to spend a third winter in their respective trenches.

The Battle of the Somme resulted in the recovery of territory which had been under German occupation since the early months of the war. It also relieved some of the pressure on the French defenders of Verdun. These achievements came, however, at a huge cost. Some three and a half million men on both sides had been thrown into the maelstrom, and a million of them had become casualties. The initial British attack on the Somme was 'probably the greatest single catastrophe of the whole war.'[54] The New Army 'pals battalions' and their Territorial counterparts contained 'the eager, devoted, physical and spiritual elite of the British nation'.[55] The huge number of casualties amongst their ranks has ensured that 1 July 1916 is remembered to this day as the defining moment of the offensive, and as a brutal testament to the futility of war. The attack on High Wood has similarly been represented as further evidence of 'hapless Tommies' sent to their inevitable deaths by incompetent and uncaring British generals. On the 15 September, however, several British divisions did in fact achieve their assigned objectives. The key villages of Courcelette, Martinpuich and Flers were captured. The once-formidable obstacle of High Wood was cleared of German defenders. Unlike 1 July, the advance on 15 September could be measured in thousands, not hundreds, of yards. Some German battalions suffered a casualty rate of fifty per cent; the impact on the morale of the survivors was such that the once-impregnable German defensive line almost collapsed in places. Churchill's 'land battleships' may 'have been let off prematurely and on a petty scale',[56] and failed to perform satisfactorily in poorly-chosen terrain, but eighteen of the new tanks had contributed to the battle and given valuable support to the advancing infantry.[57] Their ability to cross no man's land, eliminate machine gun nests and terrify the enemy was a harbinger of a more mobile form of warfare on the Western Front.

There is no denying the human cost to the divisions engaged in and around High Wood in September 1916. There were 29,376 reported British casualties on 15 September alone. On that day, the 47th Division lost over 4,000 men. Over fifty commissioned officers were killed in action or subsequently died of wounds, the great majority of them serving in the 140th and 141st Brigades, which had borne the brunt of that day's fighting.[58] Deployed in reserve initially, but soon called into front line action, the casualty figures for the 22nd Battalion – serving as part of the 142nd Brigade – clearly illustrate the consequences of throwing men time and again against well-defended positions: two of the battalion's officers were killed in action, three were wounded and one was missing; the corresponding figures for other ranks were 13, 144 and 58.[59] Despite taking High Wood, however, the 47th Division was criticized by the British High Command for 'lack of push' and wastage of men. Major General Charles Barter, Divisional Commander, was controversially removed from his post despite what he and many others regarded as the Division's greatest achievement, and on 19 September the 47th Division was replaced in the line by the 1st Division. The men who had entered the line fit and strong, full of confidence and ready to take their part in the great British offensive, 'came out, a few days later, a handful of men, muddy and tired out'.[60] For many others, the war was over. The body of Captain Albert Baswitz was discovered amongst the death and destruction of the Switch Line and carried back along the broken ground and supply lines to the makeshift cemeteries near Bazentin Ridge.

Chapter 4

Anzacs

When you think how your country is calling,
And getting, whenever she calls;
When you read who are fighting and falling,
The best from your hamlets and halls.
When you hark to the shock and the thunder
Where the corpses old Europe bestrew,
It makes you feel glad to live under
The Flag that your forefathers flew!

From 'Dryblower' (Edwin Murphy),
It's Good to Be British Today (1914).[1]

Teacher-soldiers from the Dominions also fought and died on the killing fields of the Western Front in 1916. Some were men who had seen action before, fighting for their King and Empire in the disastrous campaign against the Turks in the Dardanelles. Others were later enlistments who had yet to experience the horrors of modern warfare. Amongst the thousands of young Australians who answered the call of the 'Old Lion' (see plate 12) were Sydney Forbes and Adolph Knäble. The two men had much in common. Both were born in 1894 in Melbourne, Victoria, before moving with their families to Western Australia (WA). Like Albert Baswitz in London, they chose teaching as a career. Both began as Monitors employed by the WA Education Department in 1908, before undertaking further training at the Teachers College in the state capital Perth. There they developed their knowledge and craft, and played together in the college football team, before returning to the classroom as qualified teachers. War service interrupted their careers. Both 'young lions' had seen previous part-time military service, volunteered to fight for their King and Country, enlisted as privates and trained at Blackboy

Hill. On 19 July 1916 Sydney and Adolph both took up positions in the front line trenches and experienced the full force of the German military machine on the Western Front.

Sydney Trevorrow Forbes was born in the Hawthorn suburb of Melbourne on 1 April 1894. His parents, James and Mary (née Flett), had migrated ten years earlier from the fishing village of Findochty on the shores of the Moray Firth in Scotland. By 1898 they were living in the Perth suburb of Subiaco and Mr Forbes, a carpenter by trade, had found employment with the Public Works Department. After the death of his father in 1909, Sydney lived with his mother and siblings Mollie, Pearlie, George, Alick (Alexander) and Jim in Windsor Street in nearby Claremont. By the turn of the century Claremont counted some 800 households and boasted river approaches, new roads, recreational reserves, several churches, a college, banking facilities, a library, a chemist and a resident doctor.[2] It was a new district in a new city in a relatively new British colony. After earlier exploration of the west coast of Australia by Dutch and French naval expeditions, the area around the Swan River had been proclaimed a British colony by Captain James Stirling in 1829. Originally inhabited by the indigenous Noongar people, the territory presented a harsh environment to the first free settlers from Britain. By 1850 the non-indigenous populations of Perth and WA were still small, at just over 1,000 and 5,000 respectively.[3] Designation as a penal colony added 10,000 convicts to those figures over the next two decades. As demand for food rose, an increasing amount of land was devoted to dairy and poultry farms and to market gardening. In 1856 Queen Victoria proclaimed Perth's status as a city, although to many, even thirty years later, it 'appeared little better than a thriving village'.[4] The development of a railway line in 1881 from the port of Fremantle, where the Swan River meets the Indian Ocean, opened up more land for development. The discovery of gold deposits in 1885 had a huge impact. The exploitation of the Murchison, Coolgardie and Kalgoorlie goldfields attracted a new wave of migrants from overseas and the other Australian states. Perth benefited enormously from the mining boom: electricity generation commenced in 1893; six years later, a public tram system operated; the Perth Mint opened its doors to prospectors and investors alike. In 1900 alone, miners collectively exchanged 1,400,000 fine ounces of gold for £6,000,000 sterling. The city's population more than trebled in the decade before 1901. The same happened in the next ten years, and by 1911 Perth counted nearly 90,000 inhabitants. Initially, there were few amenities for residents living in the new sub-divisions, but increasing involvement by the State Government led to improvements, in water supply especially. Gold transformed the city and the state: 'From being a slow, backward, and practically unknown community in 1891, Western Australia in 1900 was known the world over as a country of immense wealth, of progressive ideas, and of almost boundless possibilities.'[5]

Little is known about Sydney's early life and schooling, but we do know that he attended Perth Boys' School (PBS), an institution which grew out of the original Colonial School for boys and girls established in 1830. Officially opening in September 1847, PBS enrolled 44 boys.[6] In this pioneering phase of the development of schooling in Western Australia, PBS provided free, non-denominational education to boys from all social classes: 'No one of any rank or persuasion is excluded, the object being to bring all the young public up together.'[7] The WA Board of Education had high hopes for the school. PBS was to be a 'model school' – later Normal School – which would exemplify good practice in schooling and encourage developments in education beyond the capital city. By 1854 there were six additional Government Schools for boys, in Fremantle, Guildford, Bunbury, York, Champion Bay and Pinjarra. Unlike its counterpart in London, the Board at that time wanted state-funded schooling to go beyond the provision of the 'Three Rs'. Ambitious plans for post-elementary education for all classes were scuppered, however, when Captain Arthur Kennedy, the Governor of the Colony, declared the proposals to be 'of a character far too grand for the present wants of the colony, and beyond what the public are called upon to provide'.[8] Henceforth, wealthier parents sent their children to the growing number of private schools which sprang up in Perth, whilst Government Schools catered for the rest. PBS moved to new buildings in St George's Terrace in 1854, but by the early 1890s, though still regarded by many as the principal boys' school in the colony, it was struggling to compete with the others. PBS, in fact, became little more than an elementary school; the number of enrolments had increased but were nevertheless fewer than might have been expected at a time of such rapid population growth.

In April 1896, a new headmaster was appointed. William Rooney, formerly of Crown Street School in Sydney but originally from Fremantle, was 'a young man, full of enthusiasm and with a high sense of the dignity of his profession'.[9] He was the son of a School Inspector, had trained to be a teacher at the New South Wales Training College and had studied for his degree at the University of Sydney. His arrival at PBS coincided with the erection of new school buildings in James Street and a new regime in the Education Department of WA, which intended to improve both the quantity and quality of teachers employed in state schools. PBS had previously met its staffing requirements by training monitors and pupil teachers. Mr Rooney inherited teachers who were 'underpaid, poorly dressed, careless of their responsibility and unconscious of the dignity of their profession'.[10] Many of Rooney's first appointments were deliberately made from among men of a different kind: teachers with a similar background to his own, possessing training college certificates and often university degrees, and recruited via his contacts in New South Wales in particular. PBS thrived under Rooney. Standards improved and numbers increased, due in part to boys staying longer at the school in order to take the Higher Public Examination offered by the University of Adelaide. By the time Sydney Forbes joined PBS, Mr Rooney had become a key figure in the development of Western Australia's education system, first as a School Inspector, and then as the Principal of WA's first teacher training institution.

Sydney Forbes attended the Normal School which was established within the grounds of PBS in January 1907. Like Albert Baswitz in London, he decided to become a teacher at a time when the demand for teachers was booming. Training at the state's expense gave boys and girls the opportunity to access secondary education followed by secure employment. Thomas Sten, another migrant from Melbourne and a fellow pupil at the Normal School, later stated that 'one of the best ways of getting an education was to become a teacher'.[11] Funded by the WA Education Department, Sydney entered the Normal School in 1908. He took the two-year course, followed by a year's teaching practice as a Monitor at West Leederville in Perth. A further two years at Claremont Teachers College (CTC) gave him the qualifications necessary for employment in state schools.

CTC was modelled on training institutions operating in the mother country. The founding Principal, Cecil Andrews, was an Oxford graduate and former teacher at St John's Training College in Battersea which, the *Western Mail* informed its readers in December 1900, 'is one of the best of the Training Colleges in England'. CTC began admitting trainees in January 1902. A year later, Cecil Andrews became Director of Education for WA and was succeeded by William Rooney as Principal of CTC, a post the latter held until 1927. Rooney was remembered as a 'very strong academic disciplinarian' who adopted a patriarchal style and suffered no nonsense from the young men and women who joined his college.[12] Sydney entered CTC in 1912 and took the full two-year course. Shorter courses catered for those who wanted to teach in country areas, including the single-teacher 'bush schools' which were a particular feature of WA. Preparing for a post in the larger schools in metropolitan Perth, where pupil numbers could exceed 400, Sydney's first year at CTC consisted mainly of a general education, with a particular emphasis on Mathematics, History and Geography. In Year 2 he attended lessons on Educational Studies, Psychology and Scripture taught by Principal Rooney himself. Periods of teaching practice at Claremont Practising School and PBS were reinforced by the dreaded 'Crit': teaching a lesson to a class of children on the stage of the College Hall in front of the whole student body and staff. The syllabus at CTC was in many ways more akin to that of London's Goldsmiths' College than that provided by the LDTC, where Albert Baswitz had been able to study concurrently for a degree at the University of London. Nevertheless, from 1913 CTC students were given the opportunity to attend lectures at the new West Australian University, 'with a view to extending this so that trainees might eventually be able to take degrees there'.[13] Sydney Forbes duly enrolled on several courses.

Academic study and teaching practice were only part of the wider educational and social facilities offered at CTC. The handsome building on Goldsworthy Road in Claremont, with its wonderful views across the Swan River, was only a few minutes' walk from Sydney's home. Free board and lodging in separate male and female residential dormitories were provided for all, not simply for 'country students' like Tom Sten. Sydney, however, appears to have escaped this restrictive environment and lived in a lodging house off-site with five female students – referred to, somewhat disparagingly, as 'Syd Forbes' harem'.[14] Once in college, campus routines were rigidly adhered to. Communal meals were taken by all students; there was a daily afternoon tea; evening prayers were held; all were expected to take part in sporting activities on Wednesday afternoon, when 'Old Bill' Rooney would ensure that proper sporting attire was worn.[15] Whilst Sydney was clearly not the best student at CTC – one of his college reports referred to his academic work as being of a 'desultory character' and his attainments as 'but fair' – the 'energetic' Mr Forbes clearly excelled at sport. He represented CTC at both cricket (see plate 13) and (Association) football in the Perth leagues, playing alongside young men who would later travel with 'Syd', as he was known, to foreign fields in the service of their country. With two particular mates – Walter Blair and Adolph Albrecht – Sydney gained a reputation as a sprinter; the CTC trio invariably took the prizes in the 100 yard races held at the Physical Training Annual Demonstration by Perth Schools. After graduating from CTC, Sydney and the rest of the class of 1912/13 began their careers as fully qualified teachers, giving them and their families a new status and degree of security, even if their average weekly wage was less than that of a railway porter. Having financed their education and training, the WA Education Department directed teachers to schools. Sydney's first appointment was at Oxford Street State School in Leederville, where he had been teaching for less than a year when Australia found itself at war.

Created in 1901 by the federation of the six former British colonies, the Commonwealth of Australia was a self-governing Dominion of the British Empire. The mother country, however, retained responsibility for foreign policy. King George V's imperial subjects followed the unfolding diplomatic events of 1914 with both interest and growing concern. The distance in space and time from London meant that the most recent news was always a day or two late for the citizens of Perth. The *West Australian* of Wednesday, 5 August reported that 'World-shaking events are happening in the Northern Hemisphere'. The newspaper noted British Foreign Secretary Sir Edward Grey's communications to the German government concerning Belgium but was patently still unsure whether war had been declared. The following day's edition, however, under the banner headline 'The War and the Commonwealth', reported that 'the die is cast, and the British Empire is at war.' The newspaper's editorial was fully aware of the consequences:

> Australia, far distant as it is from the centre of the conflict, will inevitably be shaken by the clash of nations in the northern hemisphere … As a member of the family of Empire the Commonwealth comes automatically into the struggle, to render the fullest aid our resources will permit, or the need of the mother country demands. No shadow of doubt rests upon the loyalty of the people.[16]

News of the British declaration of war spread quickly. Perth's newspaper vendors did a roaring trade, and crowds thronged the bulletin boards in St George's Terrace. Thousands of excited citizens cheered loudly at the latest piece of news. Many bought hastily supplied rosettes in the national colours, and traders hoisted Union Jacks on the flagpoles of their premises. Within days, organizations of all kinds had pledged their loyalty. The WA Teachers' Union postponed its Annual Conference and expressed 'the confident conviction that the State schoolteachers will be among the foremost in giving practical proof of their patriotism.'[17] The Commonwealth Government's offer of 20,000 troops, to be sent 'at the earliest opportunity',[18] was gratefully accepted by the War Office in London. As the existing permanent force and militia was constitutionally prohibited from being deployed overseas, the creation of a new expeditionary force – the Australian Imperial Force (AIF) – was set in motion. Enlistment centres opened in Perth and Fremantle and were followed by others in Albany, Bunbury, Geraldton, Kalgoorlie and elsewhere. Supply soon outstripped demand. Over 4,500 men volunteered in Perth alone in the first few days of war. Stringent medical and dental examinations ensured that the first recruits to the Dominion's new citizen army were amongst the fittest in the land.

Sydney Forbes was one of the first to volunteer. On 17 August 1914 he enlisted at the Helena Vale racecourse in Perth. So, too, did his mates Adolph Albrecht and Walter Blair. Other CTC trainees and alumni joined the initial rush to enlist. A total of fifteen were amongst the initial selection of 1,400 recruits.[19] At the training camp at Blackboy Hill outside

Perth, these teachers-turned-soldiers met up with their fellow recruits: a diverse bunch of 'bushmen and clerks, clergymen and swagmen, fathers and sons, work mates and team mates, teachers and pupils'.[20] A few of the new men – particularly a group of railway workers from Kalgoorlie nicknamed the 'Shovellers' – conformed to later depictions of Australian troops as rough-and-tough 'larrikins'.[21] Others were clerks and tradesmen, city boys who had reported for duty wearing suits and straw hats and carrying shiny suitcases. Private Forbes' Attestation Paper and Medical Report give us our first real glimpse of the teacher-soldier. He was twenty years of age, just over 5 feet 9 inches tall, weighed 145lbs and had a chest measurement of 34 inches. He had brown hair and a fair complexion, with eyes officially recorded as 'yellow'.[22] Like the great majority of the young men of his generation, he had previous military experience as a Senior Cadet and member of the Citizen Force. On 6 October he was appointed to the 11th Battalion, the first infantry unit to be raised in WA. Given the Service Number 205, he thus became one of the first men from WA who would later be lionized as 'Anzacs'. The composition of the battalion's eight rifle companies was geographically based, and Private Forbes joined B Company with men who came predominantly from Perth. The CTC sprinters were amongst the first at Blackboy Hill and with others marked out the new training facility and erected bell tents to accommodate later arrivals. Water had been laid on, but it was weeks before there were showers or proper latrines. The food, mostly stew, bread and jam, was monotonous. There was no canteen, but according to another early arrival, Thomas Louch of H Company, 'in the evenings itinerant pie merchants came to the precincts of the camp and did a roaring trade.' Uniforms consisted of

> slop-made dungarees, of the cheapest description, which fitted where they touched and stained everything blue. In addition, each man got a white rag hat, two thick flannel shirts, two pairs of long woollen underpants, an abdominal belt, two pairs of boots, one pair of socks, and a small cake of soap. The soap was not for use as it had to be produced at kit inspections which were held frequently. We were then made to send our civilian clothing home. Everyone was ashamed of the blue dungarees. Shortly afterwards we were issued with the standard AIF uniform of jacket, breeches, puttees and hat.[23]

Despite many of the new recruits having experienced some form of military service, the initial training focussed principally on basic soldiering: marching, drilling and musketry practice. Battle training consisted of repeatedly 'advancing in short rushes and flopping down on the whistle blast'.[24] On Sundays the men were granted leave, but as they were confined to camp, thousands of friends and family members travelled from the city to visit them at the training ground instead.

Before heading off to war, the 11th Battalion paraded before Sir Harry Barron, the State Governor. The city's streets were crowded with spectators who had come to witness 'The Memorable March of the First Contingent'; 'there was little cheering, however, the seriousness of war evidently weighing heavily in the minds of the onlookers, most of whom could claim relationship with the men in uniform, who were soon to depart.'[25] The troops then travelled by train to Fremantle. Schoolboys at Scotch College cheered their heroes and waved them on their way as the carriages passed the school grounds. Awaiting the 11th Battalion in port were two of His Majesty's Australian Transports (HMAT), *Ascanius* (A11) and *Medic* (A7). On 31 October 1914, A and B Companies, consisting of 6 officers and 236 other ranks, boarded the *Medic*. The other six companies, containing 26 officers and 762 men, climbed aboard the *Ascanius*. On the *Medic*, and in the same company, were Privates Forbes, Blair and Albrecht. The latter had surreptitiously changed his first name from Adolph to Frederick and had survived the early wave of anti-alien sentiment and restrictions on those of Germanic extraction. Lieutenant James Morgan, one of six teachers from PBS to enlist, was also in B Company. In A Company on the *Medic* were Lieutenant William Rockliff (a member of the first cohort at CTC in 1902 and also teaching at PBS in 1914), Sergeant Frank Matthews, Corporal Raymond Meredith and Privates Louis Telford and Fred Courtney. The other transport, HMAT *Ascanius*, carried other CTC graduates: Lieutenant Samuel Jackson (also PBS) in C Company, Private Andrew McDonald in D Company, and Sergeants Jack Archibald (PBS) and William Love and Privates Maurice O'Donohue and Walter Crossing in G Company.

The two transports sailed as soon as the last of the West Australians were on board. The ships dropped anchors just off the coast at Gage Roads, and for two days waited for their rendezvous with the rest of the convoy carrying the First Contingent of the AIF. Since 24 October a great armada had been gathering in the wide expanse of King George Sound near Albany on the southern coast of WA. HMATs – twenty-six of them – had transported 20,000 newly-trained troops (and twenty-five women from the Australian Army Nursing Service) from Brisbane, Sydney, Melbourne and Adelaide. A further twelve transports had carried 10,000 troops from New Zealand to join the convoy. The joint force steamed out of Albany on 1 November 1914, just three months since the declaration of war. In an impressive display of British imperial power, HMS *Minotaur*, the flagship of the Royal Navy's China Squadron, led the way. Following in close order were HMAS *Melbourne* and HMAT *Orvieto* (A3) carrying Major General William Throsby Bridges, Commanding Officer of the AIF. Other escort ships included HMS *Psyche* and *Pyramus* (both from the Royal Navy's New Zealand Squadron), HMAS *Sydney* and the Japanese battle-cruiser HIJMS *Ibuki*. On 2 November, the main convoy reached Fremantle and, taking the *Medic* and *Ascanius* into the line, began the long journey across the Indian Ocean.

The novelty of life on board ship was soon forgotten when, after only two days at sea, the fleet was hit by squally weather. Many men succumbed to seasickness, or 'singing practice' as some euphemistically called it. Spirits were raised at the end of the first week, however, when just after breakfast on 9 November the convoy experienced its first engagement. Nearing the Cocos Islands, the men of the 11th Battalion watched in excitement as

> HMAS *Sydney* [began] streaking off ahead of the convoy, to be followed by *Ibuki* which passed close by us belching black smoke and clearing her decks for action. Someone thought he could hear gun fire, and then at 11.30 a signal came to say that the *Sydney* had engaged the German cruiser *Emden* and put her out of action.[26]

News of the naval triumph spread like wildfire. On the *Ascanius*, Lieutenant Colonel Lyon Johnston and the officers of the 11th Battalion toasted the *Sydney*'s captain and crew. Miscreants in the ship's brig were released and all other ranks shouted a beer. The euphoria was tempered somewhat by the death of Private Fred Courtney the following day. Fred had been at CTC with Sydney Forbes in 1912 and had taught in the timber town of Manjimup before enlisting. He had apparently been seriously ill at Blackboy Hill but had not wanted to be left behind. His mates had somehow managed to keep him alive on a diet of alcohol, but this was no cure for severe pleurisy and pneumonia. He was one of eleven men who died of pneumonia and were buried at sea during the voyage.

Gradually the troops settled into a routine which was designed to keep them occupied and to develop their fitness and military skills. Officers and NCOs attended evening lectures which prepared them for leading map-reading and signalling activities the following day. Physical exercise and musketry practice on the crowded decks were difficult but necessary. Many men preferred to sleep with blankets on deck, rather than use the hammocks in the overflowing quarters below. Despite the heat of the tropics, water was rationed and there were no showers. In their spare time the West Australians played games: 'Housie-Housie which was permitted, or Crown and Anchor which was forbidden'. Others studied Morse Code and tried to make sense of the ship-to-ship signalling, or practised their schoolboy French, 'which we expected to need very soon.'[27] On deck, in the total blackout observed at night, they sat and talked of home and speculated on the future.

The convoy put in to Colombo on 15 November to take on coal and water. The harbour was 'choked with shipping and warships of the Allied Powers', including transports bringing garrison troops from Singapore, Calcutta and Bombay and Territorials from Britain.[28] 'Mosquito craft' approached the ships, and the fascinated troops watched as naked 'natives' dived to the bottom to seize the coins the men had thrown overboard.[29] The convoy then headed towards the Red Sea and refuelled at Aden, where, as at Colombo, the men were denied shore leave but did manage to buy figs and Turkish delight from the small trading boats which came alongside. The men from the Antipodes had now been at sea for a month. They were beginning to suffer in the awful heat and from lack of fruit juices and other fluids. The battle zone to which they were headed, however, was no longer as far away as they had first anticipated; on the night of 27/28 November Major General Bridges received a marconigram from the War Office in London informing him that Egypt, not England, would be the convoy's destination. Two days later, the transports began their journey through the Suez Canal. Arriving in Port Said on 2 December, the *Ascanius* carried six companies of West Australians slowly through. The troops stood on deck and perched in the rigging, cheering and waving to Indian, Sikh and Gurkha troops who were guarding the vital waterway against the possibility of attacks by Turkish forces, now that the Ottoman Empire had sided with Germany and its allies. Private Forbes and the men of A and B Companies on the *Medic* arrived at Alexandria on 13 December, then boarded trains to meet up with the rest of the battalion, which had disembarked from the *Ascanius* a week previously. For most of the young men from WA, this was their first real glimpse of the world beyond their own shores. During the five-hour rail journey to Cairo they marvelled and were appalled in equal measure at the extent of cultivated land in the Nile Delta and the squalid conditions in which most of the local population lived. From Cairo they marched to their camp at Mena, which was located at the foot of the Pyramids, 'solemn sentinels' which had stood for some 5,000 years.[30] The new AIF camp had been built from scratch on acres of sand but was soon occupied by nearly 20,000 members of an army which was following in the footsteps of military expeditions undertaken by Greek hoplites, Roman legionaries and French citizen soldiers. The New Zealanders established their camp at Zeitoun, the Australian Light Horse at Heliopolis.

Training began immediately. Marching out in extreme heat and across energy-sapping sand during the day was followed by bitterly cold nights in the open and heavy morning dew. Tents were provided eventually, but keeping the desert sandstorms out of them proved to be problematic. The men's first Christmas away from home brought some cheer, especially to the 50 per cent of the battalion who were given leave to visit Cairo after attending Church Parade on Christmas Day. No special arrangements had been made for the remainder; their meagre festive dinner consisted of tinned pineapple and bread and butter. Christmas puddings, supplied by readers of the *London Daily News*, arrived three weeks later, on the same day that the battalion posed for one of the iconic images of the Great War (see plate 14). On Sunday, 10 January 1915, 704 men from the 11th Battalion marched to the nearby Great Pyramid of Cheops at Giza for a group photograph. Historians and genealogists in WA have to date identified over 300 of the men sitting on the terraced structure, including Sydney Forbes, Fred Albrecht, Walter Blair and several of their colleagues from CTC.[31] Many of the Australians also visited other wonders of the ancient world. The Pyramids and Sphinx were especially popular, even if, as Mel Gibson and his mates in the film *Gallipoli* found to their cost, the innocents abroad were hounded by hawkers and would-be guides adept at relieving them of their *piastres*.[32] Some even travelled up the Nile to Memphis in a 'puffing, stodgy steamer'.[33] In the absence of any form of organized camp entertainment or social activity other than the YMCA, however, many men preferred the attractions of Cairo itself. Some repaired to the city's opulent Shepheard's Hotel (open to other ranks as well as officers at first) to bathe, dine and write letters home; others rushed to the notorious Wazzir (or 'Wozzer') district, which promised plentiful cheap alcohol and harlots signalling their availability. Widespread incidents of drunkenness, indiscipline, absence without leave and venereal disease indicate a problem which was far more serious than its occasional portrayal as 'typical larrikin behaviour'.[34]

The serious business of preparation for war continued. Reorganization of the AIF resulted in a military structure resembling that of the British Army. Sydney Forbes, by now an NCO, thus found himself in A Company (the original A and B Companies combined). The 11th Battalion, together with the 9th, 10th and 12th Battalions, now formed part of the 3rd Brigade in the 1st Division of ANZAC – the Australian and New Zealand Army Corps. Training continued, but the almost daily practice of frontal attacks – advancing in short rushes, then lying prone and fixing bayonets before finally charging headlong towards an imaginary enemy – often resulted in widespread confusion. By April 1915, however, the Anzacs were ready for the next stage of their military mission. The main force was to embark from Alexandria on 3 April, but despite all leave being stopped, a large number of Australians and New Zealanders decided to settle old scores with the 'gyppos'.[35] The so-called 'Battle of the Wazzir', which took place on Easter Sunday, 2 April, involved widespread acts of violence and destruction of property and left a stain on the reputation of an otherwise well-trained and disciplined force. Corporal Sydney Forbes and the 11th Battalion were not amongst the miscreants that day. The 3rd Brigade had been chosen, not for the last time, as the advance guard for the forthcoming campaign and had left Egypt four weeks earlier.

Hostilities between Britain and the Ottoman Empire had commenced as early as 2 August 1914, when the battleships *Sultan Osman* and *Reshadieh* under construction in British ports were requisitioned by the British government. On 3 November, just as the First Contingent was starting its passage across the Indian Ocean, the Royal Navy began a bombardment of Ottoman defences in the Dardanelles, the first stage of a planned assault on Constantinople. Hopes of a swift advance by sea were dashed by determined action by Ottoman gunners in forts overlooking the Straits linking the Mediterranean to the Black Sea. British and French naval operations resumed in February and March 1915 but only resulted in further losses of ships and men. The decision to use ground forces on the Gallipoli peninsula led to the creation of the Mediterranean Expeditionary Force (MEF) under General Sir Ian Hamilton. The island of Lemnos, some 60 miles away from invasion zone, was chosen as the springboard for what was, at the time, the largest amphibious operation ever undertaken. Travelling from Alexandria on SS *Suffolk*, the men of the 3rd Brigade AIF reached Mudros Harbour on 5 March. They noted how few naval vessels there were at that point, and the island's almost total lack of facilities. Corporal Forbes and his fellow West Australians lived on the *Suffolk* at first. Often cold and hungry, they did at least enjoy letters and food parcels from home; letters back to WA were strictly censored. On fine days they were rowed ashore for route marches across the island. After several weeks, and as more troops arrived, enormous tented cities sprang up at Mudros West (Anzacs) and Mudros East (British and French divisions). Training became more rigorous and included almost daily practising of beach landings and dashing for cover in nearby hills. Mudros Harbour, guarded by small patrol boats and nets at its narrow entrance, eventually contained some 200 ships and thousands of men. A young New Zealander, Ormond Burton, described the scene:

> Never in all her history had Great Britain brought together such an assemblage of ships. There were battleships, cruisers, destroyers and submarines of the British Navy; auxiliary cruisers, Channel picquet boats, tugs, river boats, oil tanks, water tanks, colliers,

store ships, quaint French men-of-war of peculiar construction, Russian [ships], and then row after row of transports crowded with fighting-men. Atlantic liners, battered tramps, boats of the Cunard line and the Castle Company were moored with the vessels of the Nord-Deutscher Lloyd, with Hamburg and Bremen boats, and with Turkish and Egyptian vessels, which in former times plied through the Straits and the Sea of Marmara. The *Gaby Deslys*, a tiny tug, buzzed busily around the harbour. The *Ark Royal* sent up her seaplanes and sometimes the yellow sausage-shaped captive balloon. The *Queen Elizabeth*, super dreadnought, magnificent, majestic, lay in state, surrounded by ships of lesser name.[36]

On 21 April General Hamilton issued a morale-boosting message to the troops:

Soldiers of France and the King. Before us lies an adventure unprecedented in modern war. Together with our comrades of the Fleet, we are about to force a landing on an open beach in the face of positions which have been vaunted by our enemies as impregnable. The whole world will be watching your progress. Let us prove ourselves worthy of the great feat of arms entrusted to us.[37]

Hamilton also made a personal visit to the *Suffolk* and informed the men of the 11th Battalion that very shortly they would be landing on the Gallipoli Peninsula. Tom Louch was one of many in the assembled ranks who thought that the landing and the march to Constantinople 'would be just like shelling peas'.[38] At 1400 hours on Saturday, 24 April 'the majestic battleships led the lines from the great harbour amidst beating of drums and ringing cheers from the crowded British and French transports.'[39] Ships dipped their flags in salute; their crews stood to attention. Naval bands struck up *Sons of the Sea* and then, somewhat incongruously, played waltz tunes. Australian troops passing French transports tried to whistle *La Marseillaise*. After seven weeks on Lemnos, the Anzacs were about to face 'the very test of themselves as soldiers'.[40]

Three battleships – HMS *London, Queen* and *Prince of Wales* – carried Colonel Ewen Sinclair-MacLagan's 3rd Brigade to Gallipoli. The men of the 11th Battalion went aboard HMS *London* on Saturday morning. A midday meal of soup, meat and vegetables was followed by pudding, tinned fruit and a choice of tea, coffee or cocoa. After a brief church service, the men found time to write their last letters home, play cards, have a smoke and enjoy an impromptu concert. The ship's crew made the West Australians particularly welcome and, according to Corporal Forbes, entertained them 'right royally'.[41] Morale was excellent. When the battalion's commander, Lieutenant Colonel Johnston, told them, 'Boys, the General informs me that it will take several battleships and destroyers to carry our brigade to Gallipoli; a barge will be sufficient to take us home again!' his men responded with resounding cheers.[42] Rifles were oiled, bayonets sharpened, wills written in paybooks and prayers said privately, before the men took some rest. In the early hours of Sunday, 25 April, as the fleet approached land, ships' portholes were blacked out and all lights extinguished. Just after midnight, Sydney Forbes, Walter Blair and Fred Albrecht joined the rest of the attacking force for a hot breakfast and a tot of rum. The teacher-soldiers from Perth had been chosen, once again, to be amongst the first wave of Anzacs and now stood ready and equipped for war. Their uniform comprised a woollen tunic, breeches, puttees and brown boots, and a greatcoat. They wore a British pattern field-service cap and webbing, although the latter was made of kangaroo leather. Bronze collar and shoulder badges – depicting the rising sun and 'Australia' respectively – displayed their origins. Their equipment, consisting of an Australian-made British SMLE rifle, 200 rounds of ammunition, entrenching tool, three empty sandbags and enough water and rations to last three days, weighed 87lbs in total.[43]

At around 0300 hours HMS *London* dropped anchor. By now the 11th Battalion had climbed down the rope ladders into small open boats. Steam pinnaces were waiting to tow them in their landing craft (or 'tows') an anticipated two miles towards the shore (see plate 15). On the order 'Full steam ahead', the tows went 'racing and bounding, dipping and rolling, now in a straight line, now in a half-circle, on through the night'.[44] Having put their greatcoats in their packs, the men shivered in the cold night air. In Number 9 tow were A Company's 1 and 2 Platoons, commanded by Major Edmund Drake Brockman, before whom Sydney Forbes had signed his Attestation Paper at Blackboy Hill, eight months previously.

Skippering the tow was a 'plucky little middy' named Churchill,[45] namesake of the British politician who was one of the key proponents of the 'Eastern' campaign in which the West Australians were now playing a major part. Behind them, in Number 10 tow, were 3 and 4 Platoons commanded by Captain Reginald Everett. Both tows approached the coast in silence, packed tight with men and their supplies. A moon which might have illuminated their approach disappeared at about 0330 hours and, despite the Ottoman searchlights which momentarily arced above the peninsula, the invaders remained undetected. Corporal Forbes, in 1 Platoon, later described how, at around 0430 hours, they were just short of the beach when

> the first shot went 'ping!' and we were under fire. About a minute after this there was a perfect fusillade. My word, they did pour the lead into us! We had to row the last 40 yards, and so we were unable to return their fire. Fortunately, no one in our boat was hit before we landed, although the bullets were flying in all directions. In fact, we did not wait to reach the land, but hopped over the side of the boat up to our waists in water and waded out.[46]

Sydney Forbes was one of the first to land on Anzac Beach. The two companies in Captain Everett's boat, which had been shot to pieces, sustaining casualties and starting to take in water before sinking, managed to get ashore further north. In fact, the whole Australian force had landed over half a mile further north than originally planned. In the darkness the tows had been unable to maintain their positions, and currents drove them diagonally, rather than directly, towards the beach. Having landed, however, the men of A Company sprinted 25 yards across the narrow strip of shingle towards the cover of the higher ground ahead of them. Corporal Forbes and 1 Platoon 'went half-way up the first hill, and lay down there to take off our packs, and try and collect the boys together.'[47] Then they continued their scramble upwards, stumbling into holes and ruts and pulling themselves up by tree roots and branches, before finally topping the hill. Bayonets helped them to secure holds on the ascent and to dispose of the enemy: 'The Turks were driven off this first ridge with the bayonet, which they do not seem to like very much.'[48]

An hour after landing, the 11th Battalion men joined forces, on what was soon to be known as Plugge's Plateau[49] (see Map 6), with other 3rd Brigade units which had beached further south. Some 4,000 men had made it ashore in just fifteen minutes,[50] but after the confusion of the landing and the ascent of Ari Burnu, the 3rd Brigade's battalions had become fragmented, then mixed. Major Drake Brockman assumed command, then ordered the hastily regrouped units towards the second ridge. Proceeding to Rest Gully, 1 Platoon met up with the rest of A Company and other units. Whilst the bulk of the 11th Battalion continued to hold the left of the Brigade's line and advanced to the second ridge, a few men now found themselves alongside 9th and 10th Battalion troops. Corporal Forbes was amongst a mixed group of Anzacs who continued to push on towards the next ridge, which the covering force had been ordered to take. He later recalled:

> I got separated from the rest of our company and found myself out on the right with another lot. We went forward about a mile and three-quarters on to a ridge, but the Turks began to come on in far superior numbers, so we had to get back as quickly as our legs would carry us. There were only about 25 of us, and there were some hundreds of Turks.[51]

This brief description refers to an incident upon which the fortunes of the campaign turned. A small group of men from 3rd Brigade under Lieutenant Noel Loutit had continued their advance through the evocatively (and later) named Shrapnel and Wire Gulleys. Loutit then rallied some other troops who had stopped to rummage through a deserted enemy encampment in Owen's Gulley. The thirty or so men under his command chased the retreating enemy through waist-high thorn scrub before climbing a 200ft spur on to Adana Ridge. At around 0900 hours they caught their first glimpses of the Narrows, their ultimate target. Their primary objective, however, the so-called 'third ridge' in the Sari Bair range, was still some 400 yards ahead. The successful invasion of the Dardanelles was predicated upon its capture. It had to be taken quickly, whatever the cost, and once captured there was to be no going back. For an hour they waited for support before advancing further, but Drake Brockman's men on the second ridge had already begun digging in. Enemy forces had regrouped and, in their hundreds, had begun advancing towards them. Under intense fire, and in danger of being encircled, Loutit ordered his men to retreat. The dash back to the second ridge resulted in further casualties, including Corporal Forbes, who suffered a shrapnel wound to his back. He was one of just eleven men who returned from Adana Ridge, and he later noted that 'the marvel is that we ever got back at all, for we had to pass over an area of cleared ground, and the Turks were firing at us all the time.'[52] Climbing the steep gulley to Johnston's Jolly and Second Ridge, the survivors from Adana turned to fight the rapidly advancing enemy troops.

By midday on 25 April the initial landing had become a full-scale battle. Ottoman artillery shells had begun to rain down from Gaba Tepe at first light. Later shelling from the third ridge provided cover for the Turkish infantry and created havoc amongst the invaders. Many of the men in the second-wave 1st and 2nd Brigades, denied the element of surprise, became casualties. So, too, did troops from the New Zealand and Australian Division (NZAD) which landed after them. Stretcher-bearers navigated the steep terrain and carried the wounded back across the exposed beach. Amidst much confusion and delay in bringing in reinforcements, landing tows evacuated hundreds of men back to the naval vessels offshore, only one of which, the *Seeangchoon*, was a designated hospital ship. In the absence of land-based artillery support until the arrival of the 26th Indian Mountain Battery around noon, HMS *Triumph*, *Bacchante* and *Queen* returned fire. For the rest of the day there was ferocious fighting, attacks and counter-attacks, all along the line. Attempts by the 11th Battalion to advance northwards beyond Baby 700 to Chunuk Bair were thwarted by the arrival in mid-morning of Lieutenant Mustafa Kemal and the 1/57th and 2/57th Battalions of the Ottoman Army's 19th Division. These 'Turks', many of whom were in fact Syrian Arabs, were determined not to let the land they knew as Çanakkale fall into enemy hands. Lulled into a false sense of superiority by wartime propaganda and the feeble initial resistance to the landing, the Anzacs were now surprised by the Ottoman riposte. Baby 700 changed hands five times before Kemal's force finally secured it and made full use of its commanding views over the first and second ridges.

Corporal Forbes, meanwhile, was still detached from his battalion and involved in action elsewhere: 'Later on in the afternoon we went forward some short distance again, and I received another little present from the Turks in the way of a pellet of shrapnel in another part of the back.'[53] He was wounded once more that day whilst taking cover near the junction of Lone Pine and 400 Plateau:

> I was in the small 'dug-outs' with another platoon, when I received a little more shrapnel in the right wrist. I had no control of my hand, in fact, I couldn't use it, so I went back about 50 yards, put a ligature round my biceps to stop the bleeding, bandaged the wrist as well as I could, and was taken on board one of the transports.[54]

The Anzacs had stopped far short of their original objective. By nightfall they were in possession of a semi-circular strip of land a mile and a half long and one mile deep. In the process of gaining no more than a toehold on enemy territory they had sustained some 2,000 casualties. Their generals began discussing the possibility of evacuation, until General Hamilton ordered them to dig in and defend their fragile bridgehead.

That night, the 3rd Brigade stubbornly held their ground against constant enemy attacks. They had been fighting for 24 hours, but 'despite their losses and in spite of their fatigue, the morning of 26 [April] found them still in good heart and as full of fight as ever.'[55] Of the fourteen original Anzacs from CTC, four had become casualties: Maurice O'Donohue was reported missing; Andrew McDonald, James Morgan and Jack Archibald were wounded, evacuated, and on their way back to hospitals in Malta and Egypt. Sydney's fellow sprinters from CTC, however, were still in action. Fred Albrecht had spent much of the first day carrying ammunition up to Walter Blair and the others engaged in the fighting around Baby 700. They were now part of an Anzac force doggedly defending rather than advancing. Their entrenched line held during the following week, aided by naval artillery fire and reinforcements from the Royal Naval Division and Royal Marines Light Infantry. Casualties mounted, and when on Sunday, 2 May an attempt was made to move the Australian line forward, '800 men were lost without advantage.'[56] Walter Blair was killed in action in yet another attempt to retake Baby 700. An unsuccessful assault on Gaba

Tepe led by Captain Raymond Leane two days later resulted in yet more casualties.[57] Lieutenant William Rockliff was shot in the abdomen, and a gunshot wound to the hand ended Corporal Forbes' first tour of duty at Anzac Cove. Amongst others seriously wounded and evacuated that day was Sydney's brother Alick, who had landed later on 25 April with the 16th Battalion. By the end of the first week at Anzac only 450 men of the 11th Battalion were still in action.[58] They continued to hang on 'by the skin of their teeth'.[59]

It was from his bed in Tigne Hospital in Malta that 'Syd' Forbes wrote to the Perth *Sunday Times* with news of the heroics at Anzac Cove. His convalescence consisted of afternoon tea with visiting ladies, beef dinners, concerts by military bands, and activities such as bridge, billiards and swimming. There were downsides, too, which included hospital bedbugs and lice, close contact with amputees and men dying from their wounds, and updates from new arrivals about mates killed at Gallipoli. After five weeks in hospital, and by the time his friends back home were reading of his exploits, Corporal Forbes was on his way back to the front. He rejoined his unit on 20 June and spent the next six weeks fighting 'Jacko', 'Abdul' and 'Johnny Turk', as the enemy were variously referred to. The earlier makeshift entrenchments had since given way to something resembling a mining settlement, its inhabitants constantly digging and hauling supplies whilst enemy shells and snipers' bullets whizzed amongst them. The newly promoted Quartermaster Sergeant Forbes faced other enemies too. Summer on the peninsula brought dust and furnace-like conditions even in the shade. Water was in short supply. Men shared their dugouts with scorpions, tarantulas and lice which were immune to the proprietary powders. Plagues of flies explored men's eyes, noses, ears and mouths. They feasted on the bloated corpses between the lines, colonized the stinking latrines and infested the men's food. The 'Gallipoli Trots' affected four men out of five. By late July the number of evacuations was exceeding the number of new arrivals. The men were worn out, and many were 'suffering from nervous breakdown'.[60] Basic pleasures, such as drinking tea and receiving letters from home, assumed a new importance. So, too, did the cleansing daily dip in the sea, even though it was often accompanied by a shower of shrapnel from an Ottoman gun battery nicknamed 'Beachy Bill'.

Sergeant Forbes' second spell at Anzac lasted forty-eight days before he was wounded again. On 6 August, whilst the 1st Brigade AIF was attacking Lone Pine and the 3rd Australian Light Horse prepared for the infamous attack at The Nek, the 11th Battalion was defending the recently captured Leane's Trench. These actions were parts of a larger strategy to break the stalemate and push on to the Sari Bair Range. But the August Offensive achieved little, and the brutal fighting continued. Serious shrapnel wounds to Sydney's right shoulder led to another speedy evacuation by sea to the 1st Australian General Hospital at Heliopolis in Egypt. By late November he was back at Sarpi Camp on Lemnos, joining hundreds of others waiting to return to the Dardanelles. It was a journey he never made. In December, the Anzacs evacuated the Gallipoli peninsula and regrouped in Egypt. Defence of the Suez Canal remained a priority, but it was also an opportunity for the AIF to reorganize. The expansion of the army also 'meant a splendid field for promotion of tried leaders and men throughout the force'.[61] In March 1916 Sydney Forbes became a commissioned officer in the now divided 11th Battalion; Fred Albrecht became an officer in its sister unit, the 51st Battalion. Fellow CTC alumni William Rockliff and Jack Archibald, recovered from their wounds, transferred to promoted posts in the 44th Battalion. Thousands of reinforcements poured in from Australia, and the first Anzacs – or Diggers as they also began to call themselves – prepared the new men for their forthcoming deployment to the Western Front.

On 29 March 1916 the men of the 11th Battalion sailed from Alexandria on HMAT *Corsican*. Landing at Marseilles eight days later, they boarded trains for the sixty-hour journey to the lines held by the BEF in Northern France. The countryside they travelled through was beautiful, in stark contrast to the harsh terrain of Egypt and parts of remote WA. They were received warmly by a French civilian population which generally shared General Haig's recently-formed opinion of the troops from the Dominions: 'Splendid, fine physique, very hard and determined looking … The Australians are also mad keen to kill Germans and to start doing it at once.'[62] Some among them may therefore have been disappointed to find that their first deployment was in the Bois Grenier sub-sector. Albert Baswitz and the 47th Division had engaged in bitter and costly fighting in the same region in 1915, amidst the broken fields and industrial slagheaps around Festubert, Loos and Lens. When the AIF took over the lines in early April 1916, however, the sector was relatively quiet and used by the British as 'The Nursery', in which troops new to the Western Front were introduced to the rigours and routines of trench warfare. Their new billets were rough and ready, reminding many of the sheep-shearing sheds back home. After the heat of Egypt and the warmth of southern France, they found their new home in Flanders decidedly cold. The nearby town of Armentières on the Franco–Belgian border, however, provided some compensations. The Australians were the BEF's highest paid troops, and they quickly patronized the local stores, tea rooms, estaminets and other attractions for men far from home. They soon became accustomed to 'omelettes' and 'pommes de terre frites', and the light 'bierre' brought to their tables by 'Marthe' or 'Lucille'. Some, for want of real action, began helping 'Madame' and 'Jeanette' on nearby farms when off duty.[63]

Throughout April and May 1916 the West Australians trained with the rest of the 3rd Brigade. They prepared for the possibility of enemy gas attacks, were taught how to use Mills bombs and spent hours at bayonet practice. On 25 April 1916, their first Anzac Day passed off quietly. After an inspection by Army Commander General Sir Hubert Plumer, the veterans and those who had since joined their ranks were issued with beer and extra rations, followed by a brigade concert in the evening. Two days later, they were inspected once again, this time by Haig. The experienced men amongst them recognized the tell-tale signs that they would soon be moving into the fighting lines. In May, parades gave way to working parties and increasing amounts of night work involving digging and cable-laying. On 20 May Second Lieutenant Forbes, with 26 fellow officers and 929 other ranks, moved up to the front line trenches near the village of Fleurbaix.[64] The men from WA were but the latest BEF contingent to fight on this battlefield. In 1914, British, Indian and French troops had fought there, attempting to halt the German advance towards Armentières. In May 1915 a full-scale attack had resulted in numerous British casualties. German defences in the area were still formidable a year later. Occupying the ridge of high ground between the villages of Aubers and Fromelles – Aubers Ridge (see Map 2) – enemy forces had a clear view of the flat plain on which the British forces were massed. Patrols and wiring parties helped to secure an otherwise vulnerable position, but the 11th Battalion was nevertheless subjected to a daily 'evening hate' of projectiles fired by German artillery and trench mortars. 'Jack Johnsons', 'coal boxes', 'rum jars', 'flying pigs', 'whizz-bangs', 'Minnies', 'woolly-bears' and 'pineapples' churned up the flat, waterlogged area in which the Australian trenches were situated and often disinterred the decomposed bodies of British servicemen who had died there in previous actions. A raid on the battalion's positions around Cordonnerie Farm on 30 May began with an intensive artillery bombardment which obliterated 60 yards of Australian line and resulted in 120 serious casualties. A party of German troops then stormed a section of the battered trenches and took several prisoners. As preparations for the launch of the major British offensive on the Somme gathered pace, however, the 11th Battalion was given the opportunity to exact revenge for its recent loss of men and dented pride. Haig encouraged the Australians to conduct a series of reciprocal raids on German positions. The Anzacs were thus to play a part in the Battle of the Somme by diverting enemy attention and resources away from the main thrust of the attacks further south near Albert. In the week which preceded the great British offensive on 1 July, and coinciding with the massive preliminary bombardment by the Royal Artillery, the 1st Division AIF mounted five raids on German positions in their sector. Five further raids took place during the first days of the offensive, including one carried out by the 11th Battalion on 2 July on the so-called Tadpole. However, as Charles Bean, the war correspondent attached to the AIF, noted, the British newspapers may have celebrated these heroic actions, but the Anzacs had yet to be really tested on the Western Front. Three weeks later, as the wider Somme offensive raged on, morale-boosting raids by the Australians gave way to involvement in devastating large-scale battles at Fromelles and Pozières. The 1st Division was ordered south on 10 July in preparation for the next great push by the BEF. The 11th Battalion's former positions in front of Aubers Ridge were occupied by the yet untested troops of the 32nd Battalion AIF. Following directly in the footsteps of Sydney Forbes was another teammate from CTC. On 16 July Adolph Knäble entered the line near Cordonnerie Farm.

* * *

Sydney Forbes and Adolph Knäble may have had many things in common, but there were some obvious differences between them. Sydney's family had originally migrated from Britain, but Adolph's origins were both British and German. His father, Adolph Michael Knäble, had been born in 1854 in Emmishofen, a German-speaking town situated near the River Rhine and some 30 miles north-east of Zürich in Switzerland. In April 1888 Adolph senior arrived in Australia from Germany, settled in Melbourne and worked as a labourer. In 1894 he married Alice George, whose father Felix had migrated from England to Victoria in the 1850s. The Knäbles' first child, Adolph junior, was born on 26 December 1894. Like the Forbes family, the Knäbles later migrated to WA. In 1896 Adolph senior found employment in the timber trade at Canning Mills near Perth. By 1900, however, he had moved to a new Canning Jarrah Timber Company enterprise at Wellington Mill, the largest private timber town in WA at the time, but still just a frontier township of only forty households in the then remote south-west region of the state. The relative anonymity of city life may explain the apparent lack of archival evidence for Sydney's early life; in stark contrast there is a wealth of information relating to Adolph's formative years. Contemporary local and regional newspapers, particularly the *Bunbury Herald* and *Southern Times*, reported on notable individuals and families committed to communal endeavour. From the 'District News' pages we discover that Mr Knäble was involved in trade union matters, representing his fellow workers at the Sawmill Employees Union conference at Jarahdale in June 1907 and being elected President of the Wellington Mill Branch of the Timber Workers' Union in 1912.

Social events were also covered by the papers. In 1904 Mr Knäble attended the Fancy Dress Ball dressed as a clown. At the Wellington Mill Sports he dead-heated for first place in the Old Buffers Hurdle Race. He helped to raise funds for the building of the Anglican church and organized entertainments for local children. Mrs Knäble played her part, too, working with other wives to prepare suppers at social events and, renowned for her rich contralto voice, was invariably called upon to perform at the community's most important social gatherings. Adolph and his younger siblings – Lillian, Constance, Joyce and Carl – also featured in local news reports. They attended Wellington State School, its grand title belying the reality of a simple wooden classroom and sole teacher providing a basic elementary education. Adolph was bright enough to be appointed as Monitor at the school. At the age of seventeen he moved to Bunbury, the regional centre some 17 miles away, where he developed his classroom craft at the State School and passed the Senior Monitor examinations. He took on wider responsibilities in 1912 and 1913, acting as assistant stage manager for the school's Annual Concert and staff steward in the Cross-Country Run. He also worked with other local teachers to organize Bunbury's 'Empire Day Celebrations', an event attended by 1,500 local schoolchildren. Adolph led a Sunday school class at St Paul's Cathedral in Bunbury, where he was a regular worshipper and member of the choir. He also made the most of sporting opportunities. He had represented Wellington State School in the Interstate Schools Cricket Competition, but his loyalties soon switched after his move to Bunbury, where he played (Association) football for Bunbury Britishers in their 4–1 defeat of Wellington Mills in June 1912. He played cricket for Bunbury Technical School, having enrolled in evening classes there soon after his change of school and ultimately achieving First, Second, and Third-Class examination passes in Commercial Arithmetic, English and Shorthand respectively in March 1913. Like his contemporaries Albert Baswitz in London and Sydney Forbes in Perth, he also trained to be a part-time soldier. When the first units of the New Australian Army paraded in Bunbury Drill Hall in August 1912, Cadet Knäble was amongst them and was officially transferred to the 86th Company of Infantry (Bunbury) as part of the new Citizen Forces which had recently been established in the Dominion. On 28 January 1913 the *Bunbury Herald* announced that 'Mr Knäble, one of the assistants at the State school, was amongst the successful candidates in a recent examination and now goes to the Training College for a period of three years.'

Adolph spent only one year at CTC. Unlike Sydney Forbes, he took the Short Course in preparation for employment in smaller schools. Once again, he combined his studies with sporting activity, playing alongside Sydney in several representative matches. Unlike many of his teammates, however, he did not respond immediately to the call to arms. Whilst Sydney and other CTC men had flocked to the colours in August 1914, Adolph waited a year before joining them. At the beginning of 1914 he had been appointed headteacher of Carine School in the northern suburbs of Perth. A year later, he was still teaching, this time at South Brunswick, a small township on the Perth to Bunbury railroad. In August 1915, however, he returned briefly to his family in Wellington Mill, having enlisted in the AIF at Northam. The reasons for this delay are unclear. Previous, albeit compulsory, training as a Cadet followed by two years' service in the Bunbury Infantry Company presumed full-time active deployment in time of war. His German name and ancestry did not automatically debar him and, in any case, having been born in Melbourne he could accurately describe himself as 'British-born'. His Swiss-born father, Adolph Knäble senior, had also followed in the footsteps of many others, including Albert Baswitz's father in London, in formally becoming a naturalized citizen of his adopted country by swearing an oath of allegiance before a magistrate in Bunbury in February 1914. Personal reasons may have played a part in young Adolph's decision-making at this time – a reluctance, perhaps, to be separated from his 'dear friend' Dorothy Lawson in Northam – but it is more likely that his leadership of a local Army Cadet Group meant that his initial war service was undertaken closer to home.[65] The imperative to follow in the footsteps of the first Anzacs may well have been the deciding factor.

Adolph enlisted in the 32nd Battalion AIF (see plate 16). Like Albert Baswitz in London and Fred Albrecht in Perth, Adolph Knäble was a young man of Germanic origin who chose to fight for the land of his birth rather than that of his ancestry. His Service Records state that Private 1603 Knäble's previous occupation was 'Schoolmaster' and his religious affiliation was 'Church of England'. Aged twenty-one years and seven months, he stood 5 feet 11 inches tall, weighed 161lbs and had fair hair and complexion and blue eyes. His Term of Service was 'to end of the war and 4 months after'.[66] After one month's training at Blackboy Hill, Adolph was awarded his corporal's stripes. A fortnight later, on 25 September 1915, he was one of the 500 men of the 32nd Battalion raised in Western Australia who sailed from the port of Fremantle.[67] After a six-day journey along the southern coast of Australia, the *Indarra* docked in Adelaide. Major Thomas Flintoff, accompanied by the Bishop of Bunbury, marched C and D Companies off the transport ship to their new quarters at the city's Cheltenham Park Racecourse. There they joined the battalion's A and B companies which had been raised in South Australia (SA). Their new training camp was known to all as 'The Soldier Factory', where 'Johnny Raw', whatever his previous military experience, was transformed into 'Tommy Brown'.[68] On their first evening in camp, however, the men from WA did at least gain some respite from what lay ahead of them, in the form of a social event organized by their new comrades from SA.

After eight more weeks of training, the composite 32nd Battalion embarked on HMAT *Geelong* on 28 November. They then made the long journey across the Southern and Indian Oceans in the wake of earlier AIF contingents, before arriving in the Egyptian port of Suez on 13 December, just days before the evacuation of Gallipoli. Now part of the 8th Brigade of the newly formed 5th Division AIF, they were initially deployed near Tel-el-Kebir, where they were given instruction in trench-digging and road-building and introduced to Lewis and Vickers machine guns and Stokes mortars. They spent six months in the Egyptian Desert, in intense heat and plagued by flies, conducting route marches and fighting mock battles. On 17 June 1916 the 32nd Battalion sailed on the *Transylvania* from Alexandria and, like the 11th Battalion before them, disembarked at Marseilles and headed north to the Western Front.

By July 1916 there were 90,000 Australian troops in France, with a further reserve of 90,000 men in training in England.[69] The 5th Division replaced the 1st Division in the 2,000 yards of line facing Aubers Ridge (see Map 2). The British 61st (South Midland) Division held a further 3,000 yards to their right. By 16 July the 32nd Battalion was assembled on the left of the British line with the rest of the Australian 8th Brigade. Already tired from the exertion of carrying all their ammunition and equipment from their billets in Fleurbaix up to the line, the new men took up their positions during heavy rain. Their so-called trenches, dug in an area where the water table was just 18 inches below the surface, began to slump and, despite the Australian's best efforts, provided little protection from the enemy. The German defenders held the high ground; the church tower at Fromelles was a key observation point. The Germans in question were, more precisely, Bavarians, and among their number was Corporal Adolf Hitler. Unlike the men of 32nd Battalion, the men of the 6th Bavarian Reserve Infantry Division (BRID) – the 16th, 20th and 21st Bavarian

Reserve Infantry Regiments (RIR) – were mostly experienced troops. Many had fought in the Battle of Aubers the previous year and had spent much of the time since strengthening the breastworks of their trenches and installing electric pumps to keep them dry. They had used weedkiller to limit the cover available to enemy attackers, deployed searchlights and star shells at night and improved their supply lines. The Wick and the Sugar Loaf, two fortified salients, ensured that the flanks of would-be assailants would be vulnerable to concentrated machine gun fire. Scattered buildings between the two trench lines also served as defensive positions and rallying points for counter-attacks.

A dense mist covered the battlefield on 17 July, and the British attack – 'Z Day' – was postponed for two days. In a letter read out to each unit in XI Corps, General Haking rallied the expectant troops by stating, 'I know you will do your best for the sake of our lads who are fighting hard down south.'[70] The first major assault on High Wood had started just days before and, at that very moment, Australian forces including the 11th Battalion were poised to attack the German defences at Pozières. As the mist lifted on Wednesday, 19 July, the British bombardment began. Nearly 400 artillery pieces and mortars opened fire on the enemy lines at 1100 hours. The Bavarians were hardly taken by surprise. They had noted the by now familiar pre-offensive signs of clogged roads and movement of men. They were also clearly aware of the presence of Australian troops, at one point in the days before the battle raising a sign reading, 'Advance Australia – if you can!'[71] A second sign had also appeared on 18 July, asking 'Why so long, you are twenty-four hours late?'[72] Both signs were duly shot down by the indignant new arrivals. Awareness of the British plans also extended to the women serving in the estaminets behind the lines. What happened next, however, has been shrouded in mystery and controversy for over a century. Despite the fact that 'the subsequent fourteen hours of vicious combat were to prove the most catastrophic of the one thousand days of Anzac presence on the Western front',[73] the precise details of the Battle of Fromelles itself – and the fate of many of the men involved in it – have only recently been brought to light.

After a good breakfast and then a midday meal, the men of the 5th Division moved up to their final jumping-off positions. Most of the Australians were in place by 1500 hours as planned, but the 32nd Battalion and the rest of the 8th Brigade arrived an hour later. The men fixed bayonets in readiness for the signal to attack. Some watched the aerial battle between fighter and reconnaissance aircraft overhead, but most kept their heads down as the artillery duel intensified. Enemy guns had responded to the British bombardment by targeting the Australians as they made their way up to the line. For the next two hours the crowded assembly trenches were shelled. Survivors later described the deafening impact of 'weird noises like thousands of iron foundries'.[74] Disastrously inaccurate firing by their own guns – 'dropshorts' from the AIF artillery – added to the large number of casualties suffered by the 32nd Battalion in particular. On four occasions the British bombardment lifted, but the ensuing raising of dummies – a repetition of the 'Chinese' attack employed by the 22nd Londons at Loos – failed to elicit a response from defenders who were patently aware of previous ruses. When the real attack materialized, the Bavarians' machine guns opened up without hesitation.

The Australians finally 'hopped the bags' at 1753 hours, just before the planned zero hour of 1800 hours. Despite its inexperience, the 32nd Battalion anchored the whole attack on the left of the British line. As Adolph Knäble and his mates entered no man's land they heard an enormous noise and felt the tremors caused by the 2nd Australian Tunnelling Company's detonation of a 1,200lb mine near Cordonnerie Farm. From their left came covering fire from the British 60th Brigade. Nib Trench, held by 21BRIR troops, was the 32nd Battalion's immediate objective. As they moved forward, an enemy lookout shouted, 'Die Engländer kommen!', and his fellow countrymen apparently cheered as they saw the Australians climbing over their parapets and heading towards them. Neither the British shelling nor the mine had destroyed the enemy's defences. In the space of the next 30 minutes, and under intense fire, the men of the 32nd Battalion advanced nearly 130 yards. On reaching the enemy's first line of trenches they quickly killed or captured the few surviving defenders, before moving on to what they believed to be the Bavarian second line. This 'line' was, in fact, a communication trench, known as the Kastenweg, which the Bavarians had constructed with mud-filled ammunition boxes, and it had become no more than a shallow ditch half full of water, mud and slime. Battalion bombers under Lieutenant Eric Chinner secured the new position, and the rest began to dig in and erect rudimentary barricades.

The capture of these enemy positions had simply drawn the 32nd Battalion further into the killing zone. The ruins of nearby Delangré Farm acted as a mustering point for Bavarian troops deliberately held back for the counter-attack. At first, attempts by 20 and 21BRIR to reclaim their territory were repulsed, but after nearly four hours of vicious fighting, the men of the 32nd Battalion had become increasingly handicapped by the mounting numbers of casualties, insufficient supplies of sandbags to rebuild their makeshift defences, soaked rifles and shortage of drinking water. A call for more materials and reinforcements at 2140 hours was answered by carriers from the 30th Battalion, some of whom decided to stay and fight rather than maintain the crucial supply chain. The light was failing. Enemy shelling intensified. Counter-attacks continued. Machine gun crews moved ever closer, covering the bombing teams which began to enter parts of the Australian line, a line that was effectively broken when the men of the 31st Battalion were ordered to fall back.

Despite the early – but illusory – gains, the attack had failed. Recognition of this fact led to the formal abandonment of offensive action early the next morning, at 0110 hours on Thursday, 20 July. Ordered to return to their original starting positions, many men broke cover and rushed back over land they had just captured. Bavarian riflemen fired at will at the fleeing Australians, and their bombers pursued them relentlessly. This mass retirement did not, however, include many of the advance guard of the 32nd Battalion, which continued to fight on in the by now even more exposed and vulnerable waterlogged ditch. By 0330 hours their position was untenable. Bavarian troops had rolled up their left flank, got behind them and begun to shower them with bombs. Lieutenant Mills gathered together some 150 men of 8th Brigade and began a fighting withdrawal back through the old Bavarian front line. By 0410 hours, and after brutal hand-to-hand fighting and running the gauntlet of machine gun fire and sniping across the original area of no man's land, the few survivors of the 32nd Battalion made it back to their own lines. Others had patently not received the order to withdraw or had received it too late. For several hours the remnants of the brigade continued to slip back through the carnage of the battlefield. By midday on 20 July, when the guns on both sides ceased firing, the Battle of Fromelles was over.

The first serious engagement by Australian forces on the Western Front had ended in humiliating and costly defeat. The pattern of limited advance, enemy counter-attack and ultimate panicked withdrawal was repeated along the rest of the British line. The enemy's defensive salients at the Sugar Loaf and the Wick stood firm, as did the rest of the Bavarian line between Fromelles and Aubers. The neighbouring British 61st Division suffered 1,547 casualties; the corresponding figure for the Australian 5th Division was 5,533, of whom nearly 2,000 were killed in action or died of their wounds.[75] The 32nd Battalion alone listed 718 casualties,[76] almost 75 per cent of the battalion's total establishment, but closer to 90 per cent of its actual fighting strength. Private Adolph Knäble was not amongst the men who responded to the 32nd Battalion's post-battle roll call. Despite enquiries during and immediately after the war by the Australian Army and family members, his fate on the battlefield at Fromelles remained unclear. A fellow soldier claimed to have seen him lying in no man's land with wounds to his face and hip, but Adolph was not amongst those recovered by his fellow Australian troops at night (see plate 17), some of whom subsequently died of their wounds. Nor was he amongst the hundreds of Australian prisoners paraded through Lille by the German authorities just days after the battle. He was one of the many hundreds of men initially classified as 'missing in action, presumed killed', his bodily remains probably left in territory reclaimed by the enemy during the flight back to the original lines. It is highly likely that he was one of the many 32nd Battalion men who had fought and died in the proximity of the Kastenweg ditch, or was possibly part of the small group who were later reported to have advanced even further into enemy territory in search of a supposed third-line trench. Confirmation of his death on the battlefield would come almost a century later.

* * *

The Battle of Fromelles was immediately followed by another major offensive involving the Australians. At a church parade attended by Sydney Forbes and the men of the 11th Battalion on Sunday, 9 July, General Birdwood had confirmed rumours that they would be travelling south to the Somme. The assembled troops received the news with great enthusiasm. Travelling by train from Armentières the following day, in trucks still dirty from their earlier equine cargo, they joined the rest of Birdwood's 1 ANZAC near

Amiens. Over 60,000 men were transported 60 miles in just a week.[77] To their rear was a city hardly touched by the conflict, its shops and cafés vibrant despite the war. Before them, however, some 25 miles to the east, was a raging battle which had already claimed thousands of casualties. The big guns could be heard rumbling in the distance, and at night flashes of light over the battlefield reminded them of the task ahead. The West Australians marched in full kit along the chalky-white roads of Picardie, stopping at Naours for yet more bayonet and bombing practice, before finally reaching their allotted bivouacs at Forceville on Tuesday, 18 July. Surplus gear was collected, and the necessary equipment for the forthcoming assault was issued: wire cutters, ammunition and signalling gear. On the afternoon of 19 July, at the very moment that his friend Adolph Knäble was about to attack the Kastenweg at Fromelles, Sydney Forbes moved up to Albert. The 11th Battalion men marched through a town whose inhabitants had fled, along cobbled streets littered with shards of glass. They passed the Golden Virgin, 'head downwards, poised imminent above the shattered city, like an avenging wraith'.[78] Some of their fellow countrymen, undaunted, had irreverently nicknamed the statue 'Fanny', after freestyle swimmer Fanny Durack who had become their country's first female Olympic champion at the Stockholm Games of 1912. Marching along the road to Bapaume they passed the machinery of modern warfare assembled in Sausage Valley, then turned at Casualty Corner into the network of communication trenches around Black Watch Alley. The British and Australian artillery had already begun their preliminary bombardment. Enemy machine guns rattled incessantly, and gas shells landed near the Australian positions. Immediately ahead of the new attacking force was a landscape devoid of distinguishing marks other than craters and heaps of churned-up earth. In the near distance, however, was their objective: the village of Pozières (see plate 19). The reputation of the Australians had preceded them. A British Tommy vacating a front line trench shouted out to them, 'If you Anzacs can take and hold Pozières, we'll believe all we've heard about you!'[79]

The Australians sat at the junction of two British armies. The main thrust of the offensive on the Somme was undertaken by the Fourth Army, which held the sector predominantly to the right of the Albert to Bapaume road. The British Reserve Army, of which 1 ANZAC formed a part, filled a secondary role in the overall campaign, awaiting the opportunity to expand operations to the north and west towards Mouquet Farm and Thiepval if circumstances permitted. Once again, as at Fromelles, the Australians were to play a subsidiary part in support of the greater strategic plan, but the capture of Pozières was not only crucial to the intended geographical extension of the offensive, but also vital for the success of the next planned assault on High Wood just four miles away to the east. The village lay on a ridge which, as at Aubers, gave its German defenders commanding views over the neighbouring countryside. British troops had failed to capture Pozières on 1 July, and all subsequent attempts to take it had failed. On 14 July, as the British 23rd Division attacked towards the village, the accompanying bombardment had reduced many of its buildings to brick dust and rubble. Still the stronghold stood defiant, its mighty Gibraltar pillbox guarding the approach from Albert and the surrounding fields in Sausage Valley and Mash Valley. This point still marked the German front line. Behind it was a second line also running at right angles to the road.

Unlike the dismal failure at Fromelles, the AIF assault at Pozières was successful. The 11th Battalion, now commanded by Lieutenant Colonel Harricks Roberts, played a crucial part in the capture of the village. Two years of war had resulted in a slow but discernible learning curve for the BEF. Hard-won experience and costly failures began to inform organizational structures, operational procedures and leadership on the battlefield. Some senior officers gradually began to take a 'more integrated approach to the basic infantry attack',[80] combining the deployment of troops on the ground with the use of auxiliary arms, aerial reconnaissance and signalling systems. Success on the battlefield still ultimately depended, however, upon the decisions and actions of smaller units and lower levels of command. During the Battle of Pozières the actions of a few individuals, including Lieutenant Sydney Forbes, made 'a material difference to the outcome of an operation in the midst of a modern, technology-driven battlefield.'[81]

The 11th Battalion waited in its front line positions for four days before the attack. The men improved their lines, brought up supplies from the nearby Gordons' Dump and took part in night patrols. They had time to watch the aerial dogfights above them and cheered when a British fighter downed a German monoplane. The British heavy artillery continued to pound the village. Red dust covered everything. The 3rd Brigade held the right of the divisional line and had orders to attack from the south-east; the 1st Brigade was to destroy the German defences to the west of the village, including the formidable Gibraltar pillbox. The 11th Battalion's trenches, some no better than the shallow drainage ditches encountered by the 32nd Battalion at Fromelles, lay at right angles to the Albert–Bapaume Road. For A and B Companies, their first objective – the Pozières Trench with its 15ft deep barbed wire defences – lay over 200 yards in front of them. Beyond that was their second objective, the OG (Old German) line, which ran parallel to the main road. C and D Companies were to secure the light railway which ran through the village. The heat of the day on Tuesday, 22 July made the final preparations even more arduous, but the men from WA were generally in good heart. Some wrote letters home, others shaved, and many shared jokes – and the rations of mates who had been wounded and evacuated. The moist evening air was shattered by disruptive German artillery barrages.

Just before midnight, in the darkness of a moonless night, Lieutenant Forbes and his men finally moved to their jumping-off positions. They were amongst the 2,000-strong attacking force now creeping towards the enemy lines, led by scouts and troops carrying wire-cutters. Some of them were within 40 yards of the enemy line when, almost simultaneously, they were illuminated by both German rocket flares and shells fired by British and Australian batteries stationed in Sausage Valley. As the two-minute hurricane bombardment subsided, whistles blew and the first wave charged forward, bayonets fixed. What happened next resembled much of what had occurred at Fromelles. Lack of clarity in brigade orders, inadequate support on the right flank from another unit (in this case the 9th Battalion) and difficulties in identifying the terrain combined to create confusion in both the 11th Battalion and the 12th Battalion which had been detailed to follow them through the enemy positions. Pozières Trench was taken but not consolidated, before a headlong rush ensued to and beyond the second, by now barely distinguishable, OG line. Once again, limited initial resistance from the enemy was simply a prelude to determined counter-attacks. Casualties mounted, particularly amongst the officers. It was at this point that the actions of a small group of officers and men from the 11th Battalion made such a difference. Having by then advanced about half a mile beyond their original jumping-off points, Captain Leon Le Nay, Captain Walter Belford and Lieutenant Sydney Forbes managed to recall their men, regroup them and then organize a new line from which to launch further attacks. Disciplined and resolute, the battalion continued its advance throughout the early hours of Wednesday morning. The fighting was fierce and ruthless. The German troops, mainly men of the 157th Regiment (117th Division, Seventh Army) had managed to defend their positions against repeated attacks. Now, those who tried to surrender were bayoneted or shot without mercy by Australians who preferred not to take prisoners. Those who refused to leave their shelters were bombed.

By dawn on 23 July the battle for Pozières appeared to be over. The 2nd Battalion had taken the Gibraltar strongpoint to the west of the village. In the east, troops of the 11th and 12th Battalion had captured Hauptmann Ponsonby Lyons, the Commandant of Pozières, whose grandfather had been an Englishman. Following reports that the Germans had evacuated the village, small parties of Australians proceeded to enter the ruins and, despite enemy sniping, began prospecting for souvenirs. Sporadic action continued, however. A small German counter-attack emanating from near the Windmill on the road to Bapaume was repulsed, but then another enemy force began to assemble in a trench in front of the positions now held by the 11th Battalion. Captain Belford, a participant in the subsequent events, later described how Lieutenants Forbes and Hallahan immediately countered the threat:

> The party advanced through the hedge on the north boundary of the village and made for the trench. When they got near, Forbes saw a number of Germans throw up their hands and heard them shout, 'Kamerad!' But an officer or NCO was seen to dash along the trench and beat down the upraised hands, and shots were fired at the patrol. Then Hallahan arranged that he should attack from his position while Forbes took his men round to the left, so as to attack the trench from two sides. The two parties again crept through the hedge and were making for their objective when a very heavy fire was directed at both parties. Lieut. Forbes and 'Tyger' Lyon were both killed and several men were wounded. Hallahan gave the order to retire.[82]

The Battle of Pozières was, in fact, far from over. In the days which followed, the 1st Division AIF pushed north and west in the face of ferocious German resistance, before finally being relieved by the Australian 2nd Division on 27 July. The village, the windmill and the strategic ridge upon which they stood had been taken, but at a terrific cost. At Pozières the Australian dead 'lay thicker there than on any other battlefield of the war.'[83] Casualty figures for the 1st Division included 181 officers and over 5,000 other ranks;[84] the 11th Battalion lost 18 officers and 512 other ranks. More men were lost in the subsequent bloody attack on Mouquet Farm, before the battalion moved north to the Ypres sector, where it spent the remainder of 1916.

News of the battle travelled fast. Whilst the Australian public had been told that the Battle of Fromelles was little more than a large raid, and the scale of defeat and cost in lives was not fully revealed, the heroic actions and names of the glorious dead at the Battle of Pozières were paraded before an audience eager to share in the Dominion's military success. On 20 August, just four weeks after the 11th Battalion had entered the line, Perth's *Sunday Times* ran as its headline Charles Bean's declaration that 'The West Australians were magnificent at Pozières.' As an introduction to its latest Roll of Honour, and to boost its pro-conscription stance, the newspaper stated:

Our West Australian soldiers have gained great glory at Pozières, but alas, they have paid the price. The long list of casualties given below tells its own tale. Within the past week or so news has been received of the death in action of Major Welch, Captains Mansfield, McCrae and Macfarlane, and Lieuts Bell, Ian, Ottaway, Levetus, Walters, Forbes, Hastings, Williams, Ellis, Nichol and Mudge. The fact that the officers have suffered so severely points to considerable losses among the rank and file, and although the death roll so far announced is not great, the list of wounded already numbers several hundreds.[85]

In early October the *Daily News*, another Perth-based newspaper, carried an article relating to the death of Lieutenant Sydney Forbes. Under the headline 'Treacherously Shot', it reported that Sydney's mother had received a letter from an 11th Battalion soldier who had been wounded at

Pozières. From the 1st General Hospital in Birmingham, Signaller Frank Waterhouse had written:

> Dear Mrs. Forbes
>
> It is with great regret that I have to confirm the death of your son, and my most faithful comrade, Lieutenant Sydney Forbes, who was most treacherously shot by a German prisoner on the night of July 25–26. He had taken several prisoners, and had just turned his head to get one of our chaps to escort them in, when one of them snapped up a rifle and shot Syd in the head.[86]

Despite the differences in date and manner of death between the letter and Captain Belford's 'official' report, this version of events was soon picked up by the *Sunday Times*, which informed its readers:

> Lieut. Syd. Forbes, who it now transpires was treacherously shot by a German prisoner whom he had in custody, was as fine a type of young Australian as one would wish to meet. A young man of no inconsiderable talents … rising in his own gritful way from private to lieutenant. It is all the more sad to think that his meritorious career of active service should be ended by an act of treachery of the most Hunnish and despicable kind.[87]

Unlike his fellow teacher and soldier Adolph Knäble, whose fate in a disastrous defeat was shrouded in mystery, Sydney Forbes (see plate 20) had entered the pantheon of young Australian men – the Anzacs – who were celebrated and revered in their own country and beyond. They were portrayed at the time and have been since as the hard-fighting products of a hard country, men with grit and determination, their lives shaped in the testing environment of the colonies. Sydney Forbes, the teacher-turned-soldier, may not have conformed to the legendary depiction of the 'bush-bred, squared-jawed' natural warrior who detested discipline and displayed 'an indifference to danger and nonchalance toward death',[88] but he was an Anzac, nevertheless.

Chapter 5

Enzeds

The Australian and New Zealand troops have indeed proved themselves worthy sons of the Empire.

King George V, quoted in C. E. W. Bean (ed.),
The Anzac Book (1916) (see plate 22).

Anzacs came in many guises. New Zealanders shared with their Australian neighbours the experiences of imperial service and national pride, of fortitude and privation, of heroism and disaster. Many were fellow travellers of Sydney Forbes and the West Australians, comrades in a military adventure which took them first to Gallipoli and then on to France. Thousands more stood alongside Albert Baswitz and the Londoners as they tried to push the Germans back at High Wood on the Somme. Amongst the ranks of these Anzacs – or 'Enzeds' as many preferred to call themselves – were men like Frank Wilson (see plate 23) from Auckland.

Frank was a 'Diehard'. One of the last men to land at Gallipoli, he was also amongst the last to leave. Frank had arrived with the 6th Reinforcements on 8 November 1915. Six weeks later, he was one of the select few left to defend the lines whilst the rest of the Auckland Battalion evacuated the peninsula. Composed of the 'bravest and the steadiest men',[1] the rearguard was essentially

> a fellowship of sacrifice … they were looked upon as the men who were to die for the sake of their comrades. None expected them to come through alive. It was a supreme act, made without fuss or show of emotion, in a fashion typically New Zealand.[2]

There had been rumours about a possible evacuation for some weeks, but few believed that such hard-won territory would be given up so easily, especially as preparations for a winter campaign appeared to be taking place. Frank Wilson's position on Rhododendron Spur was strengthened by digging deeper dugouts and adding more barbed wire in front of the fire step. The need for more comfortable and secure accommodation was especially important after the great storm of 26 November and the four days of blizzards which followed, which had left hundreds dead and thousands more suffering from frostbite. The Ottoman defenders had also noted the increased number of working parties and the movement of guns, activities which indicated that some form of attack was imminent, although debates in the British Parliament had alerted them to the possibility of an evacuation. The authorities in Constantinople, however, had judged such talk to be part of a disinformation campaign designed to mask a major offensive, and so they continued to move heavy artillery – supplied by their German allies – into the peninsula. The majority of Enzeds and Turks alike were unaware that planning for the evacuation of Gallipoli had in fact been taking place since Lord Kitchener's visit in November. Not until 16 December were the troops at Anzac officially notified, and at last they made sense of activities which had been designed to mislead the enemy. Now they could comprehend the order to refrain from firing – the 'silent stunt' they called it – on 25 and 26 November;[3] a similar 'ceasefire' would be an inevitable part of the removal of troops on the day of the evacuation itself. Similarly, they had noted the continuous patrols in the skies above them by the Royal Naval Air Service (RNAS), a strategy designed to limit aerial observation by the enemy of the necessary logistical preparations for a mass withdrawal of men and equipment. Increasing numbers of troops were now leaving Gallipoli rather than arriving . So, too, were the heavy guns and their ammunition. Tinned food, which had been carefully stored away despite the troops' urgent dietary needs, suddenly became more plentiful.

Elaborate plans were made for the final evacuation of the Dardanelles. Australian and New Zealand troops from ANZAC and British forces from Suvla Bay would leave first; the troops fighting in the south at Cape Helles would follow later. Enzed Ormond Burton, tending the wounded on a hospital ship offshore, wrote an account of what this entailed for the Auckland Battalion, observing later that 'the success of the whole movement depended on accurate timing and on everyone knowing just exactly when and where he was to move.'[4] On 16 December a small advance party left for Lemnos to prepare for the battalion's return. Two days later, on the evening of Saturday, 18 December, two parties of Aucklanders left their positions and without incident boarded the transports waiting close to the shore at Anzac Beach. The men in the remaining half of the battalion spent the whole of the next day waiting for their turn. At 0900 hours Ottoman gunners bombarded the depleted lines at Rhododendron Spur, as a matter of routine rather than as a response to what was unfolding before them. At 1800 hours, as planned, another group of men headed for the beach, followed by the penultimate party at 2100 hours. The latter, too, said, 'Goodbye, boys! See you in Cairo!' before responding to the roll call.[5] Then they

> filed down the steep slope to Chailak Dere, and there at the precise moment met the files of Wellington and Canterbury passing downward from the Apex and Cheshire Ridge. Chailak Dere had never seemed so quiet before. Scarcely a bullet fell anywhere. In the brilliant moonlight every familiar feature showed clearly out, the angles, the bends, the bracken, the scrub, and the graves of men. The lighters were ready. In half an hour all were on board.[6]

All, that is, except the Diehards. The Aucklanders' lines were now held by just four officers and thirty-nine other ranks. Private Frank Wilson was among them. So were two fellow teachers from Auckland: Lieutenant John 'Jock' MacKenzie and Company Sergeant Major Joseph 'Joe' Gasparich. The Diehards still had three hours before they could abandon their positions. They had spent the whole day with nerves on edge, expecting at any moment to face heavy fighting. Now, in the stillness of the night, each man stood alone, 30 yards away from the next man and 2,000 yards from the safety of the beach. Joe Gasparich later described how the minutes ticked away so slowly during that 'long lonely wait in the dark'.[7] The final minutes must have been excruciating:

> The rearguard stood to arms in silent, deserted trenches and waited for the sudden shout, the rush of Turks, the last bitter struggle and then Quiet Death, to whom they had given themselves that their

friends might go free. Just before their time was up a shout ran along the Turkish line. Surely the enemy were coming now? They must have seen the transports in the moonlight and the boats moving to and fro between the ships and the shore. The rearguard 'stood-to', ready to die like men.[8]

But the expected onslaught did not materialize. Instead, at 0200 hours on Monday, 20 November, Frank Wilson, Joe Gasparich, Jock MacKenzie and the final group of Aucklanders quietly made their way down the slopes to the beach, where Colonel Arthur Plugge was waiting for them. The last of the Australians, including men from the 23rd and 24th Battalions AIF holding Leane's Trench near Lone Pine, left soon after. Suvla Bay was then abandoned; the rearguard of the 6th Lancashire Battalion, led by Lieutenant Clement Attlee, the future British Prime Minister, boarded their transports and began the journey back to Lemnos. In a final act of destruction, Australian engineers detonated their mines at The Nek and the guns of the Royal Navy ignited the abandoned and fuel-soaked stores left behind by the MEF. As the few heroic remnants of a failed military adventure looked back towards Gallipoli, 'the dark mass of Sari Bair stood out clear against the sky. The outline slowly vanished. It was the last of Anzac [but] in the hour of defeat men re-consecrated themselves to victory.'[9] The Gallipoli campaign had cost the Enzeds dear. Nearly 14,000 New Zealanders had served there and 8,000 of them had become casualties. The number of those who were killed in action or died of their wounds or disease was 2,779. Of these, 252 were committed to the sea and just 344 were interred in marked graves.[10] The remains of others lay scattered in the scrub. The Auckland Battalion had left Egypt with 1,100 men and had received a similar number as reinforcements during their eight months in action. Nearly a thousand of them were wounded; 19 officers and 344 other ranks were killed.[11] Many of the 600 Aucklanders who found themselves back on Lemnos at the end of 1915 were understandably bitter at having been ordered to withdraw in the face of the enemy and thus leave their fallen 'cobbers' behind.[12]

Some of the veterans, like Joe Gasparich and Jock Mackenzie, had been at war for over a year, having responded to the 'real and imminent danger' facing the British Empire in August 1914.[13] They were amongst the first 8,574 men in the Main Body of the New Zealand Expeditionary Force (NZEF).[14] They were aboard HMNZT *Waimana* when she sailed from Albany with the First Contingent of the AIF in late October and stopped near Fremantle a few days later to allow the West Australians to join the flotilla.[15] Both continued their training in Egypt and on Lemnos before taking part in the landing at Gallipoli on 25 April. Sergeant Joe Gasparich was attached to Divisional Headquarters (HQ) as part of General Godley's bodyguard. Disembarking from the *Lutzow*, a captured German liner, Joe landed at Anzac Beach at 1000 hours. Jock MacKenzie was ashore by noon, and the Auckland Battalion led the way for the 3,100 Enzeds in the fourth and final wave of the landings. They were ordered to reinforce the 3rd Brigade AIF, which had landed in the earlier waves. Like the men from WA before them, they made their way through Shrapnel Valley before being dispersed along Plugge's Plateau and the Second Ridge. Chaos and confusion followed. They experienced 'smoke, dust, heat, the air whining, singing, trembling, with the screeching shells and the flying fragments, rifle barrels red hot with constant firing, dead and dying all around'.[16] Two weeks later, Joe and Jock were in action again, this time at Cape Helles. On witnessing the loss of 800 fellow members of the New Zealand Infantry Brigade (NZIB) attacking across the so-called Daisy Patch on 8 May, Sergeant Gasparich told General Godley, 'Sir, this is a sheer waste of good men.'[17] A gunshot wound to the arm led to Joe's evacuation to hospital in Alexandria, but Lieutenant MacKenzie fought on. In June, the Aucklanders were back at Anzac, engaged in constant attacks and counter-attacks at Quinn's Post. As part of the failed August offensive, when the Australians fought at Lone Pine and The Nek and British forces landed at Suvla Bay, the Enzeds attacked at Chunuk Bair.

Five months of 'constant hammering at the Turk' had taken its toll.[18] The arrival of the Australian 2nd Division permitted some respite, and in mid-September the veteran Anzac battalions returned to Lemnos for rest and recuperation at Sarpi Camp. Frank Wilson and the 30 officers and 1,060 men of the 6th Reinforcements from New Zealand joined them there,[19] as did Joe Gasparich and others who had recovered from their wounds. In the second week of November veterans and new men alike were transported together to Anzac and made their way to the trenches of Rhododendron Spur, the highest Enzed positions on the peninsula. Five weeks later, they learnt of the decision to abandon the campaign. Despite the ravages of combat, climate and disease, which had reduced many men to 'miserable, bent scarecrows, their faces haggard and drawn',[20] Joe Gasparich and 'Fighting Jock' MacKenzie were now fit and ready for action.[21] Their suitability for and, indeed, their right to be part of the final rearguard was indisputable. Both were seasoned soldiers, men held in the highest regard by officers and other ranks alike. The choice of Private Frank Wilson for the covering force, however, was not an obvious one. Ormond Burton noted, 'The Main Body and those who had seen much fighting were the keenest of all. They begged for a place as a privilege. They demanded it as a right. They entreated and cajoled.'[22] Frank Wilson had enlisted in the Auckland Battalion just days before the Gallipoli vanguard had landed. To many of the old hands, the late arrivals were little more than 'lead-swingers' forced to the front by the pressure of public opinion. Frank's battlefield experience was indeed recent and limited, but back home he was already 'the popular idol of every Auckland schoolboy'.[23]

*   *   *

Francis Reginald 'Frank' Wilson was born on 28 May 1885, the youngest child of John and Elizabeth (née Storey). Frank's parents came from Timolin, a small village in Co. Kildare, some 50 miles from the city of Dublin. Part of the massive Irish diaspora of the nineteenth century, they migrated to New Zealand in 1875 with their eldest children Elizabeth and Henry. Their new home was a relatively new British colony. The Treaty of Waitangi in 1840 had established an uneasy formal relationship between Māori and European settlers; the former shared the rights and privileges of British subjects, the latter arrived in ever-greater numbers and needed land. Over the following three decades disputes over land ownership led to a series of military confrontations and the confiscation of Māori property by the British Crown. By 1870 the non-Māori population had passed 250,000; by 1896 it had reached 700,000, and numbers of Māori had dropped below 40,000.[24] Some of the earlier migrants had settled around Canterbury to farm sheep, or in Dunedin to strike it rich (if they were incredibly fortunate) in the goldfields of central Otago.

Government-funded public works programmes (for railway and road construction) and assisted immigration schemes during the 1870s led to further development. Migrants from England, Ireland and Scotland were allocated farmland. Many arrived just before the economic depression of the 'Hungry Eighties' but stayed long enough to benefit from a recovery based upon the export of agricultural produce – mainly meat, butter and cheese in refrigerated ships – to Britain. Others settled near the ports and worked in the construction trades and service industries which were creating new towns and cities throughout the British Empire. The Wilsons settled in Ponsonby, a district of the city of Auckland on the North Island. For a brief period, from 1840 to 1865, Auckland was the colony's capital. With its access by river to a hinterland transformed from forests and bush to productive farmland, and magnificent harbours to facilitate overseas trade, Auckland quickly became the country's largest city. Its population rose from nearly 17,000 in 1881 to over 30,000 by the end of the century.[25] Frank's father worked as a labourer, and the family home was on Dublin Street in Ponsonby, less than two miles from the city centre and only fifteen minutes away by horse-drawn tram. Frank was part of a growing family, surrounded by siblings. The two Irish-born children, Elizabeth and Henry, were joined by New Zealand-born Violet, John, Rosa and Albert, before Frank was born. Their early days were marred by Henry's death at the age of sixteen in 1890. Frank was five years old at the time and about to begin his formal education, first at Ponsonby School, then at Auckland Grammar School (AGS). Originally endowed in 1850 by colonial Governor Sir George Grey, AGS officially opened in 1869. By 1900 this fee-paying school for boys and girls led by headmaster James Tibbs, a graduate of Keble College Oxford, was the largest and most important in New Zealand. The curriculum at AGS mirrored that of its counterparts back in the 'Old Land'. AGS was one of the first schools in New Zealand to establish a Cadet Corps based on the British public-school model, compulsory for all boys from 1899 and an integral part of Auckland's defences.

Sport was important, too. Frank, a genuine and talented all-rounder, was known throughout his own home town and beyond as a first-rate sportsman. Considered one of the fastest runners in Auckland, he won the AGS Old Boys' 150 yard sprint in 1904 with a time, apparently, of

15.20 seconds. He scored several centuries for Ponsonby Cricket Club and captained them during their championship-winning season of 1914/15. He was a strong swimmer, played tennis and organized the Boys' Gymnasium at his local church. It was the game of rugby, however, at which he excelled. Only six months after starting at AGS he received his 'Lion' (or first 'cap') as a member of the school's 'football' team.[26]After leaving AGS in 1906 he played in a few matches for Ponsonby Rugby Football Club. Frank was following in the footsteps of an even more famous sporting idol, the legendary David Gallaher. The captain of the 1905–1906 'Originals' – the first 'All Black' team to tour the British Isles – also lived in Ponsonby, shared Frank's Irish heritage and in the years before the war became a selector for the provincial and national teams. Frank continued to develop his rugby skills whilst studying at Auckland Training College (ATC) and Auckland University College (AUC). In 1914 he captained the AUC team which won the Auckland Championship. By then the speedy wing three-quarter had also played for Auckland on twenty-two occasions, for North Island, and for his country: in 1910 he became an All Black. Playing in a preliminary match before a tour of Australia, he marked his first cap by kicking a drop goal in the 26-17 win over Wellington. His second cap was gained when the All Blacks played against New South Wales in Australia, but a knee injury late in the game ended his participation in the tour and his international career.

Frank Wilson was one of twenty–eight foundation students at Auckland Training College when it opened in 1906. Principal H. A. E. Milnes, himself a sportsman of some note, described Frank as 'a student of good ability but wedded to sport'.[27] This 'man of many parts',[28] however, engaged in numerous other activities. Popular with his fellow students, he was elected ATC's first Senior Prefect. He enjoyed acting, playing the role of Thomas in ATC's 1907 production of Sheridan's *The Rivals* and performing regularly as a member of the University Glee Club. He played the piano and sang in the All Saints Church Choir. He was also a keen gardener and lover of flowers; he grew the champion rose in the Auckland Exhibition of 1914.

In 1910 Frank graduated from ATC. For the next four years he taught at Newton West, a popular elementary school just south of Ponsonby Road, whilst still finding time to pursue his many sporting activities and other interests. The British declaration of war against Germany in August 1914 did not immediately result in Frank Wilson becoming a soldier. Many Aucklanders followed the example of their fellow Britishers in cities throughout the country and the wider empire and, despite some consternation about the immediate economic consequences of war, mounted 'the usual display of patriotic ardour'.[29] Trainees and alumni from ATC were not immune from the war fever that gripped the city of Auckland. Many of them were amongst the first to flock to the colours. Jock MacKenzie and Joe Gasparich had also trained at ATC (see plate 24) and were among fifteen college alumni who departed their homeland with the Main Body of the NZEF. Most had enlisted as infantrymen in the different companies of the Auckland Regiment; others joined the Auckland Mounted Rifles, were riflemen in the New Zealand Rifle Brigade (NZRB), gunners in the New Zealand Field Artillery, medical orderlies in the hospital ships and field ambulance sections of the New Zealand Medical Corps (NZMC) or members of divisional signal and machine gun companies. Whilst other former trainees followed in the first batches of reinforcements, it was not until March 1915 that Frank Wilson enlisted. He would have been an obvious contender for a place in the Main Body but had delayed joining the NZEF until six months into the war. The reasons for his initial reticence are not clear, but they may well have related to work or even sporting commitments. The initial entries in his Service Record depict a man with fair hair, blue eyes and an athletic build. He was 5 feet 10 inches tall, weighed 164lb and had a chest measurement of 39 inches.[30] Like many men of his generation he had previous military training, having served for five years in the Public School Cadets, reaching the rank of Lieutenant. At the age of twenty-eight he now joined the thousands of reinforcements preparing to join the fray. Further training followed at Trentham Military Camp where, true to form, he combined soldiering with captaining the 6th Reinforcements' rugby team. On 14 August 1915 Frank Wilson sailed from Wellington on HMNZT *Willochra*. By the end of September, having followed in the wake of the first Anzacs to Egypt and then on to Lemnos, he joined the depleted 3rd (Auckland) Company of the Auckland Infantry Battalion at Sarpi Camp near Mudros. The veterans of Gallipoli may have been scathing about each draft of reinforcements, but the new men like Frank were fit, well trained and eager to prove themselves before the war was over. On meeting their heroes

> the 6th Reinforcement, on their part, were torn between two emotions. On the one hand they were impressed by the fame these early men had won; for in those days the name of 'Anzac' stood very high. On the other hand, it was very difficult to connect honour and fame with the handful of decrepit, homesick, thoroughly verminous and blasphemously 'fed-up' scarecrows who represented the Auckland Battalion.[31]

So it was that on 8 November Frank Wilson set out on the Anzac trail with Jock MacKenzie and Joe Gasparich and stood alongside them on the night of 19/20 December. On returning to Mudros, the Diehards were saluted by the assembled ranks of men they had protected during the evacuation from Gallipoli. The return to Egypt began early on Christmas Day. Breakfast was hurried, and a promised festive dinner on their transport, the *Marsova*, did not materialize. For many men, the prospects of spending the New Year in Cairo gave them something to look forward to. Disembarking at Alexandria, however, they boarded waiting trains which took them not to the capital but to Moascar near Ismailia. A Turkish threat to the Canal demanded their presence there, and within days the troops were under canvas. The stay in Egypt also provided an opportunity for the battered New Zealand forces, as it did for their Australian counterparts, to reorganize. The arrival of the 7th, 8th and 9th Reinforcements, and the return of hundreds of sick and wounded men from the military hospitals, permitted the creation of additional battalions and brigades, components of a New Zealand Division (NZD) which replaced the NZAD. In March 1916 Jock MacKenzie and fellow officers took up posts in the new 2nd Auckland Battalion, part of the new 2nd Brigade. Newly promoted Second Lieutenant Joe Gasparich and Sergeant Frank Wilson remained in the 1st Auckland, 1st Infantry Brigade. The troops of the Canterbury, Otago and Wellington Battalions were similarly ordered. Training, especially in the new units, continued without interruption. Rumours abounded as to where the Enzeds would be deployed next; Mesopotamia, Salonika and France were all possibilities, with the latter favoured by most of the men.

Plate 1. Captain Albert Baswitz, M.C. The 'gallant fair-haired officer' of the 22nd London Battalion (BEF) was 'generous of heart, cheery of spirit, utterly fearless'.
(King's College London Archives)

Plate 2. North End Road, Fulham. Albert Baswitz's childhood neighbourhood: noisy and crowded, vibrant and colourful – a suburb of purposeful activity and enterprise. (Blades Collection)

Plate 3. Latymer Upper School. An English secondary school with a long and justifiably proud history of providing scholarship opportunities for boys from all social classes. (LUS Archives)

Plate 4. London Day Training College. A new model for supplying trained teachers to the Board Schools of the capital. Seated, centre, are Percy Nunn (sixth from left), John Adams and Margaret Punnett. It was widely held that Dr Nunn could teach calculus to a class of whelks. (UCL Institute of Education Archives)

Plate 5. Teachers and Soldiers. Richard Garland, Herbert Handley and Edward Mount. Like their friend Albert Baswitz, all were alumni of Latymer Upper School, the London Day Training College, King's College – and the Officer Training Corps. (King's College London Archives)

Plate 6. University of London OTC. Annual Camp was the highlight of the year for these part-time soldiers. In 1914, war was declared just days after the ULOTC arrived for training at Ludgershall near Salisbury Plain. (Blades Collection)

Plate 7. William Loring.
Pictured wearing the uniform
of the Imperial Yeomanry at
the time of the Second Boer
War c.1900. He later became
the founding Warden of
Goldsmiths' College, London.
(Special Collections & Archives, Goldsmiths
University of London)

Plate 8. The Battle of Loos. Dubbed the 'The Slag Heap
Victory' by the British press, Albert Baswitz and his fellow
London Territorials attacked the German lines at Loos, in
an industrial landscape dominated by colliery towers and
'crassiers'.
The Sphere 16 October 1915 (Blades Collection)

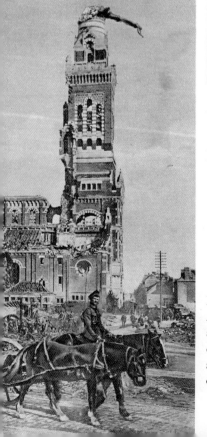

**Plate 9. The Hanging Virgin and Child of
Albert.** Hundreds of thousands of British
and Dominion troops congregated in the
city of Albert, before passing beneath the
statue's gaze on their way to the killing fields
of the Somme. (Blades Collection)

Plate 10. The Road to Bapaume. Part of the great highway of war leading to and from Albert. Despite five months of bitter fighting and huge numbers of casualties in 1916, the town of Bapaume remained in German hands. (Blades Collection)

Plate 11. Victory on the Somme. Canadian troops, assisted by a lone tank, round up German prisoners to the west of High Wood on 15 September 1916. (Blades Collection)

Plate 12. The 'Old Lion' calls to her cubs. Being 'British' extended beyond the British Isles. In the far reaches of Empire, men and women in the Dominions prepared to fight for their King and the 'old land'. (Parliamentary Recruiting Committee)

Plate 13. Claremont Teachers College Cricket XI, 1913. Pictured left to right, standing are Thomas Sten, Hugh King, Charles Griffiths, Walter Blair and two unidentified trainees. Seated on chairs are Gordon Gemmell, Sydney Forbes, Walter Crossing and one unknown. Seated fro row are Malcolm Stewart and Richard Hardwick. (Edith Cowan University Archives)

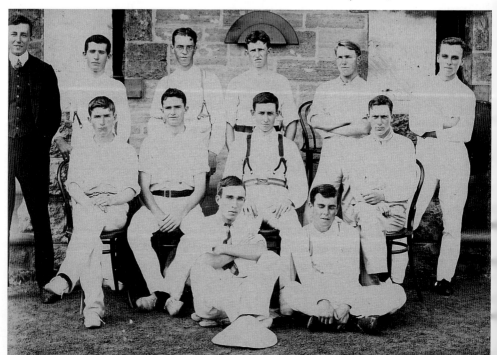

Plate 14. Anzacs in Egypt. Like thousands of tourists before and since, members of the 11th Battalion (AIF) pose for the camera at the Great Pyramid of Cheops at Giza on 10 January 1915. (West Australian Genealogical Society)

Plate 15. The Gallipoli Landings. One of the first Anzacs recalled that as they neared the shore, 'the first shot went "ping!" and we were under fire. About a minute after this there was a perfect fusillade. My word, they did pour the lead into us!' Bean (1916) *The Anzac Book.* (Blades Collection)

Photograph by C. E. W. BEAN

THE SUNRISE OF APRIL 25, 1915

The small boats taking troops to the shore can be seen beside the transports and close to the land

Plate 16. Corporal Adolph Knäble.
Originally amongst the 'Lost Legions
of Fromelles', the young Australian's
remains were later discovered in a mass
grave near Pheasant's Wood and reburied
with full military honours in a new
CWGC cemetery of the same name.
(Courtesy of Neville Green, Perth)

Plate 17. 'Don't forget me cobber!' A bronze statu
recalling the night-time recovery of the Australian
wounded at Fromelles now stands in the former n
man's land below Aubers Ridge. (Blades Collection)

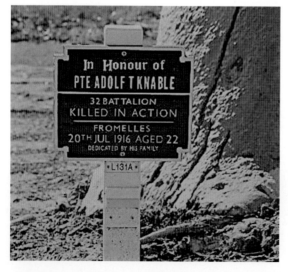

Plate 18. King's Park, Perth. The
memorials here are still the focus
of the annual 25 April 'Anzac Day'
service. The Honour Avenues contain
poignant reminders of lost comrades
and family members.
(Courtesy of Sally Jones, Perth)

Plate 19. Anzacs on the Somme. War correspondent Charles Bean reported that 'the West Australians were magnificent at Pozières'. Their capture of the German defensive lines in July 1916 paved the way for the BEF's assault on High Wood two months later. (Blades Collection)

Plate 20. Lieutenant Sydney Forbes. One of the first men ashore at Gallipoli on 25 April 1915, 'Syd' Forbes rose through the ranks of the 11th Battalion (AIF) and led his company in the decisive attack on enemy positions near the Windmill at Pozières. (Perth *Sunday Times* 20 August 1916)

Plate 21. The Fallen remembered. The Claremont Teachers College War Memorial, still standing in front of the original building which now forms part of the campus of the University of Western Australia. (Courtesy of Sally Jones, Perth)

Plate 22. 'Diggers' and 'Enzeds'. Men from Australia and New Zealand were proud to call themselves Anzacs. They fought alongside troops from Britain, India, Newfoundland, France and Africa in a campaign which ended in evacuation and humiliating defeat. Bean (1916) *The Anzac Book* (Blades Collection)

Plate 23. Sergeant Frank Wilson. Teacher, All Black, champion rose grower and 'Diehard'. The man from Auckland Training College was one of the last of the NZEF troops to leave Gallipoli. (Auckland Libraries Heritage Collections 31-W3283)

Plate 24. Auckland Training College. Principal Milnes and the 1910 ATC cohort. In the top row (third and fourth from the right) are 'Fighting Jock' MacKenzie and Joe Gasparich. Ormond Burton stands far left in the second row down. (Auckland Libraries Heritage Collections 31-WP688)

Plate 25. Second Lieutenant H.A.E. Milnes. The ATC Principal enlisted in the NZEF at the age of forty-one. 'Bert' was killed in action whilst attacking a German pillbox during the Battle of Broodseinde on 4 October 1917.

(Auckland Libraries Heritage Collections 31-M2344)

Plate 26. Tyne Cot. CWGC headstones mark the final resting places of the thousands of British and Dominion troops who fell during the advance towards Passchendaele. (Blades Collection)

Plate 27. Centenary Commemorations. Still remembered by the institution he established before the Great War: the Bert Milnes Memorial Service held on 4 October 2017 in the office of the Dean of Education at the University of Auckland.

(Courtesy of Professor Graeme Aitken, Auckland)

Ruines d'Ypres
The ruins of Ypres
Ruines des Halles aux Draps, du Beffroi
et du Portail Sud de la Cathédrale.
Ruins of the Cloth-Halls, Belfry and
Southern Portal of the Cathedral.

Plate 28. Ypres, the 'City of Fear'. The ruins of the medieval Cloth Hall in 'Wipers', a waymarker for thousands of men heading for the battlefields of the Salient. (Blades Collection)

Plate 29. The 'Tripehound'. The Sopwith Triplane was a worthy opponent of Baron Manfred von Richthofen's 'Flying Circus' in the skies above Ypres in 1917. (Blades Collection)

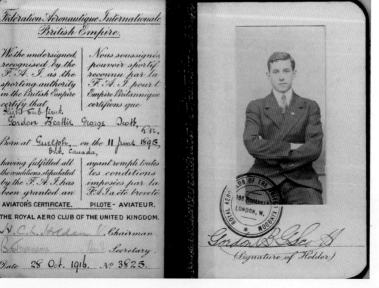

Plate 30. Sub-Lieutenant Gordon Scott. The young flier from Guelph in Ontario trained to be a teacher at the University of Toronto's Faculty of Education. He left Canada for England in 1916 and joined the Royal Naval Air Service.
(Courtesy of Marika Pirie, Ontario)

PTE. PERCY L. BARBER
EDUCATION

Plate 31. Percy Barber. The former part-time teacher-soldier enlisted in the Canadian Expeditionary Force and fought on the Somme, Vimy Ridge and Hill 70. He was killed in action at Passchendaele and was buried at Tyne Cot.
(*The Varsity War Supplement,* Toronto)

Plate 32. The Sugar Factory. This heavily-defended German position was captured by Canadian forces, including Percy Barber and the 21st (Eastern Ontario) Battalion, during the Battle of Flers-Courcelette on 15 September 1916.
(Blades Collection)

Plate 33. The Vimy Memorial. Testament to a nation's courage and loss, the magnificent Canadian Memorial looks down from Vimy Ridge to the Douai Plain and the industrial landscape of the Lens sector.
(Blades Collection)

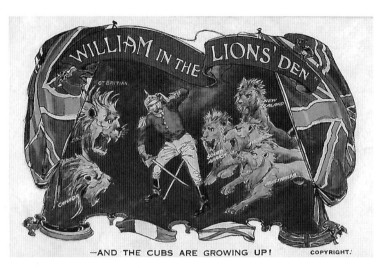

Plate 34. 'Young Lions' triumphant. The 'determined colonials' became the shock troops of the BEF, spearheading many of the major offensives of the last year of the war and contributing to the final defeat of the German Army on the Western Front.
(Blades Collection)

Plate 35. New nations forged in war. Pride in wartime achievements encouraged new 'national' rather than 'colonial' identities, and forged potent and lasting 'birth of nation' legends and mythologies.
(Blades Collection)

Plate 36. George Cline. This highly decorated senior officer in the Canadian Corps Signals enlisted in the First Contingent (CEF) at Valcartier Camp in 1914. George served throughout the war, then returned to teaching at the University of Toronto Schools. (Courtesy of Marika Pirie, Ontario)

Plate 37. Ormond Burton. An 'Enzed' of many parts: teacher, medic, soldier, officer, hero, historian and church minister. Later, as a committed pacifist, Ormond was imprisoned for his strident opposition to New Zealand's involvement in the Second World War. (Alexander Turnbull Library, Wellington, New Zealand. 1/2-152915-F)

Plate 38. Fred Albrecht. A veteran of Gallipoli and the Western Front who rose through the ranks to become a commissioned officer in the AIF. Fred returned to teaching in WA, then served in the Second World War and was imprisoned by the Japanese in Java. (Perth *Western Mail* 30 July 1915)

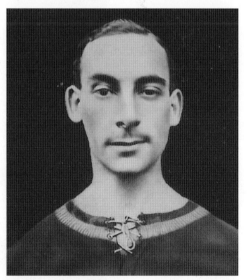

Plate 39. Ben Bateman. Preferring to play football rather than play soldiers in the OTC, Ben nevertheless enlisted in the ranks of the London Territorials and fought on the Somme in 1916. After the war he became a professional footballer with Crystal Palace F.C. (Blades Collection)

Plate 40. Flat Iron Copse.

(Blades Collection)

CAPTAIN
A. BASWITZ. M.C.
22ND BN. LONDON REGIMENT
16TH SEPTEMBER 1916 AGE 24

Sir Archibald Murray's inspection of the NZD on 3 April signalled the forthcoming move to a new battlefront. On 5 April Sergeant Wilson and the 1st Auckland Battalion entrained for Port Said and embarked on the *Franconia*. The following day, the *Ascania*, which had transported part of the 11th Battalion AIF from Fremantle at the beginning of the war, sailed from Alexandria carrying the 2nd Auckland Battalion. Frank Wilson and his fellow Aucklanders disembarked at Marseilles just a few days after Sydney Forbes and the West Australians and followed their fellow Anzacs northwards on the 60-hour rail journey through the French countryside to the Western Front.

The NZD was also sent first to 'The Nursery' on the Franco-Belgian border. By 16 April Sergeant Wilson was billeted in farm buildings near Hazebrouck. After Egypt and the South of France, the new surroundings were distinctly cold, wet and muddy. The Enzeds could hear the guns and see the flares of the battle front in the distance. Moving to Armentières in May, the 1st Auckland Battalion occupied the basement of a large factory which had previously manufactured window blinds. Nearby, the dilapidated *École Professionale* became the centre of divisional activities, housing the YMCA, church institutes, a picture house and the all-important canteen. In the town's estaminets and cafes the men could find a 'good friend' in the shape of one of the 'Mademoiselles from Armentières': Simone, Louisa, Darkie and Ginger were particular sweethearts of the men from New Zealand.[32] For the next three months the two Auckland battalions spent time in the front line: the 1st Battalion at La Chapelle d'Armentières, the 2nd Battalion near L'Épinette. Despite its reputation as a relatively quiet sector of the front, the fighting around Armentières resulted in many casualties: 1stAuckland lost 62 men killed and 203 wounded, whilst 2ndAuckland lost 22 killed and 127 wounded.[33] In late June and July 1916, as preparations for the offensive on the Somme gathered pace, the Enzeds joined the Australians in conducting trench raids on enemy lines. On the same day that the latter began their attacks at Fromelles and Pozières, the 1st Auckland Battalion carried out an unsuccessful raid from Port Egal. Lieutenant Joe Gasparich, the hero of the Daisy Patch and the evacuation, was wounded again and this time permanently incapacitated. One month later, on 18 August, the two battalions headed south. At times they travelled by train, but some of the journey involved marching along the French roads at night. They spent twelve days enjoying the green fields of Neuville-Forceville and Allery, soaking up the summer sun and eating and sleeping well. Training continued, and more men from the ranks became commissioned officers. All, including Second Lieutenant Frank Wilson, 'had seen considerable service, and without exception they were fine soldiers.'[34]

In early September, the Aucklanders reached Albert. Many of them walked into the town from their billets in Airaines and Riencourt and, like the British and Australian troops before them, marvelled at the sight of the hanging Virgin and Child. On 10 September they began the short journey to the front. The men of the 2nd Auckland Battalion, including the newly promoted Major Jock MacKenzie, led the way, moving up through Fricourt and Contalmaison to Mametz Wood. Two days later, they took up their positions in front of Green Dump, ready to play their part in the assault on High Wood. To their immediate left stood the British 47th Division; Captain Albert Baswitz and his fellow Londoners had moved up on the same day.

The Battle of Flers-Courcelette was the first major engagement on the Western Front for the men from New Zealand. The NZD was one of fifteen divisions in Rawlinson's Fourth Army which now tried to break German resistance on the Somme. On 15 September, the NZD held 900 yards of line in Caterpillar Valley. By 0600 hours the Enzeds had eaten their breakfasts and drunk their rum. Twenty minutes later, the crashing sounds of the artillery signalled the advance. The 2nd Auckland and 2nd Otago Battalions led the charge down the slope, protected by a creeping barrage ahead of them. Morale was high and the men sang as they advanced. They raced up the next slope, took Crest Trench and then pressed on towards their first key objective, the Switch Line. Ferocious hand-to-hand fighting ensued. Few prisoners were taken as the Enzeds swept through the enemy trenches and carried on relentlessly towards the Flers Line straight ahead of them. Then the Aucklanders dug in and prepared to hold their new line as other battalions, including the 4th Battalion of the NZRB, moved through to maintain the momentum of the attack. On this part of the battlefield at least, the new wonder weapon provided valuable support. The promised tanks had arrived late and had at first failed to keep up with the infantrymen. Tank D11 – His Majesty's Landship *Die Hard* no less – demonstrated the real potential of the weapon by smashing through some of the defences of the Flers Line and assisting in the capture of Flers village itself.

Second Lieutenant Frank Wilson and the 1st Auckland Battalion had, like Captain Albert Baswitz and the 22nd London Battalion, been held in reserve. On the morning of the attack they moved up from Fricourt to Mametz Wood to await their turn to join the fray. The next day, they relieved the 2nd Auckland Battalion, which had held the new line throughout the night, and then pushed on to relieve the NZRB troops in their advanced position. Then they, too, began to dig, trying to consolidate the division's left flank, which had been rendered vulnerable by the 47th Division's relatively limited advance. German resistance continued, particularly from the communication trench along Goose Alley and Drop Alley, and enemy shells fell on the exposed lines. At some point on 16 September Captain Baswitz was killed fighting near the Enzed's positions. The following day, Second Lieutenant Wilson was seriously wounded. Heavy showers of rain had turned the contested terrain into a quagmire, making the four-hour journey through the mud, wire and shell holes to the Advance Dressing Station (ADS) particularly harrowing for both the casualty and his stretcher-bearers. Frank Wilson survived his initial evacuation from the battlefield, but two days later, on 19 September, he died of his wounds at No. 45 Casualty Clearing Station at Dernancourt, a village two miles south-east of Albert.

General Haig stated that the New Zealanders 'had done all they had been asked to do and more, and had been a tower of strength to those on the right hand and on the left.'[35] Their exceptional performance came at a cost, however; 'they had gone in many and come out few.'[36] During their twenty-three days on the Somme, 2,111 men were killed in action, and thousands more were wounded.[37] Of the 1,500 men in the two Auckland battalions, some 300 were killed and nearly 700 wounded. Amongst the exhausted and filthy men who marched back to Albert was 'Fighting Jock' MacKenzie. His best friend Ormond Burton, one of the stretcher-bearers in the NZMC, had also managed to survive the victory at Flers.

*   *   *

Frank Wilson, Joe Gasparich, Jock MacKenzie and Ormond Burton had all trained to be teachers at ATC. They had been mentored and inspired by the same man: Herbert Albert Edwin Milnes, the founding Principal of the college. 'Bert', as he was known to family and friends, came from fighting and farming stock in Yorkshire. His paternal great-grandfather and great-uncles had fought in the Peninsular War against Napoleon. His father William had been born in Bradford, and after marrying Mary (née Barlow) became a 'cowkeeper' on the farm which his wife's family worked at Beeston near Leeds.[38] Bert was born in March 1875, the twelfth of thirteen children. As a young boy he enjoyed working on his small garden plot and walking in the countryside. On the death of his father in 1886, Bert and his family left the farm in somewhat straitened circumstances. His mother secured a small terraced house in nearby Beeston Hill, and Bert attended the local Higher Board School. He later transferred to Dewsbury Road School before completing his secondary schooling at the Central Higher Grade School in Leeds. Bert and four of his siblings (Orlando, Annie, Ethel and Mary) were all intent upon becoming teachers and began their careers as pupil teachers in local elementary schools.

In 1893 Bert Milnes left his beloved Yorkshire to continue his training at Borough Road College in London. Having recently moved from its original site in Southwark, the college's strong emphasis on games and physical fitness and its new gymnasium and green playing fields at Isleworth in Middlesex appealed to those who believed in combining academic study with sporting achievement. Quiet and self-reliant, Bert adopted a spartan regime of cold baths, few bedclothes and plenty of rugby. According to Arthur Burrell, the Principal of BRC at the time, Bert had a gentle voice and refrained from cursing and lewd talk. He was renowned for his hearty laugh, sporting ability and awful singing. Despite working hard at his studies, however, he was not remembered for his intellectual attainments. On completion of his teacher training Bert returned to his old school at Beeston Hill and taught under the tutelage of his former headteacher Mr Fairbrother, himself an 'Old B'.[39] During that time Bert trained the school team which won the Leeds Schools Football Championship. He left after four years to attend the Royal College of Science in London, determined to gain further academic qualifications.

He passed the University of London Intermediate Examination and shortly afterwards returned to BRC as a member of staff. Mr Milnes lived on campus and embraced all that the institution offered. He taught his trainees at the same time as studying (and struggling) alongside them to gain his Bachelor of Science (BSc.) degree from the University of London in 1904. By now he was a burly, larger-than-life figure whose laugh could shake a chair. As an experienced teacher he was soon promoted to House Tutor and then Assistant Master of Method. Unlike Dr Percy Nunn at the London Day Training College, however, Milnes was impatient with all educational theory, preferring instead to develop the practical all-rounder who could combine classroom practice with sporting prowess. 'This mass of steady rock against all waves, a cheerful lighthouse in all storms' practised what he preached and was the star player in the Old Bs rugby team.[40]

In 1905 Bert Milnes applied for the post of Principal of ATC. The 32-year-old was soon to be married to Louisa Heath Haler, a fellow teacher and daughter of a Schools Inspector. One of Bert's reasons for applying for the post was a belief that a change of climate might benefit Louisa, who suffered repeated bouts of ill health. He was one of seventy applicants who responded to advertisements placed in the New Zealand, Australian and British newspapers. Strongly supported by BRC, Bert was one of only five candidates considered by the New Zealand Education Department. In November 1905 he was appointed as Principal at the Training College and, concurrently, Lecturer in Education at Auckland University College. Before he had even set sail for the far-flung Dominion, the *Auckland Star* reported on his appointment and informed its readers of the academic and professional qualifications (including those in drill and 'ambulance') of this expert from the old country whose services they were fortunate to have secured.[41] Four months later, on 5 February 1906, the *Star* reported that the new Principal and his wife had arrived in Auckland via the SS *Manuka*. Mr and Mrs Milnes had married in Ilkley in December, shortly before departing for New Zealand. The Principal-designate had spent the weeks at sea considering the challenge ahead of him; characteristically, he had also found time to fight the ship's boxing champion.

One of the newspaper's reporters caught up with the new arrival on landing and managed to interview him. Once again, his qualifications and experience were discussed, but the self-described Yorkshireman was also eager to stress his interest in athletic sports of all kinds, and especially his experience of the 'Northern Union of England' version of rugby.[42] He also managed to state some of his fundamental beliefs about education: the crucial importance of developing 'the man of tomorrow' to counter the threat from Germany and France to British supremacy; the creation of good order and attendance in schools without resort to corporal punishment; the training and deployment of teachers 'full of zeal [and] ready to do their best for the nation's youth'. Trained teachers were the rock upon which the whole system of schooling depended but, the new Principal noted, 'to one just out from Home, it is somewhat astonishing to land in Auckland and find virgin school in the matter of one very important branch of education – the training of our primary school teachers.'[43] The report concluded by noting that Principal Milnes would be visiting the training college's (temporary) buildings at the state school on Wellesley Street in two days' time. Bert Milnes, the 'man of action',[44] was obviously keen to get started and make his mark in a new land.

The development of schooling in New Zealand was characterized by the adaptation of developments in the old country to the context and needs of the new Dominion. In Britain, Forster's 1870 Education Act had addressed the contentious issues of school supply, funding and administration. Deciding upon the respective responsibilities of central and local government was crucial to the development of a national system of schooling. In 1877 New Zealand established its own Department of Education, with powers to direct provincial authorities to provide suitable forms of educational provision. The Auckland Board of Education had until then spent less on education than any other province. From 1872 children aged five and above had been able to attend secular Common Schools without paying fees. The Education Act of 1877 made attendance at an elementary school compulsory. The rapid expansion of school places, however, depended upon the recruitment of enough teachers. As in Britain, the use of pupil teachers offered a relatively inexpensive solution to the problem of teacher supply. The Auckland Board started to employ pupil teachers in 1869, basing their system on that introduced in Otago (the British model) seven years earlier. The limitations and often poor quality of many pupil teachers led to discussions in Auckland about the possibility of a 'Normal' or 'Model School'. Dunedin (1876), Christchurch (1877) and Wellington (1880) had all opened training colleges to provide teachers for the ever-expanding school population. In 1881 the first incarnation of ATC opened under the leadership of Mr Alexander McArthur on the site of the Wellington Street School. The latter institution, opened four years earlier, catered for 1,100 pupils. The training college enrolled just six female pupil teachers in its foundation year. By 1885, however, ATC numbers had increased to 104, of whom 99 were women.[45] Three years later, the widespread economic recession in New Zealand led to reduced government expenditure generally, and the closure of ATC. By the time Bert Milnes arrived in Auckland, however, attitudes towards the importance of formal teacher training had changed dramatically. From 1899 the driving force at the New Zealand Department of Education was Sir George Hogben. In stark contrast to general and professional opinion at the time, the former Inspector-General of Schools and now Secretary of Education wanted schools to place more emphasis on practical and technical training and less on academic learning. He disliked the renewed reliance upon the pupil-teacher system and was a major influence on the 1903 Royal Commission's recommendation to introduce a national system of teacher training. In 1905 *The Training College and Pupil Teacher Regulations* empowered provincial Boards of Education to establish training colleges offering two-year courses and the possibility of part-time study at an associated university.

The appointment of Bert Milnes as Principal of ATC epitomized the new approach to teacher training. Unfortunately, official support for his new mission was not matched, initially at least, by the facilities and resources it required. The disappointment the new Principal may well have felt on his first visit to Wellesley Street was not recorded at the time. To say that his new institution lacked the resources of the specialist training colleges in London would be a gross understatement. Bert Milnes immediately insisted on the provision of new buildings, but for the first few years he and his trainees had to make the most of what they had. On 5 March 1906, just four weeks after arriving in New Zealand, the Principal welcomed twenty-eight students (nineteen women and nine men) to the new, if somewhat impoverished, Auckland Training College. These foundation students were aged between eighteen and twenty-three, and most had been pupil teachers. Frank Wilson, a young man who shared many of the personal qualities and ideals of his new mentor Bert Milnes, was among them. There were, however, some compensations and many opportunities in starting from scratch. In this new world, Principal Milnes was given a degree of independence unheard of back in England. He responded to this relative freedom from bureaucratic control by making his own staffing appointments, including that of the like-minded Herbert Cousins as headteacher of the Normal School at Wellesley Street. He was also able to imprint his own ideas on the new building, which opened in November 1908. The facilities included those with which he was familiar back in England: dedicated spaces for lectures and individual study, specialist rooms for science teaching, a library and a museum. A central hall and student common rooms, albeit separate ones for men and women, helped to foster corporate activities. Over the new building's main entrance was the motto *Totis Viribus* ('With All One's Might'). More than simply a mission statement, this was a direct instruction and expectation. Potential entrants to ATC were required to produce character and health references, and to commit themselves to a period of at least two years teaching service on completion of their training. They were expected to make the most of the additional, and often compulsory, programmes which the Principal had negotiated with partner institutions. The emphasis was often on practical work: Auckland Technical School provided courses in manual subjects and helped to develop blackboard drawing skills; Newton East Manual Training Centre provided classes in woodwork and cookery. Trainees undertook degree-level courses at Auckland University College, which had been founded in 1883. Exempt from course fees, they had to work especially hard; evening lectures at AUC followed a full day of training at ATC.

By the time Ormond Burton, Joe Gasparich, Jock MacKenzie and the rest of the 1910 cohort began their training, ATC was firmly established and well respected. Most of its trainees were women – a reflection of the gender imbalance in the teaching profession nationally – but increasing numbers of young men had begun to see teaching as a worthwhile occupation. ATC provided preparation for employment in elementary schools. It built a model Country School on its premises to prepare trainees for the hundreds of rural (or 'backblock') schools which were run by sole teachers. Spending alternate weeks in college and on school placements, trainees observed demonstrations of classroom craft given by the Principal (and Mr Cousins and his staff from the Normal School) and then applied their learning to real classroom settings. True to form, Bert Milnes insisted that every trainee take part in sporting activity of some kind. Despite his disparaging comments about Frank Wilson's addiction to sport, he was a firm believer in the cult of 'athleticism' and placed great emphasis on the physical health and development of his charges.[46] In his 1907 Principal's Report he stated: 'Good health means better work all round, it means happier lives; and happier teachers mean happier students.'[47] Principal Milnes acquired a weighing machine and recorded the height and weight of all trainees. He personally supervised the compulsory daily Physical Education lesson for the men and appointed trained PE teachers for the women. All trainees were encouraged to take part in swimming and classes in lifesaving and first aid. Competitive sport included tennis, hockey, basketball, netball and boxing. There were rarely enough male trainees to form a rugby team, but they were able to play alongside Bert Milnes (a front-row forward) in the University College XV. The Principal also trained the AUC athletics team. He could be harsh on those who did not live up to the sporting ideal. In the last cohort before the war, 104 of the 108 trainees were playing some form of sport; the four absentees, according to Milnes ,were 'weakly' and should never have passed the entrance medical examination. He went on to say that 'a student unable to take part in a game is not in my opinion suited to school teaching.'[48] For male trainees, 'athleticism' was combined with the notion of 'manliness', increasingly so after the establishment of the college's OTC in 1910. The Department of Education encouraged the development of school cadet forces throughout New Zealand, and in 1911 added Physical Drill to the curriculum for teacher training. At ATC, the male trainees drilled once a week, practised their shooting on a miniature rifle range in the museum room and attended camp at the end of the academic year.

Trainees at ATC received an annual allowance of £30 plus, for those living away from home, an additional £30 to pay the rent in approved lodgings. One of Principal Milnes' regrets was that no residential accommodation existed on the ATC campus. He and his wife Louisa did all they could, however, to involve their students in the corporate life of the college. Much of what the young Bert Milnes had experienced and valued at Borough Road College was imported directly into the wider curriculum of ATC. As such he was emulating, in his own distinctive style, the similar efforts of contemporaries such as Percy Nunn and William Loring in London, and William Rooney in Perth, in creating an institutional ethos and spirit which permeated the whole training environment. Sporting activity was central to this process, but so too were other activities which bound together the student and staff body and gave everyone a sense of exclusivity and identity. They included the familiar 'classes' adopted elsewhere in Britain and the Dominions to develop well-rounded students: music and debating societies, Bible Study and reading circles, the Glee Club, a college orchestra, dramatic productions and a Ruskin Society, the latter organized by Louisa Milnes. There were 'Socials' on alternate Saturday evenings, organized outings to nearby scenic spots such as Mount Eden or places of interest such as ostrich farms, flour mills and hat factories. The annual end-of-year picnic excursion included a communal rendition of *Forty Years On*, a song originally from Harrow School which Bert Milnes had sung as a trainee at BRC. College colours appeared on badges, caps and scarves. A college magazine was published, the *Manuka*, named after the ship which had transported Bert and Louisa to Auckland. Reunions of former trainees were always popular: the Old As modelled themselves on the Old Bs at BRC.

Bert Milnes also made a name for himself more widely in Auckland society as both a public speaker and a sportsman. The *New Zealand Herald* published details of many of the talks he gave to fellow professionals and the wider public, noting that 'his school ideas were modern and unconventional and quite in keeping with his general character.'[49] Addressing a meeting of the Country Teachers' Association in 1912, he advocated the introduction of moveable walls and described the advantage they offered of fresh air during good weather. He recognized the expense this might involve, but argued it was 'simply a matter of getting the authorities out of the old grooves'.[50] An open lecture on 'Schoolroom Humour' was accompanied by an exhibition of teaching diagrams and models,[51] whilst his talk on 'Muscular Christianity' to the YMCA was, the *Herald* reported, 'full of good advice to young men and was much appreciated'.[52] On the sporting front, Bert Milnes was a popular member of the Auckland Tennis Club and competed regularly in its men's singles and doubles tournaments. In 1913 he represented the club in the New Zealand Tennis Association Dominion Championships, playing alongside Miss F. Woodroffe in the mixed doubles. He was also the founder and President of the Auckland Basketball Association and President of the Auckland Ladies' Hockey Association.

Much of what has been written about this man verges on the hagiographic. Contemporaries excused his limitations, were charmed by his no-nonsense approach and were impressed by his charismatic leadership and the influence he exerted on all who met him. Many of the ideals he espoused are no longer fashionable, or even acceptable to modern-day sensibilities. Principal Milnes was, however, a role model at the time to many of his male trainees and idolized, apparently, by the female students. His reputation was further enhanced when, at the age of forty-one, he enlisted for service in the New Zealand Army.

By the time Bert Milnes began his training as part of the 32nd Reinforcements, just over a hundred of his former students had enlisted; Gasparich, Mackenzie and Burton were amongst eighteen members of the 1910 cohort alone who were already with the NZEF. Men from ATC had landed at Anzac Cove on 25 April 1915 and fought on the Daisy Patch against 'Johnny Turk'. All had suffered the privations of Gallipoli, and several had been wounded and hospitalized. All but one had managed to survive the campaign; Sergeant William Wells of the 15th North Auckland Company was killed in action on 19 November, the first man from the college to die for his country. In March 1916, Bert Milnes signed up as a private in the NZEF. The *Auckland Star* reported that the ATC Principal felt that 'although his duties at home were important, he could render even better service to his country as a soldier.' He later told a fellow officer that 'he could not look the Old As in the face if he had not been "out there" to lend a hand with them.'[53] His former trainees had set an example of service, as he had done previously for them, which he now felt obliged to follow. He had read the letters and newspaper reports about their exploits and seen photographs of their time in Egypt and Gallipoli sent to the *Auckland Weekly News* by former trainee Robert Steele. The war was far from over, and his young protégés were at that very moment preparing for their next deployment, quite possibly to the trenches of the Western Front. The New Zealand Government continued to call for men to join the Army and, unlike its counterpart in Australia, was about to introduce conscription. The Military Services Act of 1916, which post-dated its British equivalent by seven months, made all non-Māori men aged twenty to forty-five liable for call up. Bert was by now a widower. His wife Louisa had died in October 1913, having struggled with ill health throughout their eight years of married life together in Auckland, and he no longer had family commitments which might have kept him at home. The avowed man of action chose to enlist rather than be conscripted. Herbert Cousins was appointed Acting Principal and was instructed to hold the fort at ATC during the Principal's absence.

Bert Milnes began his military training at Trentham Camp on 7 March 1916. In terms of age and physique, he was hardly the 'average' recruit. Soldier Number 22525 was double the age of most of the young recruits, and his bulky frame meant he had great difficulty in getting a military greatcoat that fitted him. Under the heading 'Religion' on his attestation form he wrote 'Church of England – and Yorkshire'.[54] Within a week of joining the army Private Milnes was promoted to corporal, and eight weeks later to sergeant. From Trentham, which in the first year of war had become seriously overcrowded and rife with contagious and often fatal diseases, he moved to Featherston Camp. Established in early 1916, Featherston trained men for the 10th to 43rd Reinforcements; a Māori contingent of 16 officers and 500 other ranks had trained separately at Avondale Camp in Auckland.[55] The 16-week programme at Featherston made soldiers of civilians. From the outset, the recruits concentrated on physical fitness and military drill, followed by musketry in week 3 and bayonet work in week 4. The real rite of passage, however, took place in week 14, when the new platoons undertook a three-day march over the nearby Rimutaka Hills. Camping out, night marches and a mock attack at dawn were followed by a finale on the shooting range, firing fifteen rounds in a 'mad minute'. Sergeant Milnes became something of a father figure to the men in his platoon; some even referred to the caring NCO as 'Dad'. Both he and his superior officers knew, however, that his civilian experience and leadership skills marked him out as a potential commissioned officer. On 11 August 1916, having passed the necessary formal examination, Bert Milnes received his commission and prepared for deployment (see plate 25). At the end of the year Principal Milnes returned to ATC to attend a reception given by his colleagues and, proudly wearing his military uniform, sat for a group photograph with the trainees. He then visited his wife's grave at Waikumete Cemetery.

On 13 January 1917 Second Lieutenant Milnes was taken on the strength of the Auckland Regiment. He embarked from Wellington a week later aboard HMNZT *Waimata*. Unlike the men who had sailed from New Zealand in 1914, the later reinforcements had a much better idea of what awaited them in France and Flanders. Their sea journey also took a different and much longer route. The first Enzeds to go overseas had assumed, erroneously as it transpired, that they were headed for the 'old country', only to land in Egypt. The reinforcements of 1917, on the other hand, set sail directly for England. As the on-board Adjutant, the newly commissioned officer was kept extremely busy during the long voyage via Cape Town and the Atlantic Ocean. This latest batch of Aucklanders arrived in Plymouth, disembarking on Bert's birthday, 28 March. It was not the first time he had been back to the old country. In May 1908, the *Observer* had noted the return of the college principal from a trip home, just months before the death of his mother Mary in October of that year. His new home in spring 1917, however, was Sling Camp near Bulford on Salisbury Plain, where the latest Enzeds were to undergo a further two months of training before being committed to the Western Front. In May, Second Lieutenant Milnes was posted to the 3rd Auckland Battalion, part of the New Zealand Division's (NZD) newly formed 4th Brigade. The brigade also contained experienced officers and NCOs whose remit was to season and stiffen the new formation. After being reviewed by King George V, the 4th Brigade finally proceeded overseas and landed at Le Havre on 29 May. They were not the first troops to be glad to see the back of Sling Camp, and the first days in France came as a welcome, if short-lived, relief. In bivouacs near Boulogne, many of the Aucklanders spent their evenings in the local shops, restaurants and estaminets. After their spell at the Second Army Reinforcement Camp, however, they then entrained for Étaples and the infamous Bull Ring. For a further two weeks they were treated as new recruits, whatever their previous background or experience. Second Lieutenant Milnes had enlisted some fourteen months earlier, but he and his men were nevertheless subjected to the Bull Ring's regime of intensive training and iron discipline in readiness for the battle to come. By June the latest batch of Enzeds were ready to join the rest of the NZD. Instead of travelling through France to the Somme, however, they headed north into Belgium and the battlefields around Ypres.

The market town of Ypres – 'Wipers', as it was known to British and Dominion troops, or 'Ieper' to its mainly Flemish inhabitants – was steeped in history. Situated in the province of West Flanders, Ypres was renowned during the Middle Ages for its linen trade with England. The town's fortifications bore witness to successive military incursions by English, Spanish and French forces over the centuries. In 1914, German forces, following the Schlieffen Plan, entered neutral Belgian territory and advanced towards Ypres, surrounding the town on three sides and subjecting it to artillery bombardment. The First Battle of Ypres (19 October to 22 November 1914) succeeded in securing the town for the combined Belgian, British and French forces, but created a salient vulnerable to attack for the duration of the Great War. The Germans launched another offensive in 1915, using poison gas for the first time as a prelude to the Second Battle of Ypres (22 April to 25 May). British and French forces (including imperial units from Canada and India, and Senegal and Algeria respectively) stood firm alongside the remnants of the Belgian Army. In 1917, and after two years of static trench warfare in Flanders, a major operation to break out from the salient became part of a wider strategic plan. The British High Command decided to launch a series of offensives at Arras, Lens and Ypres. Haig and his generals – Plumer, Rawlinson and Gough – debated the merits of different modes of attack. The Somme had exposed the limitations of large-scale set-piece battles; now they considered 'a method for making a surprisingly rapid succession of violent blows'.[56] In an attempt to counter the German tactics of flexible defence, the former ambitious command to 'break through and advance' was to be replaced, initially at least, with a more cautious one of 'bite and hold' as a prelude to the final breakthrough. The efficacy of the new approach was first demonstrated by the NZD when, on 7 June 1917, three of its brigades stormed Messines Ridge, captured Messines village and consolidated the new positions. This was bite-and-hold in action, a clear indication to the British generals, and to the German forces entrenched around the salient, that the defensive grey wall could be both breached *and* subsequently held by the BEF.

The Third Battle of Ypres is the collective name for the four distinct, but related, offensives by British and Dominion forces which took place in the second half of 1917, namely the Battles of the Menin Road, Polygon Wood, Broodseinde and Passchendaele (see Map 7). Third Ypres is sometimes, but erroneously, known simply by the name of the last engagement. More generally, the battlefield is recalled in the popular imagination as one in which incompetent generals sent thousands of brave men to die in a sea of mud in Flanders fields. The conditions at Passchendaele were certainly atrocious towards the end of the battle, but when the initial assaults took place the weather was relatively settled and dry; some soldiers even complained about dust and lack of water. On 20 September the BEF began its attack on the Menin Road. Supported by a 'colossal artillery presence – greater again than anything yet employed',[57] British and Australian troops from the Second Army (X Corps and 1 ANZAC respectively) attacked across the broken land in the vicinity of Glencorse Wood and Inverness Copse. They advanced towards the villages of Zonnebeke and Gheluvelt, consolidating groups of fortified shell holes into a new forward line.

Six days later, they took the second major step. The Battle of Polygon Wood also took place in dry and fine autumn conditions and followed a similar pattern to the previous assault along the Menin Road. A ferocious attack by troops of the Australian 5th Division cleared the wood's shredded remains of its German defenders and helped move the line forward a further 1,200 yards. BEF casualty rates, however, increased with each step forward; the cost per square mile at Polygon Wood was 4,440 men.[58] The bite-and-hold tactics inflicted heavy losses on the enemy, too, however, and Haig believed that the German forces were beginning to falter. There was no lull in the fighting between the distinct offensives. As the BEF began its final preparations for the third major assault, General Sixt von Armin, Commander of the German Fourth Army, continued his 'frenzied efforts to regain the Menin Gate and Polygon Wood'.[59] Haig believed that one more strictly limited advance might finally prise open Sixt von Armin's defences.

By the summer of 1917 the NZD had recovered from the losses it had sustained on the Somme; its three divisions were at full strength and in peak condition, and a fourth was in the final stages of training. The stunning success at the Battle of Messines, however, had cost the division nearly 4,000 casualties. The 1st Auckland Battalion alone lost 290 men, including three officers and thirty-nine other ranks killed in action.[60]At the beginning of October all four brigades of the NZD marched north from Messines ready to take part in the third great strike eastwards. Fighting alongside a further eleven British and Australian divisions, their orders were to secure the Gheluvelt Plateau. The 1st and 4th Brigades were to take the Broodseinde Ridge and the Gravenstafel Spur; the 2nd and 3rd Brigades were to advance towards the village of Passchendaele. During August and September Second Lieutenant Milnes and the 3rd Auckland Battalion had completed their training. The Battle of the Somme had demonstrated the importance of preparing some battalions to attack over specific terrains, such as the heavily fortified woods and copses at Mametz, the Bazentins and High Wood. Other units trained specifically to counter the threat from new defensive obstacles. For the Aucklanders, the final training programme concentrated on capturing pillboxes. Since 1915 the Germans had been using concrete in huge quantities, not for reinforcing their trenches (the water table was too near the surface to dig trenches of any great depth) but for constructing mini-fortresses. There were some 2,000 of these compact and camouflaged pillboxes in the salient,[61] virtually all built by the Germans; the policy of maintaining an offensive attitude at all times precluded their use by British forces. Massive pre-cast concrete blocks were used to build the walls and roofs. Laid out in a chequerboard pattern or in echelons, and supported by machine gun nests and entanglements of barbed wire, they presented a far more deadly barrier to attacking troops than the linear defences previously employed. Milnes and his men in the 3rd Company worked in small groups – platoons and sections – practising ways in which the pillboxes might be neutralized.

After weeks of intensive training came the familiar signal for impending action: a formal review by the 'top brass'. In brilliant sunshine in a large field outside Fromentelles, the platoons and battalions of the 1st, 2nd and 4th Brigades of the NZD saluted and marched past Field Marshal

Sir Douglas Haig and his guest, the Rt Hon. Winston Churchill. The weather was still swelteringly hot when the 4th Brigade left Lumbres on 26 September and headed towards the staging area north of Hazebrouk. Foot-slogging twenty miles each day along hard and dusty roads, they encountered increasing amounts of traffic and the materiel of war. On 1 October, all three Auckland Battalions marched along the crowded highroad from Poperinghe to Vlamertinghe and on to Ypres, the City of Fear. The town of Albert had been the gateway to the battlefields of the Somme; Ypres served the same purpose in Flanders. Some who marched through the ruins described the 'pitiable sight' before them and noted the once-magnificent Cloth Hall (see plate 28) 'looking stark and naked with one wall standing'.[62] For Ormond Burton, however, the town's historic building was – like the hanging Virgin and Child in Albert – a potent symbol of survival and determination:

> The broken tower of the ruined Cloth Hall had its appeal, even to the most unimaginative. In its glory of desolation and ruin it typified the splendid valour and steadfastness that had saved Europe. It stood foursquare, battered, but still standing, the wall against which the Old Army had set its back and fought to the death. Now it pointed to the skies and spoke of victory. Ypres was no longer the gate bolted and barred against the invader; it was a wide-open way through which poured the rising tide of triumph.[63]

Burton's final point was made with the benefit of hindsight. The German invaders, secure in their pillboxes, now blocked the route out of the salient. The Aucklanders marched past the Cloth Hall, then through the town's ramparts and over its moat. The Zonnebeke Road, littered with the debris of war, led up to the line. Here they were at their most vulnerable. The supply line had been subject to bombing raids by German aircraft, especially since the arrival in the skies above the salient of Manfred von Richthofen and his 'Flying Circus'. The Germans were also aided by a change in the weather. When the Aucklanders began their move from Ypres to the reserve trenches on 1 October, and then on to the front line the following day, they did so in fine dry weather. On 3 October, 'after a fortnight of perfect skies',[64] the weather broke and a blustery drizzle and chilly westerly wind set in. Heavy rain followed and continued for the rest of the campaign. Crouching in trenches beginning to fill with water and slime, and wearing uniforms which were soaked through despite the makeshift covering of oilskin sheets, the 3rd Auckland Battalion waited for the signal to attack. With nerves on edge, men ate their breakfast of bully beef and dry bread and received final instructions from their immediate superiors. The drizzle eased temporarily as zero hour approached on 4 October, but visibility was poor. Had Second Lieutenant Milnes been able to see through the darkness and early morning mist the battlefield in front of him, he would have observed a landscape which was 'dismal and war-scarred to a degree exceeding even the desolation of the Somme'.[65] A wide expanse of dull, dreary, brown land hid within it a hideous pockmarked terrain full of shell-holes and gaping craters. The debris of modern warfare lay all around or protruded through the mud: 'tangled heaps of rusty wire, broken rifles, smashed field guns, rotting pieces of equipment, filthy and torn clothing, empty shell-cases, old tins, riven helmets'.[66] A cold wind carrying the stench of residual gas and dead men was a better indicator of what lay ahead of them in no man's land. Maps no longer accurately depicted the realities of the battlefield. The 4th Brigade had been ordered to attack the Gravenstafel Spur, one of the two ridges which projected from the Passchendaele Ridge. On its crest was a small rise known as the Abraham Heights, their designated objective, some 800 yards away from their lines. The nearby village of Broodseinde would give its name to the battle. Maps indicated that the Enzeds would have to cross one of the many small streams that ran across this part of Flanders. What their maps did not show was that the Hanebeek had been transformed into a quagmire, and on the site of the building labelled Otto Farm now stood a German pillbox. The Enzeds were also unaware of the fact that they were not the only force getting ready to attack that day. General Sixt von Armin was about to launch Operation High Storm in a bid to recapture land lost during the Battles of the Menin Road and Polygon Wood. German troops from 212th Reserve Infantry Regiment (45th Reserve Division) and fresh reinforcements from the 4th Guards Division were at that very moment moving with bayonets fixed into their own front line positions. Just 30 minutes before the British and Dominion troops were scheduled to attack, the German artillery unleashed their own bombardment on the closely-packed BEF units.

The NZD held a front of some 2,000 yards. The Aucklanders stood on the extreme right of the Enzed line. To their right were units from the 3rd, 2nd and 1st Australian Divisions. Immediately to their left were the men of the 3rd Otago Battalion, with the 3rd Canterbury and Wellington Battalions behind them in support. Further to the left stood the 1st Brigade NZEF, with Ormond Burton and the 2nd Brigade in support. It was exactly a year to the day since the former medical orderly had marched back from Flers to Albert. The veteran of Gallipoli and the Somme had since transferred from the NZMC and was now a front line combatant. Corporal Burton's two old friends from the 1910 ATC cohort, however, were no longer at the front. The wounds suffered by Joseph Gasparich the previous year in France were so severe that he had been returned to New Zealand and ultimately discharged from the NZEF. Jock MacKenzie had been killed in action near Estaires in February 1917. On the extreme left of the attacking line were the British 48th Division; their objective was the Bellevue Spur in front of Passchendaele. At 0600 hours the British guns commenced a hurricane bombardment and creeping barrage. Shells from hundreds of 18-pounders and 4.5 inch howitzers smashed into the pillboxes and killed their garrisons. Machine gun bullets whined as they passed over the heads of the advancing Enzeds. Battle-hardened German soldiers later admitted that they had never experienced enemy fire of such intensity. According to a later official history 'the whole earth of Flanders shook and seemed to be on fire.'[67] The creeping barrage lifted every three minutes to allow the advancing troops to regroup in the half-dark and smoke of battle and to limit the possibility of casualties caused by friendly fire. Enemy gunners had been quick to respond, however, and soon the attackers were showered with stinking mud and water as shells exploded all around them. The noise was terrific. With 100 yards still to go before they reached the Hanebeek, the Enzeds were subjected to fire from machine guns and rifles. In low cloud and with wind and driving rain on their backs they continued to push on across the treacherous swamp-like terrain. The defences at Duchy Farm and Riverside were quickly overcome by the designated teams of men who had done their training at Lumbres, but the pillbox at Otto Farm took longer to subdue. As dawn finally broke, the Enzeds and the Australians to their right pushed on to their objectives. Lewis gunners and battalion bombers wreaked havoc on the increasingly confused and dispirited enemy forces. Fresh battalions leapfrogged the first wave and maintained the momentum of the advance. Mangled pillboxes ran with the blood of their mutilated defenders. Thousands of prisoners were taken, but many more were denied the opportunity to surrender and were bayoneted or bludgeoned to death during vicious hand-to-hand combat. After their losses at Polygon Wood, the Australians in particular were in no mood to spare the broken German Guards Division. In what has been described as 'the massacre in the mist',[68] many of the Australians became 'stabbing, firing furies'.[69] The Enzeds, too, used their bayonets on some who pleaded for mercy.

By 0900 hours the combined force of Anzacs – fighting alongside each other for the first time since the attack at Sari Bair on Gallipoli two years earlier – had reached the crest of the Gravenstafel Spur. On the left of the line, British forces, supported by tanks operating on firmer ground, had advanced towards Poelcappelle. Most of the BEF's objectives were secured by 1200 hours. The men dug in, as they had done previously at the Menin Road and Polygon Wood. The battle was won. There was no grand counter-attack, and the victors made good their foothold on the approaches to Passchendaele. General Plumer declared that the victory at Broodseinde was the greatest since the First Battle of the Marne in 1914. The German Fourth Army's 'Daily Report' stated somewhat disingenuously that the BEF had gained no more than 'a narrow strip of territory ... totally disproportionate to the heavy casualties' they had sustained;[70] later German official histories referred to the defeat as the Black Day of 4 October.

The British strategy for the Third Battle of Ypres, with its progressive bite-and-hold advances, appeared to be working to plan, but if there was a 'cohesive unity' it was surely one which few of the men on the ground could have perceived at the time.[71] The individual soldier's contribution varied once the attack began, and his chances of survival were essentially down to luck. This was particularly the case with Bert Milnes at the Battle of Broodseinde. This was his first – and only – experience of battle. He had apparently been in good spirits as he readied the men of the 3rd Company of the 3rd Auckland Battalion in the final minutes before they went over the top. Directly ahead of them lay the pillbox at Otto Farm. No sooner had he led his men forward, however, than an enemy shell landed at his feet. He was killed instantly, the blast of the explosion leaving no evident injuries on his body.

Bert Milnes was one of 1,600 Enzed casualties on 4 October.[72] So too was Lieutenant Kenneth White, one of the ATC Principal's former trainees, serving with the 1st Aucklands. Sergeant David Gallaher of the 2nd Aucklands, the All Black rugby legend who had been such an inspiration to the young Frank Wilson, was also killed in action that day. The NZD remained in the Ypres Salient for a further week, during which several days of heavy rain turned the whole battlefield between the Gravenstafel and Passchendaele Ridges into a quagmire. A further planned advance around Poelcapelle and the Bellevue Spur on the 9 October was checked by the Flanders mud, yet more pillboxes and masses of barbed wire, but still the BEF maintained its offensive posture. Three days later, the Enzeds experienced their worst single day in the Great War when they failed to break through to Passchendaele. The number of casualties on 12 October was almost double that of 4 October. Transferred from the front line to the relatively safe area to the south of Polygon Wood, the NZD lost more men over the next three months. Field Marshal Haig praised the men from New Zealand; on the Somme and now at Ypres, he wrote, 'they always did more than they were asked to do.'[73] The season for great battles was still not over, however. In early November, another force from the Dominions – the Canadian Expeditionary Force – moved into the battered lines facing Passchendaele Ridge and readied themselves for one more great push forward.

Chapter 6

Canucks

In Flanders fields the poppies blow
Between the crosses, row on row,
That mark our place; and in the sky
The larks, still bravely singing, fly
Scarce heard amid the guns below.

From John McCrae, *In Flanders Fields* (1915)

O n the morning of 2 September 1917, a young Canadian airman
wrote a final letter to his parents. Sub-Lieutenant Gordon Scott
had just returned to base after a dawn patrol over 'Hunland'.
His letter made no mention of any contact with enemy aircraft. Instead,
the 22-year-old Royal Naval Air Service (RNAS) pilot described the rich
colouring of the clouds as the sun rose and he descended through the
cloudbank beneath him:

> [The clouds] were ten thousand feet thick and full of rain and hail.
> It seemed an age before I got through although I was diving from
> ninety to a hundred knots. A cloud is very dark and nothing can
> guide you except your instruments. The hail stung somewhat. I
> came out at three thousand feet, a little back of the Hun trenches,
> but soon got back to our spot.[1]

This description of the conditions in which the pioneers of aerial warfare
conducted their operations offers a corrective to the traditional and often
glamorous depictions of flying cavalrymen and air 'aces' conducting
duels in the skies above no man's land. The reality was far more prosaic,
but just as deadly. Sub-Lieutenant Scott was flying a 'Tripehound' (see
plate 29), one of the most advanced aircraft of its kind and noted for

its speed and manoeuvrability. Indeed, the Sopwith Triplane's recent success rate in combat had led German technicians and pilots, including the famed Manfred von Richthofen, to develop their own version of it. These new flying machines, invented little more than a decade previously, were still experimental works in progress. The development of lighter than air vessels by inventors (the Wright Brothers and Samuel Franklin Cody), pilots (Louis Blériot) and military organizations (the Royal Navy) had added a new dimension to warfare. Nevertheless, even state-of-the-art aircraft such as the Sopwith were still constructed of wire, plywood and fabric. The Clerget Rotary engine, which developed 130 bhp, was less powerful than the engines of many standard production cars today. For the men patrolling the skies above them, the daily decision to fly was weather-dependent. Even in fine conditions, pilots sitting in their cramped cockpits were open to the elements. The standard khaki army service dress worn by RNAS pilots in France offered little protection against the cold; additional layers of leather or fur overcoats, plus protective goggles and helmets, made flying at high altitudes more bearable. There was little respite from the noise and fumes of the engine, but at least the dashing white silk scarf favoured by many airmen could be used to wipe away the oil which routinely spattered man, cockpit and the few instruments fitted to the aeroplane. Projectiles fired by the enemy might easily destroy these relatively flimsy craft. Crossing enemy lines below 2,000ft was particularly hazardous as it brought the airman within the range of ground-based machine guns. With a relatively light armament (a single synchronized Vickers machine gun), a reputation for structural weakness and difficult to repair, the Sopwith was nevertheless designed specifically for an aggressive role. It was a fighter plane, with an exceptional rate of climb and high service ceiling, designed for the young knights of the air to seek out enemy machines and destroy them.

The Great War was into its third year before Gordon Scott enlisted in the armed forces of the British Empire. Many of his fellow students and teachers at the University of Toronto had rushed to the colours in 1914. They, and later recruits like his fellow trainee Percy Barber, had since taken part in the Canadian Expeditionary Force (CEF) deployments on the Somme, Vimy Ridge and Hill 70. Unlike many of his contemporaries, Gordon chose to fight in the air rather than in the trenches. Entering the infantry was subject to the customary health and fitness checks; becoming an airman, not surprisingly, required official validation of training undertaken and flight hours completed. When Gordon Scott entered the RNAS in October 1916, he did so with a recommendation from the Curtiss Air School based at Long Branch Aerodrome in Toronto. There he undertook his preliminary lessons, flying the Curtiss JN trainer biplanes. Versions of the 'Jenny' built in Canada were nicknamed the 'Canuck', a name also applied to soldiers of the CEF. Having completed his initial training, he moved to England. On 28 October he gained his 'ticket' – the Aviator's Certificate from the Royal Aero Club of the United Kingdom (see plate 30) – and simultaneously enlisted as a Probationary Flight Officer in the RNAS. Further training ensued at Crystal Palace in London in November 1916 and at Vendôme in France in February 1917. In June that year he graduated from the new RNAS Training Establishment at Cranwell, having been formally examined in Flying Ability (2nd Class) and Aerial Engines, Navigation, Gunnery and Photography (all 2nd Class, with scores of 70, 78, 71 and 66 per cent respectively). In his graduation report Gordon Scott was judged to be a 'V.G. Pilot. Good & very keen Officer'. Despite being formally 'Recommended for Scout Seaplanes', the newly commissioned Temporary Flight Sub-Lieutenant subsequently joined one of the most prestigious and successful air units on the Western Front. On 6 July 1917 he reported for duty at Bailleul Asylum Ground in France, the operational base of the 1st Squadron RNAS.

In August 1914 the newly formed RNAS comprised 95 aircraft, 7 airships and 655 serving personnel.[2] When it merged with the Royal Flying Corps (RFC) in April 1918 to form the Royal Air Force (RAF), the respective figures for machines and men were 3,000, 100 and 55,000.[3] Rapid technological advances during these formative years resulted in the development of specialist machines for reconnaissance, artillery ranging, bombing and aerial combat. Gordon Scott joined a squadron which had been the first to be established by the RNAS, in October 1914. Its pilots and mechanics had experienced the creation of a new military force at first hand. They could also point to some famous victories in the period before the young 'Canuck' joined them: on 7 June 1915 Flight Sub-Lieutenant Rex Warneford shot down a German airship (Zeppelin

LZ37) and was awarded the Victoria Cross. The Dominions were also well represented amongst the 1st Squadron's stars. The New Zealand air ace Thomas Culling, who had lived in Auckland before the war, had been shot down four weeks before Gordon joined the squadron. The legendary Stan Dallas, an Australian ace with over thirty confirmed victories before he too was shot down and killed in June 1918, was Commanding Officer of what he called 'the first fighting squadron in the Navy'.⁴ Dallas had flown the prototype Sopwith Triplane in June 1916 and had already written some of the earliest treatises on aerial warfare. He was also renowned for the care he showed to new pilots, shepherding them in the air and inducting them into their new roles as airborne fighters. This was partly out of self-interest; the new men, ironically nicknamed the 'Young Huns' by an experienced fellow officer,⁵ were a danger not only to themselves but to the rest of the flight. For young fliers like Gordon Scott, it was considered a great honour to be one of the dozen or so men under Dallas's command.

Gordon Scott joined his new squadron just as preparations for the great offensive in Flanders in 1917 were gathering pace. British aircraft had caused severe damage to the German lines. They had assisted the ground forces with artillery ranging and mounted their own ground strafing and rear area bombing campaign. To do this they needed command of the skies and the necessary fighter aircraft to limit the enemy's own aerial threat. The 1st Squadron RNAS had been loaned to the RFC since February that year and was stationed with No. 1 Squadron RFC as part of 11 Wing at Bailleul in France, close to the Belgian border. The town of Ypres lay no more than 11 miles to the north-east, and Messines Ridge, which the New Zealand Division had attacked so effectively in June, was only 10 miles away. Both squadrons adopted an aggressive stance, taking the war to the enemy over his own territory. The Germans responded by using their own aircraft to bomb Bailleul and to deploy their *Jagdstaffel* (or *Jasta*) squadrons to intercept the British raiders. *Jastas* 4, 6, 10 and 11, led by Manfred von Richthofen, were based at Marckebeeke near Kortrijk, some 18 miles due east of Ypres and only 25 miles from Bailleul. Both Stan Dallas and Thomas Culling of 1st Squadron had fought against von Richthofen's Jasta. The so-called 'Red Baron' described himself as a 'professional chaser'.⁶ His distinctive red-painted Albatross D.III biplane had wreaked havoc during its engagements with the RFC in 'Bloody April' 1917 but was generally regarded as an inferior fighting machine to the Sopwith Triplane. The self-styled *Rote Kampfflieger* believed, however, that pilot skill and experience could overcome technical inferiority, stating that 'the quality of the box matters little … success depends upon the man who sits in it'.[7] From late July 1917 von Richthofen's 'Flying Circus' and other German squadrons continued to engage in aerial dogfights with the Sopwith Triplanes of the RNAS and the Nieuport 17 Scouts of the RFC. German aerial tactics resembled those of their countrymen in the trenches below. They adopted a defensive posture, waiting for the enemy to come to them, before launching their own devastating counter-attack from the air above their own territory whenever possible. As each side endeavoured to gain a technological advantage and aerial superiority, new aircraft entered the arena. Some RNAS squadrons – but not Dallas's – had received the latest Sopwith, the Camel. In the first days of September, von Richthofen, with fifty-nine confirmed 'kills' to his name already, began flying over the Salient in a prototype Fokker F.I Triplane.

Gordon Scott's letter of 2 September may have been intended to allay any fears his parents might have had about the very real risks he was facing. Each squadron flew hundreds of patrols, many without incident and most without serious losses of men or machinery. But it took time for new men to 'see' things in the air, and they had to learn quickly. Unlike the infantrymen below him, Gordon's battlefield was huge, measured in miles rather than yards. Likewise, the threat was not simply in front, but all around him. In this hostile and unforgiving environment, inexperience and simple mistakes often proved fatal. By September 1917, however, Gordon had been patrolling the skies above the Salient for over two months. Unlike many of the thousands of men in the watery swamp below, he had escaped death or serious injury. Any illusions Mr and Mrs Scott might have had about their son's wartime experience, however, were shattered on 4 September when they received a telegram via trans-Atlantic cable notifying them that their son had been reported missing in action the previous day. The official report in Sub-Lieutenant Scott's Service Record states: '3 Sept 1917. Missing. Last seen at 9.20 a.m. E. of Zandvoorde during a fight between two triplanes and six scouts.'[8] The young airman was believed to have been shot down behind enemy lines.

His body was never recovered. The last letter to his parents was delivered to the Scott family home on Cork Street in Guelph, Ontario, some three weeks later.

* * *

Gordon Beattie George Scott was a Canadian by birth, as were his parents. His father Andrew Scott had been born in 1862 and his mother Margaret (née Hadden) was born the following year, both in Ontario. In the 1901 Census of Canada the family described their 'Racial or Tribal Origin' as 'Scotch'. Three generations of the Scott family – Andrew's parents George and Marion, his grandparents Robert and Jane, and his older brother George – had migrated from Jedburgh in the Scottish county of Roxburghshire in early 1851. They were part of a considerable diaspora: 185,000 Scottish migrants settled in Canada between the years 1770 and 1870.[9] Earlier migrants had made their homes in the Maritimes; later arrivals moved westwards to Ontario, attracted by the millions of acres of Crown Lands which could be bought cheaply and on easy terms. The Scotts made a living farming productive lands around Eramosa in the Wellington district. The Haddens, Gordon's mother's side of the family, also claimed Scots ancestry, having migrated from Kincardineshire. Robert Hadden married Alice Coleman (Canadian-born but of Irish descent) in Ontario in 1851 and set up home in Guelph. It was there that their daughter Margaret and Andrew Scott lived after their marriage in 1892, and where they in turn raised three children: Lily (born 1893), Gordon (1895) and Alice (1897).

Guelph – 'The Royal City' – was founded on 23 April (St George's Day) 1827, in territory originally settled by the First Nation community of Attawandarons. The London-based Canada Company was responsible for the colonization of Upper Canada, and John Galt, a Scottish novelist and the Company's Superintendent, established its headquarters there. Galt planned the new settlement on European lines, building squares and broad main streets – named after English counties and British towns and cities – radiating from the Speed River. Designed to attract settlers from Britain, and especially farmers like the Scott family, Guelph grew steadily at the centre of a highly productive agricultural area. In 1856 the

Grand Trunk Railroad linked the town to Toronto, some 62 miles to the east. Guelph was proclaimed a city in 1879, its civic coat of arms proudly displaying the figure of Britannia. Money and livelihoods were made from lumber and flour mills and breweries, but by the turn of the century manufacturing businesses such as the Bell Piano & Organ Company began to dominate the local economy. Census returns illustrate the changing nature of employment opportunities in the district. Gordon's uncle George Scott, for example, described his occupation as 'farmer' in 1891 and 'factory labourer' in 1901. Gordon's father Andrew Scott stated that he was first a 'dry goods clerk' (1891) and later a 'merchant' (1901), reflecting a change in status rather than change of job. He was employed by E. R. Bollert and Co., Importer of Staple and Fancy Dry Goods, Millinery and Clothing. Selling items such as 'Gentlemen's Scotch and Canadian Grand Value' underclothing, Bollert's department store catered for an expatriate community that still thought of Britain as 'home'. By 1903 Andrew Scott had risen through the ranks to become co-proprietor of a company employing sixty staff. Messrs Bollert and Scott were described (probably by themselves) in the local trade directory as 'live, wide awake business men … they are honourable and reliable, and have won a lot of friends here'.[10] As befitted the wife of such a prominent citizen, Margaret (or Mrs Andrew) Scott was listed in Guelph's *Social Register*.

Gordon Scott's early years revolved around family, church and school. Their home on Cork Street gave Gordon and his sisters easy access to other family members: Uncle George, Aunty Sarah and cousin George Jnr. lived on the same street. The attractions of the city centre, less than half a mile away, were also within easy walking distance. So too was Exhibition Park on London Road. The family had, like many Scottish migrants to Canada, taken their Protestant faith with them and were regular worshippers at the Knox Presbyterian Church on Dublin Street. Gordon's first school, the Central Public School (CPS), was also on Dublin Street. Guelph CPS had opened in 1877, during a decade in which provincial legislation made elementary schooling in Public Schools (formerly known as Common Schools) available to all children. Abolition of fees and mandatory attendance duly followed. Under Principal David Young, CPS became a highly successful institution. By the turn of the century it was essentially a confederation of six schools across the city, its thirty teachers educating as many as 2,000 pupils at any one time.[11] It was one of the first schools in Canada to introduce Physical Training and also employed a Drill Instructor. Classrooms were bright and inviting and decorated with pictures and plants. In common with schools throughout Ontario, it celebrated its links with Britain, observing key dates such as Empire Day, Dominion Day and the King's Birthday. After 1904 CPS placed greater emphasis on manual subjects, enabling pupils to leave school at the age of fourteen better prepared for the local employment market. Increasing numbers, including Gordon Scott, began to leave CPS for a secondary school education. He passed the examination for admission to Guelph Collegiate Institute (GCI), situated not far from home on the Paisley Road. GCI was the oldest public high school in the city, having been founded in 1886 upon predecessor institutions known as Guelph Grammar School and Guelph High School. GCI's curriculum combined elements of 'grammar' (Latin and Greek) and 'commercial' subjects (Book-keeping, Stenography, Typewriting). Calisthenics, Gymnastics, Drill and a Highland Cadet Corps helped to develop individual physique and corporate pride. Numbers on the roll at GCI increased under Principal James Davison, and whilst most of its leavers found employment in local trades and industries, others were able to proceed to university. Some, like Gordon Scott, chose to undertake further education and training to become schoolteachers.

A career in teaching would not have been an obvious choice for earlier generations of the Scott family in Canada. The first settlers built their houses, worked the land and gradually established small townships. William Briggs, author of one of the standard texts on the history of education used by trainee teachers in Ontario, noted that:

> The condition of general education among the people in Canada was at that time very low. Merely to make a living was a strenuous task. The people were crude in their manners and intolerant in their opinions, but they were full of courage and manly independence.[12]

As early as 1816, settlers were permitted to set up their own Common Schools. Their children were taught in rudimentary schoolhouses, in most cases by individuals for whom the term 'teacher' was inappropriate. Travelling through Ontario in 1835, Anna Jamieson asked

> who that could earn a subsistence in any other way would be a schoolmaster in the wilds of Upper Canada? Ill-fed, ill-clothed, ill-paid or not paid at all, boarded at the homes of different farmers in turn, I found indeed some few men, poor creatures! Always either Scotch or Americans – and totally unfit for the office they had undertaken.[13]

The status of teaching was far higher by the time Gordon Scott chose it as a career. As in Britain and in other overseas Dominions, the pressure of population growth, combined with a burgeoning recognition of the social and economic importance of elementary and secondary schooling, resulted in demands for more and better teachers. In 1844 Ontario's Superintendent of Education, Egerton Ryerson, toured Europe and the United States to investigate different models of education provision, before championing a series of reforms back in his own province. Subsequent debates about how to secure both quantity and (at the same time) quality in the teaching force in Ontario assumed a pattern familiar to educators and administrators in other parts of the British Empire. The key issues were common to all, namely *where* teachers should train, *what* knowledge and skills they required and *how* they should acquire both. The relative merits of schools, colleges and universities as the location for teacher training led to experimentation, in Ontario as elsewhere in Canada, with different forms of 'scholarship and professional training'.[14] Two general developments gradually emerged and still resonate today: local control yielded to central direction and regulation, and apprenticeship models of training eventually gave way to professional learning, qualifications and status.

The earliest, and later most widespread, form of teacher training in Canada was provided by Normal Schools. The Toronto Normal School (TNS) was established in 1847, just one year after the Common Schools Act. TNS prepared prospective teachers, some as young as sixteen, by focussing on classroom method according to a an accepted – or 'normal' – set of rules. Entry qualifications included demonstrable skill in reading, writing and arithmetic, and a moral character reference from a clergyman. Extensive subject knowledge was not a prerequisite, nor was it developed in training. Other Canadian provinces followed Ontario's example and opened their own Normal Schools, for example in New Brunswick in 1848 and Manitoba in 1882. TNS also became the template for teacher training elsewhere in Ontario. Ottawa opened its Normal School in 1875, and others were established in London (1900), Peterborough (1908), Stratford (1908) and North Bay (1909). By the beginning of the twentieth century Ontario had 5,654 public schools and 130 grammar and collegiate schools, their teachers numbering 8,321 and 568 respectively.[15] Collectively, the province's Normal Schools trained over 1,000 young men and women each year.[16]

Other experiments included the introduction of County Model Schools. These operated an apprenticeship model, whereby senior pupils (pupil teachers in all but name) taught whole classes under the supervision of certificated teachers. This short-term fix for a teacher shortage problem did little to enhance the status of the teaching profession. Most 'model school' graduates never progressed beyond elementary levels of teaching. The introduction of 14-week training schemes at Collegiate Institutes in the late 1880s also attracted many local candidates but did little to address teacher quality. After leaving GCI in 1912, Gordon Scott began his teacher training at Guelph Model School (GMS), which was based in the familiar surroundings of the Central Public School and was also led by Principal David Young. Gordon was one of twenty-eight trainees, twenty-one of whom were young women. This gender disparity had been evident in earlier GMS cohorts, was also the case in TNS and other Normal Schools in the province and, according to the province's Minister for Education, was a reflection of the numerous alternative employment opportunities available to young men at the time. GMS gave the young Mr Scott plenty of classroom experience and provided tuition in subjects such as art, music, writing and manual work which would help prepare him for employment in the Public Schools. The one-year programme at GMS also provided leavers with a progression route to one of the Normal Schools in Stratford, Hamilton or Toronto. Gordon moved to the provincial capital in 1914, but did not enrol at TNS as might have been expected.

The young man from Guelph joined thousands of other migrants in a city which had doubled its population every fifteen years during the nineteenth century. With 341,991 recorded inhabitants in 1911, the great majority of them of British origin, Toronto's population was over twenty times greater than that of Gordon's home city.[17] Toronto had been 'a place of meeting' for indigenous peoples long before the first French trading settlement was established there in 1749. Located on the northern shore of Lake Ontario, it had become a communications hub for the province, first by water and later by rail. As in Perth in Western Australia and Auckland in New Zealand, infrastructure projects such as street railways and landscaped parks marked the gradual transition from pioneering past to modern civic culture. The old and the new co-existed. At the Canadian National Exhibition held in the city in 1913, the province's increasing shift from agricultural to industrial production was exemplified by displays of emerging technologies such as telephones and car tyres. Most of Toronto's transport system, however, still relied upon animal power; the city's fire brigade used horses (and in winter, sleighs) to pull their engines and other trucks. The city also boasted more taverns (110) than schools (78),[18] but for ambitious young men and women training to be teachers, Toronto offered opportunities for employment and career advancement. The city's elected Board of Education provided schooling for over 50,000 children and employed over 1,000 teachers.[19] There was an additional incentive; the salaries of teachers employed in Toronto's schools were often twice that of their counterparts in rural areas.

By the time Gordon Scott arrived in Toronto, the Normal School had served the city and the province well for over sixty years; its reputation was firmly established and celebrated by a large alumni body working in the schools of Ontario. TNS, however, was no longer the only teacher training institution in the capital city. The University of Toronto, founded in 1853 just six years after TNS, had educated the province's scientific, medical and legal professionals and other leaders. Now it intended to do the same for the teaching profession. In 1907 it opened a Faculty of Education (UTFE), the joint product of a Royal Commission and a provincial restructuring of teacher training provision. UTFE described itself as 'a professional school of education'[20] and offered a General Course for graduates – and others with suitable qualifications and experience – intending to teach in the city's schools. From the outset, the new institution attracted hundreds of trainees each year. Just as Albert Baswitz had chosen the London Day Training College for the access it gave him to an institute of higher education (the University of London), so Gordon Scott chose the more academic and higher status programme on offer at UTFE rather than that at TNS. This would not necessarily make him a better teacher – the debate about where best to acquire subject knowledge, pedagogic knowledge and practical skills still resonates today – but it would enhance his professional standing and improve his career prospects. Gordon met the admission requirements for UTFE: he was nineteen years of age (the minimum age for entry), provided a reference from a member of the clergy and a medical certificate, and his prior training and teaching experience was sufficient, in lieu of a degree, for a full certificate of entrance. Most importantly, he was a British citizen, and the University of Toronto prided itself on upholding British heritage and traditions. Indeed, its official songbook included such patriotic favourites as *Rule Britannia*, *Men of Harlech* and *Scots Wha Hae*.

The UTFE General Course lasted a full academic year. For the 1914/15 cohort the year began on 29 September 1914 with a lecture in the Assembly Hall in the new Faculty building on the corner of Bloor Street and Spadina Avenue. The largest cohort in UTFE's short history had been drawn from Toronto and over forty different counties in the province.[21] The majority of the 412 students in attendance that day were young women, mostly aged between twenty-one and twenty-three.[22] Little had changed since May 1907, when Dean William Pakenham had written to Dr Robert Falconer, the President of the University of Toronto, claiming that 'man passes from the ranks of the teachers; the woman is now dominant.'[23]Amongst the 158 male students sitting alongside Gordon Scott were Gordon Forsyth from Toronto, and fellow provincials Percy Barber from Picton, William Buchanan from Omemee and Wilfred Durant from Chesterville. From further afield, and one of the few to hold a university degree, was Hedley Goodyear from Grand Falls, Newfoundland. Together they worked their way through the three key components of the General Course during the autumn term of 1914 and the spring and summer terms of 1915. They attended lectures on the history, philosophy and psychology of education, and others on school law and administration. They conducted academic and professional evaluations of the curriculum operating in Ontario's elementary and secondary schools. Finally, the theory from lectures on classroom methodology was put into practice during school placements consisting of fifty days of observation and twenty school periods of teaching. The latter took place in 'the school of instruction by practice',[24] or 'Model Schools', as institutions working with Normal Schools and faculties of education were generally known. Gordon and his fellow students practised their craft under the watchful eyes of teachers known as Assistant Supervisors at nearby Ryerson (Public) School and Jarvis Street Collegiate Institute, and Instructors at the University of Toronto Schools (UTS). The latter institution was a dedicated teacher-training school, independent of the Board of Education and governed by the Dean of UTFE. Originally intended to comprise two separate schools devoted to a 'general' and 'technical' curriculum respectively for both boys and girls, when it opened in 1910 it taught boys in the higher primary and secondary grades only. UTS taught both children and students; official policy gave priority to the latter, recognizing the schools' importance as 'the laboratories of the Faculty of Education'.[25] Nevertheless, the school's emphasis on 'the virtues of honest work, fair play, polite manners, and good morals' made it popular with parents and attracted staff of high calibre.[26] Instructor in Science George Alton Cline, for example, had graduated with Bachelor and Master of Arts degrees from the University of Toronto and had then undertaken the General Course at UTFE in 1911.

Gordon and his fellow trainees were certainly kept busy during their year at UTFE. As members of the wider university they also had the opportunity to take part in its numerous sporting, cultural and social activities. Of the young men from UTFE mentioned above, only Hedley Goodyear gets a mention (for his involvement in the Literary and Dramatic Societies) in the pages of the university magazine, *The Varsity*. Their counterparts in Perth and Auckland experienced far less competition for places in teams and productions than those attending a university with over 4,000 fellow trainees and undergraduates; the Department of History alone enrolled nearly twice as many students as the Faculty of Education.[27] There may also have been a gulf between college undergraduates and faculty trainees; the *Torontonensis*, the annual Year Book record of student activity and achievements for the constituent colleges (such as University, Victoria, and Knox) and professional faculties (such as Medicine and Applied Science), did not include a section on UTFE.

Meanwhile, the rest of the world was at war. As in Australia and New Zealand, Canada went to war 'because Britain went to war'.[28] On 4 August 1914 bands played, small boys paraded with flags and drums, and men began queuing to enlist at the Armouries in Toronto. In a city in which eighty-five per cent of the population claimed British ancestral ties, it was hardly surprising that the declaration of war against Germany should prompt the waving of Union Jacks and renditions of *God Save the King* and *Rule Britannia*. Similar scenes were enacted throughout Ontario. The citizens of Guelph, for example, hung out flags and bunting and placed photographs of King George V and Lord Kitchener in shop windows. Initial euphoria was soon reinforced by the *Guelph Mercury* in its 'Follow the Flag' editorials and patriotic cartoons featuring 'Jack Canuck'.[29] War fever gripped a nation in which over fifty per cent of the population were under the age of twenty-five.[30] The University of Toronto went to war immediately. Describing the forthcoming conflict as 'the greatest of moral struggles',[31] President Robert Falconer mobilized his institution in defence of British culture and values. On the very day that Gordon Scott began his studies at UTFE, *The Varsity* proclaimed on its front page that the 'University of Toronto Will Do Its Share'.[32] Another article was entitled 'President Falconer Scores Prussian Culture',[33] whilst the magazine's editorial drummed up support for the cause:

The University reopens amid the gloom of a world-wide calamity. Never, we believe, have British forces crossed the sea in so just a cause, and surely never have Britons stood so united in support of any government. Meanwhile there is no reason for the cessation of any student activity, except that of mere frivolity. Though the present may be dark, the future is bright for the University, for Canada and for the Empire.[34]

On the very next day, 30 September, the magazine reported 'Arrangements Made for Thorough Training in Defence of Empire',[35] a reference to the organization of a Canadian Officers' Training Corps (COTC) to be based at the University of Toronto. By then, Britain had already accepted the Canadian government's offer of 25,000 Dominion troops, and many university alumni – including UTS Instructor George Cline – had 'heard their country's call and gone to the front'.[36] By the end of the academic year in June 1915 President Falconer was able to report that the university's roll of honour boasted over a thousand names: 668 alumni had already enlisted, as had 484 undergraduates and 71 members of staff.[37] Few of the male trainees in the 1914/1915 UTFE cohort enlisted in 1914. Many did, however, join the COTC. The university authorities had been considering the establishment of an OTC since 1912, and in the meantime its Rifle Association (UTRA) had been actively training some students for war. As soon as the new term started, the UTRA began enrolling staff and students and organizing companies and squad drills. Early encouragement was soon overtaken by strong pressure to sign up. On 21 October (Trafalgar Day) classes were cancelled so that students could hear President Falconer's appeal for more recruits for the proposed Corps. Two weeks later, the university received authorization to form a contingent of the COTC. By that point 'the whole vicinity of the University in the afternoon after four o'clock was alive with military activity.'[38] Enrolments in the UTRA had reached 1,868, including 'a strong company' of sixty, including Gordon Scott, from UTFE.[39] Membership of the COTC may well have been the reason why the men from UTFE were inconspicuous in the wider aspects of university life. As new recruits in M Company they were kept busy with church parades, musketry instruction, drill, lectures and field days on the outskirts of the city. They were still without uniforms and some equipment, however, when the two battalions of the Corps – some 1,450 men – were inspected by the Governor General of Canada, the Duke of Connaught, on 22 January 1915 at the Toronto Armouries.[40] President Falconer continued in his attempts to inspire and to motivate the university community. Addressing his young charges at the start of the spring term, he reminded them of their individual responsibility and corporate duty:

> You will tell those who come after you of the drilling, the enlistment, the departure for the front, your comrades who went, those who won distinction in the field, those who fell, and those who returned. You will tell how the women worked and wept and endured while

the men were at the front. You will tell how the sons of Britain the wide world round leaped forth to do their share, how the country grimly endured and saw the awful time through.[41]

Gordon Scott continued his teacher training and, at the same time, prepared to serve his country. Unlike many of the young men in the university, he resisted the temptation and institutional pressure to enlist at the earliest opportunity. Instead, he completed his studies. He sat the Annual Examinations in early May and was awarded a First Class Certificate for teaching. His place at UTFE had been conditional upon a commitment to teach in one of Ontario's schools for at least the first year after completion of training, and Mr Scott was duly appointed to the staff of Winchester Street Public School, serving the community of Cabbagetown, just a few miles from the historic city centre of Toronto. Over the year that followed he learned to fly, then left for England and joined the RNAS.

* * *

Fellow UTFE trainee Percy Barber (see plate 31) also completed his UTFE course and gained a First Class Certificate. He, too, had joined the COTC and had also completed one of the courses provided for those intending to secure commissions in the Canadian Expeditionary Force. His records state that he then taught briefly at Essex Street School in Toronto. On 12 June 1915 he formally enlisted and was briefly 'On Active Service' as a Lieutenant in the 2nd University Company attached to Princess Patricia's Canadian Light Infantry.[42] Within a few days he was transferred to the 38th Battalion CEF and then, a month later, to the 59th Battalion. His Officer's Declaration, signed on 6 February 1916 at Brockville, Ontario, includes reference to his earlier military training in the 16th Prince Edward Regiment, one of Canada's county militia formations. Percy's final medical examination before proceeding overseas recorded his height as 5 feet 11 inches, his weight as 170lbs and his chest measurement (expanded) as 39 inches. On 2 April 1916 Lieutenant Barber boarded the SS *Olympic* at Halifax, Nova Scotia, and began the long voyage back to the land of his birth.

Percy's father, Frederick Barber, had been born in the English county of Suffolk in 1861, and his mother Florence was born in the London Borough of Woolwich three years later. Frederick's work as a Police Court Missionary and Lay Preacher had taken the family to Birmingham, where their first son Frank had been born in 1887, and then on to Southport in Lancashire where Percy and his sister Doreen were born in 1893 and 1899, respectively. In September 1903, the Barbers made the momentous move from England to Canada, crossing the Atlantic from Liverpool to Montreal in nine days aboard the *Bavarian*. The Barber family appear to have settled, initially at least, in Bobcaygeon, a village in Victoria County in Central Ontario. There, Frederick continued his work as a 'clergyman'.[43] Percy attended a local private establishment known as Hill Croft School, before continuing his education at the Collegiate Institute in Lindsay, some 19 miles away. By the time of Percy's enlistment, however, the family had moved to Picton in Prince Edward County, Eastern Ontario. This small town was originally named Hallowell by a group of Loyalists from the Thirteen Colonies who had settled there in the wake of the American War of Independence; it was later renamed in honour of Sir Thomas Picton, Wellington's second-in-command at the Battle of Waterloo. Revd Barber and his family took up residence in The Rectory, while Percy attended Picton Collegiate Institute and then began his teaching career back at his old school – Hill Croft in Bobcaygeon. After short spells of employment in County Schools in Toronto and Prince Edward County he had, by the time the Great War broke out, moved to Toronto and begun the General Course at UTFE.

A year later, and Mr Barber the teacher was now Lieutenant Barber of the CEF. Like many young Canadians of his generation he was returning to the mother country. The British public had eagerly awaited the arrival of troops from the imperial Dominion in North America. *The Illustrated War News* reported excitedly how 'The lion whelps are coming to the fray: Canadian troops who are answering the "Call-to-Arms".'[44] Sir Robert Borden, the Canadian Prime Minister, believed that 'the honour of Canada' demanded that military forces be sent to Britain. With a Permanent Active Militia of only 3,000 men and a further part-time force of some 60,000 'weekend warriors',[45] the raising of a Canadian Expeditionary Force necessitated extraordinary measures. Samuel

Hughes, the Minister of Militia and Defence in the Borden cabinet, stepped forward to mobilize the troops. Described at the time (and since) as bombastic, conceited and even insane, this controversial and polarizing figure had once been a schoolteacher. He had trained at the Toronto Normal School, studied at the University of Toronto and then taught at the Grammar School in Toronto from 1875 to 1885. At the age of thirty-two Sam Hughes left teaching, moved to Lindsay and bought the local newspaper, the *Victoria Warder*. Active in politics and the militia, in 1892 he was elected Member of Parliament for Victoria North and in 1899–1900 saw action in the Boer War. In August 1914 he effectively bypassed the existing militia organization and called for volunteers to make their way to a new military training camp to be established at Valcartier, some 15 miles north of Quebec City. Chaos ensued as thousands of volunteers from across the Dominion arrived at a camp that barely warranted the name. Shortages of tented accommodation, uniforms and equipment were exacerbated by Hughes' belligerent and authoritarian manner towards the troops and their officers; but if, in times of war, the end justifies the means, then even Sam Hughes' most vociferous critics could not deny his achievement in creating the 1st Canadian Division. In just eight weeks, this body of 31,000 officers and men, consisting of twelve numbered infantry battalions plus Signals, Engineer, Artillery and Cavalry units, stood ready to leave for England, all proudly wearing their bronze maple leaf insignia.[46] In late September Sam Hughes' 'new army' marched to the docks at Quebec City. On 3 October they began their journey, the cheers of thousands of well-wishers ringing in their ears. They crossed the Atlantic in a fleet of thirty luxury liners,[47] each in its newly painted livery of wartime grey and escorted by Royal Navy vessels on the lookout for German U-boats.

The first Canadian troops may well have disappointed some amongst the crowd which flocked to Plymouth Harbour to welcome the new comrades-in-arms, the 'wild men from a frozen Dominion'.[48] Few of the Canucks conformed to the popular *Boy's Own* stereotypes of pioneering voyagers, hunters and backwoodsmen living on the edges of civilization. Some of the first recruits had been farmers, but many others were city boys (albeit with an average age of twenty-seven) who had earned their livings as clerks, bankers, students and manual labourers. The majority could claim descent from British families; only in later divisions of the CEF would one encounter predominantly 'French' battalions, or numbers of Canadian soldiers of First Nation, African, Indian or Japanese heritage. Many of the Canadians were, like Percy Barber later, returning home, having been amongst the hundreds of thousands of new and very recent migrants to the Dominion. Indeed, around half of the men in the first two Canadian contingents were born in Britain.[49] Some of these had already served in the British Army and, together with men with prior experience in the Canadian Militia, provided an important pool of potential officers and NCOs.

The 1st Canadian Division spent the winter of 1914/1915 in tents and huts and trained on the muddy terrain of Salisbury Plain. On 16 February 1915 they landed at St Nazaire in France, before moving to Armentières for further instruction. After a spell in the front line at Fleurbaix they headed north to Ypres. In April 1915 – the month in which Dominion forces from Australia and New Zealand also experienced their baptism of fire at Gallipoli – the 1st Division took part in the Second Battle of Ypres. On the night of 22 April, the Germans attacked in the Salient using chlorine gas for the first time. French forces wavered, but the Canadians counter-attacked. In four days of fighting near the village of St Julien they lost over 6,000 men, of whom 2,000 were killed in action or died of their wounds.[50] The 2nd Canadian Division arrived in England the following month and trained at Shorncliffe Camp before proceeding to France in mid-September and then forming part of the newly created Canadian Corps in the Salient. The 3rd Canadian Division was formed in France in December. Regular officers from the British Army held most of the key commands during the early days of the CEF. Lieutenant General E. A. H. Alderson commanded the 1st Canadian Division in 1914 and then the new Canadian Corps in 1915. His successor in May 1916 was also British. General Sir Julian Byng had only recently overseen the remarkable evacuation of British, Australian and New Zealand troops from the Gallipoli Peninsula, yet despite that experience was somewhat bemused at the prospect of taking charge of another Dominion force. By that point, however, some Canadian officers had been promoted to senior leadership positions. The man in charge of the 1st Canadian Division was Brigadier-General Arthur Currie. He had been born in Southern

Ontario, the grandson of Irish migrant farmers. He was educated at local common schools and then at the Strathroy Collegiate Institute, where he gained a Third Class Teacher's Certificate. Unable to find employment, in 1894 he moved to British Columbia. He taught for a while at Victoria High School, the oldest institution of its kind in the province. Like Sam Hughes before him, however, he experienced teaching as little more than a poorly-paid temporary 'job' rather than a 'profession' and resigned his post in 1900. Few members of this transient workforce went on to such great things. A less than glittering career as an insurance salesman was followed by the highs and lows of real estate speculation. During this period, however, Currie was assiduously cultivating a parallel career in the Canadian Militia, rising through the ranks of the part-timers to become commanding officer of the 50th (Gordon Highlanders) Regiment by 1914. In September of that year he was promoted to Brigadier-General and took command of the newly formed 2nd Canadian Infantry Brigade at Valcartier. He sailed to England with the First Contingent, led his men at the Second Battle of Ypres and was subsequently promoted to command of the 1st Division.

The first Canadian forces had performed well, both in the Salient in 1915 and then in their first engagements on the Somme the following year. The CEF continued to expand, but as each new battalion, brigade and division entered the line it began to haemorrhage men. A steady stream of reinforcements from home was desperately needed to replace the 8,340 men killed, wounded or missing in the spring and summer of 1916.[51] Men like Percy Barber would fill the gaps left by 'originals' who could no longer fight. They would be transported first to England and then, after a suitable induction into the complexities of war on the Western Front, sent to their units in France. On 11 April 1916 Percy Barber reached Liverpool, the port from which he had sailed to Canada as a young boy some thirteen years before. His first months back in the old country were spent preparing for his part in the next great offensive on the Somme. This included attendance at the Entrenching School at Bramshott and the Musketry Courses at Bessborough and Hythe. Lieutenant Barber finally crossed the English Channel and reported to the 39th Battalion CEF, a reserve unit which provided reinforcements for battalions already in the field. On 3 August he was taken on the strength of the 21st (Eastern Ontario) Battalion, a unit which had been raised in Kingston and included other volunteers from Prince Edward County.

The hoped-for breakthrough on the Somme had not materialized. The BEF had suffered huge numbers of casualties on 1 July, including thousands of men from the Newfoundland Regiment in their attack at Beaumont Hamel. Three more weeks of fighting had still failed to achieve the original objectives for day one of the great offensive. Haig decided to deploy more forces from the Dominions in a series of battles within a battle. The Australians pushed the line further forward by taking Pozières on 23 July. The Canadian Corps would take part in the next set-piece, planned for mid-September, by mounting an attack from the former Anzac positions. On 10 September the 21st Battalion, together with their fellow Ontarians in the 4th Canadian Infantry Brigade, assembled in Albert, the town which had become the springboard for the major Allied offensive of 1916. Percy Barber joined Albert Baswitz and Frank Wilson and the thousands of other men from Britain and its Dominions who were making their final preparations for the Battle of Flers-Courcelette. Lieutenant Barber had experienced his first spell in the front line trenches in early August and had spent the next six weeks with his men in an intensive training regime which included familiarization with their new Lee Enfields, replacements for the Canadian-manufactured Ross rifle. The battalion had then travelled south, by the familiar combination of entrainment and foot-slogging, to billets at Vadencourt, before moving into makeshift accommodation in the desolate Brickfields area on the western outskirts of Albert in readiness for the move up to the front line. They, too, took the same well-worn route out of Albert, passing the Hanging Virgin and marching on through the town's ruined streets to the battlefield assembly zone. The men from Ontario headed towards their designated positions beyond the devastated village of Pozières. They stopped and took shelter in shallow dugouts, the remains of earlier German defensive lines. Most of the battalion's officers then moved forward, assisted by Australian guides, to observe the terrain over which they would soon be attacking. In warm sunshine the other ranks prepared themselves as best they could, listened to the exchanges of artillery fire and watched the occasional aerial dogfight above them. One enemy aircraft was brought down behind the Canadian lines by a British fighter plane. The entry in the Battalion War Diary for that day noted simply and without emotion: 'Hun machine set on fire coming down and pilot and plane were completely burned on reaching ground.'[52]

By 0200 hours on 15 September the 21st Battalion had taken up its final positions on the battlefield. Like Captain Albert Baswitz of the 22nd London Battalion and Lieutenant Sydney Forbes of the 11th Battalion AIF, Lieutenant Percy Barber had made his way through the 'crawling mass of men and horses and motor vehicles' in Happy Valley and the Bazentins, part of the 'mighty host' of Kitchener's Fourth Army.[53] Finally, he reached the section of line allocated to the 4th Canadian Infantry Brigade. The Canucks straddled the Albert–Bapaume Road; the 21st Battalion occupied the same spot near the Windmill on Pozières Ridge which Sydney Forbes and the West Australians had taken three weeks earlier. Directly to their left, stretching all the way to Mouquet Farm, stood the Canadian 6th and 8th Brigades. To their right were hundreds of thousands of men, including the Scots and Londoners facing Martinpuich and High Wood, and the Aucklanders ready to advance on Flers. In front of them was the Canadian Corps' designated objective, the village of Courcelette, its approach guarded by two major defensive obstacles: the German front line trench and, some 500 yards beyond it, the heavily defended Sugar Factory (see plate 32). When the British artillery barrage at 0620 signalled zero hour, the 21st Battalion began its advance. Covered by heavy machine gun fire, the Canucks captured what remained of the enemy trench, took prisoners and dealt with others who refused to surrender. Despite encountering determined resistance, and losing several officers to machine gun fire and snipers, the battalion continued its advance towards the Sugar Factory. In stark contrast to what was happening at the same time in the hell of High Wood, this enemy strong point was taken with relative ease. As the Battalion War Diary entry for the day noted, 'Our Artillery fire had been very accurate, and we did not receive as much opposition as was anticipated.'[54] All that remained of the refinery buildings was a mass of crushed masonry and the last pockets of enemy resistance. German troops were bombed out of their deep dugouts and over 150 prisoners were taken. By 0703 hours the 21st Battalion had secured its planned 'Final Objective' for the day, and dug in. Advanced positions manned by Lewis Gun teams were established 150 yards ahead in the Sunken Road. The new tanks, which had been intended to support the advance, arrived at the Sugar Factory after it had been captured. Ordered to hold on whilst other attacking waves passed through them, the battalion was subjected to continuous enemy shelling and sustained further casualties. By 1800 hours Canadian infantry units had captured Courcelette. Two days later, as the battle raged on and claimed more lives without any sustained breakthrough, the 21st Battalion returned to the brickyards of Albert and then retired to their billets at Vadencourt.

In the course of the action on 15 September, Lieutenant Barber had been one of the battalion's 405 casualties.[55] A high explosive shell had inflicted multiple wounds to his scalp, face, hands and left thigh; according to a later medical report he had been 'peppered' by shrapnel. He was treated at No. 49 Casualty Clearing Station the following day and then transferred to No. 11 Ambulance Transport unit for evacuation from the battle zone. On 17 September he was admitted to No. 20 General Hospital in Étaples. His wounds, and the associated symptoms of shock, were sufficiently serious for him to be sent back to England four days later aboard the hospital ship *Stad Antwerpen*. He was admitted to Anstie Grange Hospital in Holmwood, Surrey, where he spent the next six weeks rehabilitating. A series of Medical Boards determined that the wounds were slight and had caused no permanent damage, and on 6 November declared him fit for general service. Lieutenant Barber made the journey back across the English Channel on 14 December and rejoined the 21st Battalion in the field five days later. During his absence the battalion had been engaged in further costly actions on the Somme, including the assaults by the Canadian Corps on Regina Trench in late September and early October. His men had since moved north to positions in the Lens sector, and the returning officer spent Christmas 1916 and the New Year of 1917 with them in the front line at Bully Grenay. For the next three months the men from Ontario did what scores of other battalions had done in the area before them, alternating spells in the trenches with periods of rest and attending courses in the billeting and training areas behind the lines. By the time spring arrived, the stage was set for another great offensive.

Russia and France, Britain's allies in the Triple Entente, were chiefly responsible for the strategic direction of the war on land at this point. The former was embroiled in revolution and could no longer be relied upon to keep the German forces on the Eastern Front occupied. Britain's chief ally, France, had stemmed the German advance on Verdun in 1916, and now its army was ready to go on the offensive. General Robert Nivelle's planned assault on German lines in the Champagne region depended upon preventing the enemy from bringing up reinforcements from elsewhere. Hence the timing of the offensive – it was to take place in April before the Russian Army collapsed completely – and the requirement for diversionary attacks by British forces north of Arras.

Despite numerous previous failed attempts by French forces, the BEF planned to seize Vimy Ridge (see Map 8). This five-mile-long escarpment on its northwest-southeast axis dominated the landscape. The enemy was entrenched on the highest ground in the sector and had sweeping views across the Douai Plain with its collieries and slag heaps around the town of Lens. More importantly, the Bavarian and Prussian troops looked down upon the trenches at the base of the ridge from which any assault would be launched. For three years they had held this strategic strong point, time spent adding more barbed wire and concrete machine gun pits to its fortifications and constructing underground chambers and tunnels for shelter from hostile artillery. Previous attempts to take Vimy Ridge, including one timed to coincide with the BEF attack at Loos in September 1915, had cost the French Army some 100,000 casualties. Now it was the turn of the Canadian Corps to attempt to break the stalemate.[56] In March 1917 the Canucks occupied a waterlogged area littered with corpses and devastated by continuous fighting, their positions hardly conducive to offensive operations. German gunners did their best to disrupt the preparations by firing shrapnel shells into the Canadian lines. For the next four weeks the Corps and its various British and Canadian support units undertook a massive infrastructure project to the west of the ridge, building roads and light railways, laying pipes and cables, and fitting electric lighting and first aid facilities in the protective underground caverns and tunnels which they added to or excavated. Meticulous preparation – one of Arthur Currie's mantras – was the order of the day. Infantrymen rehearsed their assaults, practised their specialist roles as bombers or Lewis Gun team members, and raided the enemy lines at night. In the skies above them the RFC's 16th Squadron took aerial photographs of the latest enemy troop dispositions, trench defences and artillery batteries. Beneath them, tunnellers pushed forward under no man's land and constructed advanced jumping-off points. The imparting of information to all involved in the assault became a key feature of pre-battle planning. Each individual combatant was briefed – using maps, models and detailed reports – to an extent rarely experienced before. Whilst these men were still expected to follow orders and to 'do or die', they were also encouraged to show initiative, to think for themselves and to assume command of others in the heat of battle.

On the morning of Easter Monday, 9 April 1917, the 100,000 men of the Canadian Corps stood ready to attack Vimy Ridge. It was the first operation in which the four CEF Divisions had been under one unified command. It is not clear whether Lieutenant Barber was amongst the assault troops that morning. His battalion was certainly in the front line trenches, but his name is not among the officers listed in the Unit War Diary entry for the day. He may well have been allocated to support duties instead, part of a small number of men who were necessarily 'left out of the action in order that their services might contribute to the success of re-organization.'[57] The attacking strength of the 21st Battalion amounted to exactly 700 officers and other ranks.[58] For the previous week they had watched and waited as nearly a thousand heavy guns had fired over a million shells at the defenders on the ridge.[59] Now they were assembled just east of Neuville St Vaast in muddy trenches near Mill Street, in the centre of the 2nd Division line and at the very heart of the attacking force. To their immediate right were the 18th and 19th Battalions who would comprise the 4th Brigade's first wave. Beyond them was Currie's 1st Division, with troops from the British 51st Division holding the final line of attack on the southern flank. To the left were the 5th Brigade and then, moving northwards along the line, the 3rd and 4th Canadian Infantry Divisions. The weather was truly awful. Snow, sleet and hail had swept across the battlefield, but at least it had helped to screen their final preparations from the enemy. At 0530 hours the roar of artillery and the rattle of machine guns propelled the men forward. Following the creeping barrage, which the 4th Brigade CFA War Diary later described as 'perfect',[60] the leading wave reached the first of three German lines which by now existed in outline only. They met resistance from machine gunners who had survived the bombardment. Fierce hand-to-hand fighting ensued. Then, just after 0600 hours, the 21st Battalion went over the top. By 0630 hours they too had reached the 4th Brigade's key objective, the Black Line, before pushing through and advancing with bayonets fixed for a further 500 yards. In just thirty minutes, and with massive support from their own artillery, they took the village of Les Tilleuls and reached the designated Red Line. Enemy machine gun posts were rushed and eliminated, just as they had been in training. It was a similar story of steady advance along much of the line; German forces were pushed back as far as four miles in several places. By late afternoon most of Vimy Ridge was occupied by the Canadians. Only the defences at Hill 145 and the so-called 'Pimple' held out, and both positions were finally taken after three further days of fighting.

The action at Vimy Ridge was indeed a spectacular and virtually unprecedented breakthrough, demonstrating the efficacy of through preparation, innovative thinking and sheer determination and bravery on the part of the Canadian forces. Four Victoria Crosses were awarded, and the Canucks continued to build a reputation as the 'storm-troops' of the BEF. The victory had come at a cost of over 10,000 casualties, including the 21st Battalion's Commanding Officer, Lieutenant Colonel E. W. Jones, who was seriously wounded. The enemy, however, had suffered twice that number and lost 4,000 men as prisoners of war.[61] The battle was over, but the war continued. The Canadians now held the ridge, but they still faced thousands of entrenched Germans on the other side. On 13 April the 21st Battalion was still in the line, establishing new positions near the railway track in front of Vimy Village, sending more patrols into the new no man's land and awaiting orders for the next great advance. After several weeks of beautiful weather and rest in the Divisional Support Area, the battalion relieved the 22nd Battalion (the French 'Van Doos') and took up positions on the 'Third Line (Railway Embankment)'.[62] Lieutenant Barber was certainly at Vimy, even if he was not directly involved in the initial four-day assault on the Ridge. On the night of 7 May he was ordered to 'proceed in advance [to the Embankment] and arrange the disposition of Companies and Sections'.[63] As the rest of the battalion moved into their designated positions, enemy gas shells caused numerous casualties. Two days later, in dull and rainy weather, the battalion moved forward once again and relieved the 19th Battalion in the front line. Artillery exchanges throughout the day on 9 April led to further casualties: 'two officers wounded, Lieut. P. Barber and Lieut. J.B. Gourley, and about 50 ORs killed and wounded'.[64] Percy's wounds were relatively minor – slight shrapnel injuries to the face – but nevertheless resulted in treatment at No. 14 Canadian Field Ambulance before transfer to the Casualty Clearing Station at nearby Aubigny. The following day, he was admitted to No. 3 General Hospital at Le Tréport. He spent two weeks in hospital and then reported to No. 2 Canadian Infantry Base Depot and the 1st Army School for further training. Then he returned to the trenches and prepared for yet another frontal assault on the enemy.

The capture of Vimy Ridge has come to define the Canadian experience of the Great War. It has overshadowed all other engagements and contributions, including the successful capture of Courcelette by the CEF a year earlier. Until recently, the understandable fascination with 'Vimy' has obscured subsequent key actions in which the Canucks distinguished themselves. The capture of Hill 70 in the summer of 1917 is a case in point. If Vimy is of symbolic importance, a notion to which most Canadians subscribe, then so, too, is Hill 70. At Vimy Ridge the Canadian Corps fought as an autonomous unit for the first time, but under the command of a British general. At Hill 70 it was led by a Canadian. General Arthur Currie had succeeded Sir Julian Byng as Corps Commander in June 1917. In both battles the Canadians managed to achieve what previous forces had failed to do, namely take and hold supposedly impregnable enemy defensive positions. The planned operation at Hill 70 was also, like Vimy Ridge, a diversionary action intended to relieve pressure elsewhere, in this instance designed to draw German forces away from the Ypres Salient, where the major British offensive of 1917 had already begun. At Hill 70, six Victoria Crosses were awarded for gallantry, two more than at Vimy. If the storming of Vimy Ridge heralded the prowess of Canadian troops, then the capture of Hill 70 cemented their reputation as some of the finest soldiers in the BEF.

Currie was initially asked to capture Lens, but convinced Haig that securing more high ground in the sector was an essential prerequisite.

Two Canadian Divisions, the 1st and the 2nd, found themselves 'fronting Hill 70's shell-swept slope, with the dull dead plain in our rear'.[65] Their orders were no different to those given two years earlier to Captain Baswitz and the London Territorials stationed in the same treeless wasteland of slag heaps and shell craters: capture the hill and hold it. Heroic actions would be necessary and casualties high. For Lieutenant Percy Barber, however, the battle began with a far more banal and less than glorious incident. As the 21st Battalion moved to their assembly positions in front of the lines on the eve of the battle, Lieutenant Barber fell and was injured. There is no evidence that he required medical treatment, but he was nevertheless relieved of his command of D Company. The written record suggests, once again, that he was *at* the battle but not necessarily directly involved *in* it. The rest of the men in the battalion were 'keen and in the highest of spirit' as they attacked in the first wave at 0425 hours on 15 August.[66] They were 'piped' over the parapet by the battalion Pipe Band. There was also the familiar accompaniment of artillery and machine gun fire, initiated by their own gunners but quickly countered by the enemy's own barrage. Missiles in the shape of drums of burning oil, supplied by the BEF's Royal Engineers, produced a smoke screen through which the Canadians advanced. By dawn, Battalion HQ began receiving reports stating, for example, that 'final objective had been gained, casualties slight, and scores of prisoners'.[67] German forces had begun retiring towards Lens. The Canadians had taken the hill and now they had to secure it against the 'repeated attempts of the Hun to re-establish his position'.[68] Over the next four days they resisted twenty-one enemy counter-attacks. The 21st Battalion lost nearly half of its fighting strength: a post-battle summary reported 40 men (including two officers) killed in action and a further 208 wounded and 23 missing.[69] The successful capture of a second key strategic position in the Lens sector had challenged the maxim that determined defence was superior to offensive action. The action at Hill 70 demonstrated that the Canadian Corps, led by a Canadian general, was proficient in both attack and defence. Some observers at the time and since have equated the victories at Vimy Ridge and Hill 70 with the birth of an independent Canadian nation. The 21st Battalion's Unit War Diary stated, simply, that 'our Battalion highly appreciates the honour of participating in this British success. We feel that it has again taken no small part in the destruction of the forces of the Kaiser.'[70]

By the autumn of 1917 Lieutenant Barber had spent eighteen months on the Western Front. He had undertaken numerous spells in the trenches, pre-occupied with the routine madness of holding the lines and participating in reciprocal acts of violence. He had survived three major CEF engagements and had emerged relatively unscathed from each. He and his men now needed time to recuperate. September and October were spent in the trenches and billets near Vimy, a relatively uneventful posting which permitted periods of rest and leave for officers and other ranks alike. At the end of October, however, the 21st Battalion began its journey north to the Salient. Canadian forces had fought there in 1915. Some of their fellow countrymen, including RNAS pilot Gordon Scott, had been engaged more recently in the third major offensive to bear the name of Ypres. In the Battles of the Menin Road, Polygon Wood and Broodseinde, the massed battalions of Britain, Australia and New Zealand had succeeded in pushing the German line back. The BEF had stumbled, however, on the muddy approaches to yet another heavily defended ridge. On 26 October 1917 the Second Battle of Passchendaele began, spearheaded by the newly arrived Canadian Corps, with British and Anzac forces in support. Lieutenant General Currie was determined to take the ridge, despite the appalling conditions his men faced, and made his usual thorough preparations. The construction of wooden plank roads and duckboards enabled guns and men to get nearer to the enemy. The 3rd and 4th Divisions were first to attack. They advanced, inch by inch, through a morass of mud and captured the enemy strong point of Crest Farm. Then the 1st and 2nd Divisions moved up to the front, separated by the quagmire that was once the valley of the Ravebeek. On 6 November Canadian troops – men from the 27th (City of Winnipeg) Battalion – entered the village of Passchendaele and, in doing so, added another name to the honour roll of the Dominion. By 10 November the Third Battle of Ypres was over.

Lieutenant Percy Barber fought in the battle, but did not live to see the victory. The 21st Battalion had arrived by train to join the rest of the 4th Canadian Infantry Brigade at Potijze, an area to the east of Ypres, on the evening of 2 November. After a hot meal, the men of A, C and D Companies set out at 1830 hours to relieve the 72nd Canadian Battalion on the left of the 4th Divisional Front. Carrying their arms, ammunition, bombs, rations and two full water bottles, it took Barber and his men over five hours to move up to the line near Crest farm. The relief was completed by 0215 hours on the morning of 3 November. German forces opposite the Canadians – men from the 126th and 132nd Regiments of the 39th Infantry Division – believed the battlefield was 'swampier than ever', contained 'countless shell holes, some containing water up to the armpits',[71] and was thus virtually impossible to traverse. Nevertheless, they decided upon pre-emptive action against their newly-arrived opponents. An artillery barrage opened up at 0445 hours, followed by an attack by one of their new 'Storm Battalions'. Lieutenant Barber and the men of D Company were temporarily dislodged from their trenches, but subsequently retook their positions. A further assault was beaten back by Lewis Gun and rifle fire. Later, with the line consolidated, and under the cover of darkness, Lieutenant Barber led a small party of men into no man's land. There, some 75 to 120 yards in front of their own lines, they began to establish a series of outposts. The Casualty Record in Lieutenant Percy Barber's military service file states what happened next:

> 'Killed in Action'
> This officer was returning from a personal reconnaissance of the ground in front of the line his Battalion was occupying, when he was instantly killed by the bullet from the rifle of an enemy sniper.[72]

The action at Passchendaele cost the 21st Battalion dearly. In 48 hours it suffered over 130 casualties, including 43 officers and men killed in action, and its fighting strength was reduced to just 307 men.[73] The number of Canadians killed and wounded in two weeks of combat amounted to 15,654. The total number of BEF casualties during the Third Battle of Ypres as a whole has been estimated at 275,000.[74]

Chapter 7

Victory ... and a New World

So now the war was over. I was home again fit and well. So what was to be done? I was a man whose developing thinking had been frozen by four years of intense and continuous fighting and yet in whom ideas were surging again as a result of a new freedom. I was a student who had been without books for four years; an efficient and established soldier coming back as an inexperienced teacher.

Ormond Burton, *The Silent Division* (1935)

The Allied capture of Passchendaele Ridge had much in common with previous victories. The BEF and Dominion forces could justifiably point to similar successes at Loos, Pozières, Flers-Courcelette, Vimy Ridge and Hill 70. In each assault on an entrenched and determined enemy they had taken strong points, captured territory and achieved their operational objectives. Overall, however, little had changed. Major offensives and set-piece battles had resulted in huge numbers of casualties but had failed to inflict a decisive blow by routing the German Army. Trenches were taken but more were constructed. The great breakthrough remained an illusion. On the Western Front at least, the stalemate continued. The Third Battle of Ypres had failed, like the Battle of the Somme before it. Many of the survivors of both great offensives spent a fourth wartime Christmas in the trenches; the New Year of 1918 similarly brought little cheer. Few soldiers, or their families back home, anticipated that this would be the year in which the war would end, although millions hoped that it would be.

The German Spring Offensive, or *Kaiserschlacht* (Kaiser's Battle), which began in the last week of March 1918, seriously dented any such hopes. German armies, reinforced by some fifty additional divisions released by the cessation of fighting on the Eastern Front, quickly smashed through the Allied lines on the Somme and regained in days territory which had taken the BEF months to capture. Men from Britain and its Dominions were caught up in a maelstrom. Their desperate retreat made a nonsense of earlier limited gains and huge sacrifices. They fought over much of the same ground, and ceded positions which Albert Baswitz, Sydney Forbes, Frank Wilson and Percy Barber, and many thousands of other servicemen, had fought and died for. For a while it seemed that the war might indeed end in 1918 – but with a German victory. Eventually, the Allied line held in front of the city of Amiens, 19 miles south-west of the BEF's former operational base at Albert. General Ludendorff's great offensive had failed to strike a death blow, and had seriously depleted the reserves of the German Army.

In early August, the BEF was finally poised to resume offensive action. Once again, an enormous army assembled on the Somme. General Sir Henry Rawlinson's Fourth Army stood just a few miles to the east of Amiens. This mighty host contained Tommies, Diggers and Canucks; the Enzeds would be committed later that month. It had been four years – almost to the day – since the old British imperial lion had called the young lions from the Dominions of Australia, Canada and New Zealand. The young cubs had since come of age (see plate 34). They were no longer small-scale bands of 'determined colonials',[1] but seasoned battalions, brigades, divisions and semi-autonomous corps, all increasingly conscious of their distinct heritages and new military identities (see plate 35). Hardened and disciplined by their experiences at Gallipoli, Lens, Ypres and the Somme, and bearing the physical and psychological scars of war from previous encounters with 'Abdul' and 'Fritz', the Australian and Canadian troops now formed the 'shock armies' of the BEF.[2] Reinforcements had been sent to fill the depleted ranks. The 'Diggers', as many of the Australians now referred to themselves,[3] were still all volunteers, unlike some of the new recruits from the other Dominions sent to the front by way of conscription rather than enlistment. The Australian Corps, commanded by Lieutenant General Sir John Monash, comprised five divisions. Its battalions – nearly sixty in all – were made up of men from every state. Each division contained at least one battalion raised in Western Australia. Men who had fought alongside Adolph Knäble (32nd AIF) at Fromelles and Sydney Forbes (11th AIF) at Pozières now lined up with mates in the

16th, 28th, 44th, 48th and 51st Battalions. Currie's Canadian Corps, with four divisions and forty-eight battalions, also reflected the contribution of the country's many provinces and major cities. No fewer than fourteen battalions contained the words 'Ontario' or 'Toronto' in their official titles, including Percy Barber's 21st (Eastern Ontario) Battalion. There were six British divisions: the 12th, 17th, 18th and 32nd Divisions contained battalions originally raised in the Home and Southern Counties, the East Midlands, East Anglia, Yorkshire, Lancashire, Dorset and on both sides of the Scottish border. Many now included men from different parts of the country who had been transferred from other battalions to fill the gaps after the Somme and Passchendaele. The London Territorials were there too: the 47th Division, which included the 22nd London Battalion and others which had stormed High Wood in 1916, and the 58th Division containing the second-line battalions of the 56th Division. Supporting the infantry were the specialists: motor machine gun brigades, tank and armoured car battalions, cavalry regiments, batteries of artillery and companies of engineers and signallers.

The Battle of Amiens commenced on 8 August 1918. Described by the victors as the 'Day We Won the War' and by the vanquished as the 'Black Day of the German Army',[4] the advance from Amiens marked a major turning point in the war. The BEF's concerted all-forces and all-arms assault, based upon learning from past experience and 'neglect nothing' preparation,[5] restored confidence and initiated a war of movement which was later termed the 'March to Victory'. British and Dominion forces advanced once more over the shattered battlefields of the Somme; the French First and Third Armies attacked to the south of them. The German Army, which only four months previously had so nearly dealt the BEF a fatal blow, spent the next 'Hundred Days' in retreat. Even the much-vaunted defences of the Hindenburg Line failed to stop the Allied advance. The victorious armies included thousands of alumni from the training colleges and universities mentioned in earlier chapters. Some of the young lions who had enlisted in 1914 had managed to survive the relentless vicissitudes of war, unlike friends and fellow teacher-soldiers whose stories form the central core of this book. George Cline, Ormond Burton, Fred Albrecht and Ben Bateman all took part in the final actions of the Great War and lived to see in the new post-war world.

George Cline (see plate 36) had been an inadvertent role model to the teacher trainees at the University of Toronto. There is no evidence that Gordon Scott and Percy Barber or the other young men who began their studies at UTFE in 1914 ever met him, but they would certainly have heard of him. Instructor Cline's wartime career – his early enlistment, deployments, promotions and decorations – was followed with great interest by members of the university community. At the age of twenty-six, and single, he had responded to Sam Hughes' clarion call by leaving his employment at the University of Toronto Schools and travelling to Valcartier Camp. A teacher for three years, he was also the archetypal teacher-soldier, having already served part-time for eight years in the Militia (20th Regiment Canadian Engineers). George was an expert wireless operator, and at Valcartier joined the 1st Canadian Divisional Signal Company (CDSC). His previous military experience – and two degrees from the University of Toronto – were sufficient for the award of a commission in the CEF. Captain Cline had been born in Appleby, Ontario, but when he sailed to war with the First Contingent it was to fight against the country of his paternal forefathers. George's father Miles, despite also being born in Ontario, routinely informed the census enumerators of his 'German' ancestry.

George Cline's military career mirrors almost exactly the Canadian involvement in the Great War. He arrived in England in 1914, landed in France in February 1915 and then took part in the Battle of St Julien (Second Battle of Ypres), during which he was struck by shrapnel but uninjured. In August 1916 he took command of the 2nd CDSC in time for the attack a few weeks later at Courcelette on the Somme.

Returning to the 1st CDSC in March 1917 as Acting Major and Officer Commanding, he and his signallers were fully engaged in supporting Lieutenant Percy Barber and his fellow infantrymen at Vimy Ridge, Hill 70 and Passchendaele. After a posting to England in January 1918 as Chief Instructor at the Canadian Engineer Training Depot, a period on the Staff at Canadian Corps Headquarters and further promotion to Lieutenant Colonel, George Cline returned to the field and commanded all Canadian Corps Signals units for the rest of the war. He led his men at Amiens in August, Arras in September and Cambrai in October. George Cline's wartime service was recognized by the award of the Distinguished

Service Order (DSO) and the Légion d'Honneur Croix de Chevalier. Few of the men and women listed in the University of Toronto Roll of Service could match such an impressive wartime record. The *Toronto Star* duly noted how George Cline and his fellow officers were 'maintaining British traditions'.[6]

Ormond Burton (see plate 37) was still with the New Zealand Division (NZD) when it launched its assaults near Bapaume in August 1918. In 1914, the 21-year-old son of English migrant farmers from County Durham and graduate of Auckland Training College had been running his own single-classroom school at Ahuroa in the Northland. He, too, had previous military experience: two years in the Territorial Force (15th North Auckland Regiment) and two years in the Officer Training Corps at ATC. On enlistment, however, he was assigned a non-combatant role in the New Zealand Medical Corps (NZMC). Private Burton left New Zealand with the 3rd Reinforcements and made the long journey – which he later described in great detail – to Egypt and then Lemnos. He arrived in time to sail to Gallipoli with the first attacking force. On 25 April 1915 he was at Anzac Cove, tending the wounded, and two days later escorted them back to Alexandria on board the *Lutzow*, the ship from which the Auckland Battalion had disembarked. Private Burton later went ashore as a stretcher bearer, ferrying the wounded from the front line down the treacherous makeshift paths to Anzac Beach. Whilst his friends from college – Jock MacKenzie and Joe Gasparich – fought at the Daisy Patch and elsewhere, Ormond continued to care for fallen comrades right up to the final evacuation from Gallipoli.

When the NZD moved to the Western Front in 1916, Private Burton was serving with the 2nd New Zealand Field Ambulance attached to the 2nd Battalion of the Auckland Regiment. He was at Flers in September, when former ATC alumnus Frank Wilson was killed attacking the Switch Line, and it was during this time on the Somme that he made the momentous decision to take up arms and join the infantry. In February 1917 he was with his fellow Aucklanders in the front line near Armentières. His actions during a raid on an enemy trench led to the award of the Military Medal (MM) – for rescuing his wounded friend and superior officer 'Fighting Jock' MacKenzie. Ormond managed to get Jock back to the Enzed lines, but the young Major died of his wounds shortly afterwards.

Eight months later, Corporal Burton was in the NZD lines near Ypres, in position not far from another ATC man, both awaiting the signal to attack across the swamps in front of Broodseinde. Unlike his former college principal Second Lieutenant Bert Milnes, Ormond Burton survived the assault on 4 October, but only just. He received bullet wounds to the left shoulder and chest, the latter fortunately deflected by a copy of the Bible in his tunic pocket. He was more seriously wounded during the German Spring Offensive in March 1918, but this man who steadfastly spurned every opportunity to go on leave also refused to be sent back to England for medical treatment and was hospitalized instead at the 3rd Canadian Hospital at Boulogne. In August Sergeant Burton 'led his platoon with undiminished dash' during the 2nd Auckland Battalion's successful advance towards Bapaume from their positions near the village of Grévillers.[7] Wounded for a third time, he was evacuated to hospital in Rouen. He returned to his unit on 4 October, exactly a year since the Aucklanders had triumphed at Broodseinde. In his absence the battalion had broken through the German defences but had suffered heavy casualties in doing so. More commissioned officers were needed to fill the gaps. Just a few days later, Ormond Burton left the front for the last time and headed for England, and a posting to the 5th Officer Cadet Battalion at Trinity College, Cambridge. By the time Second Lieutenant Burton received his commission the war had ended.

Fred Albrecht (see plate 38) took part in the Battle of Amiens and the subsequent operations of the Australian Corps. He had risen through the ranks to become a Captain in the 51st Battalion AIF. His war had started in August 1914 when, with Sydney Forbes and Walter Blair, the champion sprinters from Claremont Teachers College, he had enlisted in Perth and trained at Blackboy Hill. The three friends had sailed together from Fremantle, readied themselves for battle in Egypt and Lemnos and landed at Anzac Cove on 25 April 1915. Fred was wounded in June and returned to Egypt for medical treatment at the 1st Australian General Hospital in Heliopolis. The son of a butcher from Lower Saxony, his migrant ancestry, and hence his loyalty, had been questioned by some back home, but as the Perth *Sunday Times* noted at the time, he had now 'sealed his devotion to his King and country with his blood'.[8] Fred Albrecht returned to Anzac in August and was promoted to Sergeant.

Fred and Sydney were finally evacuated from Gallipoli in December of that year, leaving their mate Walter Blair amongst the dead at Lone Pine.

Back in Egypt, both men received commissions as part of the reorganization of the AIF, but in different battalions. Second Lieutenant Albrecht joined the newly created 51st Battalion, and then spent most of 1916 on secondment to other new battalions helping to train the reinforcements arriving from Australia. He landed in France in December, six months after Sydney's death and his own battalion's subsequent operations around Pozières and Mouquet Farm. By the time Captain Albrecht reached Amiens nearly two years later, he was a veteran of the Ypres Salient, having fought on the Menin Road and at Polygon Wood. He now wore spectacles, having received wounds to his eyes in October 1917 when an enemy shell burst on the dugout he was sheltering in. He became the battalion's Adjutant just as General Ludendorff launched his great offensive in March 1918. On 5 April the 51st Battalion were at Dernancourt near Albert, where they successfully repelled a major enemy assault on their lines. Twenty days later – on 'Anzac Day', the third anniversary of the landing at Gallipoli – Captain Albrecht and his fellow West Australians were amongst the victorious forces at Villers-Bretonneux, the action which signalled the end of the Spring Offensive. On the day of the Allied counter-offensive at Amiens, the 51st Battalion was billeted near Longeau, having been relieved in the front line by units from the Canadian 8th and 9th Brigades. With the German Army subsequently retreating, however, the battalion was involved in mopping-up operations, clearing captured villages and securing crossing points on the River Somme. They spent time on a front line which was no longer static, taking turns with the troops from the United States 131st Infantry Regiment and the French 59th and 332nd Infantry Regiments. By September Captain Albrecht and his men had reached positions near the Peronne–St Quentin railway line. On 18 September they took part in the 4th Division (AIF) attack on German positions in front of the Hindenburg Line at Épehy, but thereafter played no further part in direct military action. The 51st Battalion spent the final weeks of the war resting and training near Amiens, and Captain Albrecht went on leave to Paris.

The 56th (London) Division also took part in the final offensives. Ben Bateman (see plate 39) of the 2nd London Battalion was still in its ranks.[9] Four of the young men who had travelled with him from Latymer Upper School to the London Day Training College, however, were dead. Herbert Handley, Edward Mount, Richard Garland and Albert Baswitz had all been killed in action in the British offensives of 1915 and 1916. Like Ben, they had left their studies prematurely to enlist in the London Regiment. Unlike Ben, they had joined the Army as commissioned officers. His status as one of the 'other ranks' may explain why details of his military service are more difficult to confirm than those of his college counterparts. Ben's early life and later career, on the other hand, are relatively well documented. The National Census provides information relating to his family and domicile: Ben lived with his father James (a policeman, originally from Wales), mother Emma (born in Derby) and siblings Dorothea, Fanny and James in Hammersmith (1901) and later Kensington (1911). School and college admissions registers tell us about his academic qualifications and scholarships (Student Teacher bursaries), teaching placements (at Saunders Road Board School) and sporting prowess (playing football for Crystal Palace and the England Amateur team). The Unit War Diary for the 2nd Londons, however, makes no mention of Ben Bateman, at least not by name. Instead, the details of his wartime contribution and experience are subsumed within the references to 'ORs' – other ranks. The battalion's Service Medal and Award Roll, however, does give dates for when he was serving in particular 'theatres of war'.[10] His early enlistment did not take him to the Western Front with the rest of the London Territorials. Instead, in December 1914, he travelled to Malta to take up garrison duties with a second line battalion – the 2/2nd Londons. In late August 1915 the Londoners moved to Egypt, the major staging point for the British forces fighting in the Dardanelles. The battalion then made the sea journey familiar to so many other British and Anzac units and landed at Cape Helles with the Royal Naval Division on 13 October. Six weeks later, the battalion returned to Egypt, part of the strategic withdrawal of troops from the Gallipoli Peninsula, before landing in France in April 1916. Following the reorganization of the London Regiment in June, Private Bateman joined the ranks of the 1/2nd London Battalion. Unlike his friend Captain Richard Garland, he survived the battalion's sacrificial assault on the first day of the Battle of the Somme when 'the field of

Gommecourt [was] heaped with the bodies of Londoners'.[11] He may well have been wounded in the subsequent fighting,[12] as he was not with the battalion when it took part in the Battle of Flers-Courcelette, ten weeks later. As a Physical Training Instructor, however, his absence might also be explained by the possibility of his having been recalled to England and employed in a training role for much of the following two years. He did not return to the front until the end of March 1918, when the BEF, and his battalion trying to hold the line at Gavrelle, needed every available man to counter the German Spring Offensive. The 1/2nd Londons spent the following months training new drafts and practising for the open warfare which, the High Command anticipated, would follow the BEF's next great offensive. Sergeant Bateman was not with his battalion, however, when it took part in the assault on the Hindenburg Line and the bloody confrontations at Bullecourt and the Canal du Nord. Instead, he had been one of a select group of NCOs which had left the 2nd Londons in August and returned to England.

The Armistice of November 1918, sudden and unexpected as it was to most people, prompted both individual and institutional reflection. The almae matres of our teacher-soldiers had responded to the demands of total war and had been preoccupied by its demands. In Toronto, Auckland, Perth and London, presidents and principals weighed their Rolls of Honour against the long and saddening lists of 'The Fallen'. In Canada, Robert Falconer's annual President's Report quantified the wartime contribution of students and alumni from the University of Toronto. In 1916 he had reported that over 3,000 members of his community had joined the colours. A year later, that figure stood at over 4,000, and by the time of the Armistice it was over 5,000.[13] Collectively, their wartime service had taken them to every theatre of war and to every major battlefield. The university was represented in units throughout the Canadian Corps, many of the BEF's 'British' battalions and in the Air Force and Navy. By the end of the war over 70 per cent of them – already graduates and professionals or working towards such qualifications and status – had been commissioned; of these, fewer than 20 per cent were promoted from the ranks. These numbers include the trainee teachers. By 1916 the President could report that 'The Faculty of Education had a strong company of the Officers Training Corps and gave its share of recruits.'[14] His Report for 1918 stated that 159 UTFE trainees were known to have served. The *University of Toronto Roll of Service 1914–1918*, published in 1921, listed 185. Once again, these teacher-soldiers were represented in all branches of the armed forces. Just over 42 per cent of them held commissions, a figure which mainly reflects their non-degree qualifications. In Gordon Scott and Percy Barber's year group, thirty-seven trainees joined the forces, and fifteen became officers.[15] Some had joined specialist units established on the university campus. The University of Toronto (67th) Battery, Canadian Field Artillery (CFA), was established in 1916, and the Royal Flying Corps (RFC) set up a training facility in 1917 at the Faculty of Applied Science. By the end of that year nearly a hundred students had taken commissions in the RNAS and RFC. As increasing numbers of male students left for military service, their female counterparts also did their bit for the war effort. In 1915 the university had formed its own medical unit, No. 4 Canadian General Hospital (University of Toronto). Staffed by tutors and students, mainly from the Faculty of Medicine, the fully equipped hospital provided 1,000 hospital beds for casualties in Salonika.[16] None of the trainees from UTFE joined the unit, but Barbara Ross and Lilly Keys, from the 1909 and 1913 cohorts respectively, became Nursing Sisters in the Canadian Army Medical Corps. Barbara served in France, at the 8th Canadian Stationary Hospital; Lilly worked in the Sandford Fleming Military Hospital in Ottawa. Back in Toronto, the University Women's Hospital Supply Association supported the front line work in Salonika. In January 1916, female trainees in the Faculty of Education set up their own auxiliary branch of the Red Cross to support the relief efforts. With many men having enlisted or been conscripted, by 1917 women outnumbered their male counterparts at UTFE by 247 to 72.[17] War accelerated the feminization of the teaching profession in Ontario; by 1920, women teachers held just over 50 per cent of all secondary school teaching posts in the province. This change was not simply a reflection of the number of wartime casualties amongst the male teaching force. Instead, it tells the story of increasing numbers of girls attending secondary schools and young women going on to university.

The true cost of the war in human lives was considerable. By 1916 university publications began to feature the names of the dead and wounded. The *Torontonensis* proudly listed those 'On Active Service', but also started to put together an Honour Roll with photographic images of those who had fallen. The war had produced a new set of role models: an accompanying note from President Falconer declared that the lost alumni would become 'a concrete standard for their successors, a traditional conscience for public service'.[18] The *Varsity Supplement* of 1918, printed after hostilities had ended but fully aware that all casualty figures were provisional at this stage, contained a listing of 'Pro Patria Mori'; 604 of the 5,651 alumni who had served had not returned.[19] Amongst the hundreds of names were those of thirty former UTFE trainees.[20] The cohort of 1914–15 lost Gordon Scott, Percy Barber and five of their classmates. Lance Corporal Edward Morgan of the 4th Canadian Mounted Regiment was killed at Ypres on 2 June 1916. Corporal William Buchanan, serving with the 75th Battalion, had been killed in action during a midnight advance towards Lens from Vimy Ridge on 8 June 1917. Lieutenant William Durant, who had learned to fly at the university's flying school, served in both the RNAS and the newly formed RAF (29 Squadron) and was shot down over Ypres on 2 July 1918. Lieutenant Hedley Goodyear MC was with the 102nd Battalion CEF at Amiens on 8 August 1918, but was killed by a machine gun bullet two weeks later near Le Quesnel. Lieutenant Gordon Forsyth left the University Training Company in 1917 to take up a commission in the Imperial Machine Gun Corps and was killed in action at Le Cateau on 10 October, just a month before the war ended. By then the German Army was beaten, only to be superseded by another deadly opponent. The 'Spanish Lady' – a particularly virulent strain of influenza – was no respecter of age, gender, class or military service record. At this late stage in the Great War, the virus crossed the Atlantic, possibly carried by returning service personnel. One of the estimated 55,000 Canadians victims of the pandemic – a figure just short of the number of Canadians killed in the war itself – was Sister Lilly Keys, who died in Toronto on 28 September 1918.[21]

Auckland Training College also shared in the experience of a world turned upside down by war. The number of ATC men who served their country is similar to that of UTFE. Over 150 former trainees joined the NZEF and NZD.[22] The great majority were infantrymen, members of the various battalions of the Auckland Regiment or the NZRB. Some joined as cavalrymen in the Mounted Rifles. Others followed Ormond Burton's example; at least twenty ATC men joined the NZMC and worked in field ambulances or on hospital ships. The convoy which sailed from Albany in 1914 carried twelve former ATC trainees to Egypt, men who were amongst the first to land at Anzac Beach on 25 April 1915.[23] Others joined them later at Gallipoli, or on the Western Front; thirty-seven of the forty-three Reinforcements from New Zealand carried men who had trained under Principal Milnes at ATC. Most fought against the Germans on the battlefields of France and Flanders, at Flers, Messines, Broodseinde and Grévillers, but a few served in some of the less well known theatres of war. Corporal Donald Jack of the NZRB, for example, was part of the Samoan Expeditionary Force, New Zealand's first overseas military deployment of the war. Lieutenant William Johns of the 4th Waikato Mounted Rifles fought the Ottoman forces in Palestine, as did Trooper Rupert McKenzie of the 16th Imperial Camel Corps. By the end of the war thirty-four had been commissioned, exactly half of whom had been promoted from the ranks.

Over 60 per cent of the men from ATC became casualties: thirty-four were killed in action, ten died of wounds and a further forty were wounded but survived the war.[24] The Fallen included some of those named above. Donald Jack was killed at Flers on 16 September 1915, William Johns at the Battle of Beersheba near Gaza on 1 November 1917 and Rupert McKenzie at Amman on 30 March 1918. Despite the Enzeds' baptism of fire at Gallipoli, only one ATC former trainee – Sergeant William Wells of the 15th North Auckland Company – was killed there. Fighting on the Western Front proved to be far deadlier. The campaign on the Somme in 1916 resulted in five deaths, with another six fatalities at Messines and Passchendaele in 1917 and five more in the final Allied advances of 1918.[25] Each reported death had an impact on the college community back in Auckland. None was quite so traumatic, however, as that of Second Lieutenant Bert Milnes. News of the Principal's death reached ATC at 1500 hours on Friday, 12 October 1917, just eight days after he had been killed at Broodseinde. Mr Cousins, the Acting Principal, called the student community to the Assembly Hall and read out the telegram he had just received. He then went to the playground to inform the staff and pupils of the Normal School, before closing both school and college until the following Tuesday in honour of their lost mentor and leader. *The Kiwi*, the magazine of Auckland University College, later reported that the telegram

> threw the whole Training College into the deepest gloom. The news soon spread, and those who had never known Mr Milnes wondered at the grief of those who felt that they had lost a friend who was almost a father. During the short ten years of his work in Auckland, he had made his influence felt on the lives of hundreds of young men and women who regarded him with unstinted affection and admiration.[26]

Herbert Cousins continued as Acting Principal until his appointment to the permanent position in December 1919. He did his best to keep the college focussed on its academic learning and vocational training and, at the same time, to contribute to the war effort. Students worked with Old As, knitting garments, raising money and sending parcels to their fellows serving overseas. In April 1918 they wore sprigs of rosemary and attended a memorial service at St Matthew's Church. Six months later, with Auckland and much of the rest of the world in the grip of the influenza pandemic, they left their studies early to help in local hospitals. In November of that year the 'Spanish Lady' added the name of Lance Corporal Daniel O'Brien – one of the wounded survivors of the Gallipoli campaign who had been transported back to New Zealand in 1916 – to the long lists of The Fallen.

Claremont Teachers College in Perth contributed just over 170 alumni to the BEF in the Great War.[27] For Australians, the conflict will forever be remembered for the initial landings at Anzac Cove on 25 April 1915. Twelve of the original Anzacs came from CTC: men like Sydney Forbes, Walter Blair and Fred Albrecht, whose endeavours at Gallipoli exemplified the martial spirit of an emerging nation. The college's roll of honour contains the names of a further twelve men who were sent as reinforcements to the Dardanelles. The great majority of CTC men, however, never fought against Johnny Turk. Instead, like the majority of other Australian servicemen, they took part in the great offensives against the Germans on the Western Front. Most of the CTC men were infantrymen: twenty-eight served in the original 11th Battalion and a further eighty-two joined units which also contained large numbers of West Australians. Unlike their counterparts at UTFE in Canada, relatively few CTC men enlisted in other services, although eleven joined the famous 10th Light Horse. Trooper John Regan served at Gallipoli and died after the amputation of both legs. Captain James Rodstead, a member of the first cohort at CTC in 1902, died of wounds just days after the Battle of Beersheba. Walter Crossing's remarkable military career included action with a new form of mechanized 'horse'. Whilst convalescing in the Bethnal Green Military Hospital in London in September 1915, this veteran of the 11th Battalion's landing at Anzac transferred to the Royal Naval Volunteer Reserve. Temporary Sub-Lieutenant Crossing joined a specialist RNAS squadron of armoured cars which landed at the Russian port of Archangel on the White Sea and then travelled some 1,200 miles south to the Black Sea to support Russian troops fighting against the Turks. After the fall of the Tsarist regime in 1917 he was transferred to the British Army, promoted to Captain and served in the Middle East. Walter Crossing DSO, DSC was one of the most highly decorated Australians of the Great War. Myrtle Edwards, the only woman from CTC to leave Australia for overseas service, was one of seven former trainees who spent the war tending the wounded. Myrtle began teaching as a monitor in Kalgoorlie in 1905, before enrolling on a short course at CTC four years later. Principal Rooney described her as 'a very good type. Believe could manage a large class in a big school. Earnest as a student, vigorous and thoughtful as a teacher and should prove a capital asset in any school.'[28] After CTC, Myrtle returned to the Goldfields and taught there until 1916, when she was granted leave without pay to take up nursing in military hospitals in England. Twice engaged to men who were killed or died in the war, she returned to Western Australia in 1919 and resumed her teaching career.

Only two of the CTC men who enlisted in 1914 were commissioned officers when they began their military service, namely Lieutenant William Rockliff and Second Lieutenant James Morgan. At least six of the veterans of Gallipoli were later promoted from the ranks. By the end of the war, forty former trainees had been commissioned; at least fifty others served as NCOs at some point in their military career. The casualty rate, 65 per cent of those who served, was high: thirty-eight men were killed or died of their wounds or sickness, and a further seventy-eight were wounded. None of those who enlisted in 1914 returned home unscathed: eleven were dead and the rest had been wounded by the time the Armistice was signed in November 1918. The thirty-eight trainees who attended CTC during 1912 and 1913 were particularly hard hit by the war: nine were killed in action, three died of their wounds and a further thirteen were wounded. Members of the 1913 Cricket XI were amongst the casualties. Of the nine players identified by name on the team photograph of that year (see plate 13), five were wounded and four were killed in action. They fell in locations which collectively chart some of the major Australian engagements of the war: Walter Blair at Lone Pine, Sydney Forbes at Pozières, Malcolm Stewart at Passchendaele and Gordon Gemmell at Amiens.

Back in London, Dr Percy Nunn followed the wartime careers of his former charges very closely. He continued to add notes to the LDTC Admissions Register, using information received directly from the individuals themselves or from fellow alumni reporting news of their friends' whereabouts, great deeds and misadventures. In 1920 this data was used by the *Londinian* to produce a Roll of Honour of those who 'Served in H.M. Forces'.[29] Of the 590 male trainees admitted between 1902 and 1918, at least 320 enlisted or were conscripted. Collectively they served in over fifty different regiments. One in four (seventy-eight men) joined one of the many battalions raised in the capital, such as the City and County of London Regiments, the Royal Fusiliers, the Middlesex Regiment and the Honourable Artillery Company. Many joined specialist units: twenty-three served in the Royal Artillery, twenty-eight in the Royal Engineers and twenty-three in the Royal Army Medical Corps. At least nine joined the Royal Navy and ten were in the RFC/RAF. Men from LDTC were present in all the sectors defended by the BEF on the Western Front, whilst others fought in its campaigns in the Dardanelles, the Middle East, and Russia. Albert Baswitz was one of eighteen trainees from the 1911 cohort who responded to the call to arms in 1914; a further nineteen followed, via enlistment or conscription, by the end of the war. Over 60 per cent of the men from this year group, many with links to the

University of London OTC, were awarded commissions; the proportion for men from LDTC as a whole was 48 per cent. Percy Nunn recorded the deaths of thirty-three of his former students, a number similar to that of each of the training colleges in Perth, Auckland and Toronto, but one which represented a far smaller proportion of the number of alumni who served.

The impact of war on the LDTC was particularly evident in the dramatic reduction in the number of male trainees. The outbreak of war virtually put an end to teacher training for men in the capital and elsewhere. By January 1915 almost half the country's trainee teachers had enlisted. The 1916 conscription regulations ensured that men fit for military service would not be accepted for teacher training. Only 16 of the 211 trainees in the September 1916 cohort were men, and most of these had been pronounced medically unfit for military service.[30] Some of the women students left to work in munitions factories or entered other forms of paid employment. Several male staff enlisted or were conscripted and were replaced by female lecturers on temporary contracts. The social life of the college was also affected. The Lent Term 1915 edition of the *Londinian* noted plenty of women's hockey matches but only one men's football match. Nearly every society report began with the same proclamation: 'Owing to the National Crisis we have been obliged greatly to curtail our activities.'

It was a similar story at other training colleges in London. Nearly 800 students, former students and tutors from Borough Road College served in the Great War, and over 100 lost their lives.[31] The college was forced to move in 1916 after its premises were requisitioned by the War Office and used by the Army Service Corps. The few remaining students were transferred to Richmond Theological College. St Mark's College in Chelsea moved in with St John's College in Battersea after its buildings were taken over by the Second London General Hospital. At Goldsmiths' College over 600 'Old Smiths' undertook some form of war service.[32] Caroline Graveson wrote later that the war 'was a period of constant emergencies and new adjustments (and) turned Goldsmiths' into an almost purely women's college'; by the autumn of 1918 only fifteen male trainees were in attendance.[33] Those who remained contributed to the war effort by raising funds for the Save the Children Society, helping local refugees, and growing potatoes on the college grounds. Once again, the casualty rate amongst those serving was high: ninety-two former Smiths lost their lives.[34]Amongst them was the Warden, William Loring. Captain Loring had spent the first year of the war on home duty with the 2nd Scottish Horse in Northumberland. Writing to his wife in August 1915 about rumours of a possible deployment to the Middle East he commented, 'We may see no more active service than we see in Morpeth.' Three weeks later, he landed at Suvla Bay. On 21 October he received a gunshot wound to his thigh and was taken on board HMHS *Devanha*. Three days later, he died of his wounds and was buried at sea in the Aegean.

*   *   *

William Loring was among the millions of combatants who were killed in the Great War. Most of those who served, however, survived the ordeal. For the 'soldier from the wars returning',[35] it was a new world. War was the great disruptor, and many of the returnees may well have believed that nothing could possibly be the same again. Before the war they had been teachers. During the war they had been warriors of various descriptions and expertise, and had experienced the myriad faces of war at first hand. Four years of fighting had left scars, both physical and emotional. All could count friends and colleagues who had not survived the conflict. Personal reflection was tempered by the need to pack up and pick up, to prepare for demobilization and the return to civilian life and meaningful employment. This was easier said than done, however. Some, like Henry Wulff (CTC, 1913), were so badly wounded and traumatized that they were hospitalized on their return home and died shortly afterwards. Others were no longer capable of returning to the rigours of the classroom or, like Harry Jones (LDTC, 1913), carried on teaching despite the reservations expressed by Percy Nunn:

> It is clear that he has suffered a great deal from the hardships of his military service, but it is impossible to persuade him to take things easily or to be absent from his post even when he was obviously not fit for work.[36]

Limbs lost in action, nerves shattered by repeated exposure to danger and minds and behaviour conditioned by military discipline attracted the attention of disconcerted pupils and colleagues alike.

The majority of the teachers returning home did so directly, and resumed their careers without undue fuss or ceremony. There were some official attempts to ease the transition from war to peace and to ensure that schools were fully staffed. In England, qualified teachers were amongst the high priority categories for demobilization. The Board of Education encouraged training colleges to organize refresher courses, to permit 'interrupted' students to resume their studies and to introduce flexible arrangements for other ex-servicemen to embark upon a career in teaching. Training colleges in Perth, Auckland and Toronto welcomed back the 'soldier-students', and numbers on rolls soon recovered. Enrolments at the LDTC increased from 199 in 1918 to 487 in 1919.[37] The young men of 1914 returned from the war as mature, experienced and, in many cases, more assertive adults. They were joined in London by other seasoned warriors. In March 1919, a class of sixty Australians, which included CTC alumnus Captain Roy Potts MC, held a 'Diggers Night'. They performed *The Diggers' College Song*, which referenced both John Adams and Percy Nunn.[38] The latter succeeded the former as Principal in 1922 and went on to lay the foundations upon which today's University College London Institute of Education was built. His influence and renown as an educator extended beyond the capital. When William Rooney retired as Principal of CTC in 1927, the University of Western Australia commissioned Professor Nunn to evaluate the British applicants for the post.

Ben Bateman was one of the first to return to LDTC. The declaration of war in 1914 had prematurely ended his training to be a teacher. Even before that, however, there had been signs that other interests were taking priority over academic work and classroom preparation. He had been 'Interviewed by Faculty' on at least three occasions, having raised concerns about lack of work, disappointing examination results and several unexplained absences. The reason for this poor performance was his involvement in sport. Whilst still at college he had signed for Crystal Palace, then playing in the Southern League, and made over thirty first team appearances. The flying winger had also been selected for the England Amateur Football Team, had played international matches against Ireland and the Netherlands and had toured Scandinavia. The return to LDTC, however, was successful. Percy Nunn duly wrote a testimonial for him on completion of the course:

> Mr Bateman returned to us in January 1919, for a shortened course of professional training, and taught on four mornings a week in a Central School. His teaching of general subjects is above the average; he manages his boys well, selects his matter suitably and treats it vigorously, and he makes good use of illustration and questioning. Thus, he would a valuable man even as an ordinary class-master. But he would be especially valuable in a post where he would have wide scope in connexion with games and physical exercises. As an international footballer and as an Instructor in the army his qualifications for such work are exceptionally high, and he has shewn outstanding ability in dealing with it in school.[39]

Ben Bateman's return to teaching was short-lived, however. When Crystal Palace joined the newly created Third Division of the English Football League in 1920, Ben signed full-time professional terms and was a regular member of the side that won the division championship that season. He made over 170 appearances and scored 10 goals for Crystal Palace before his transfer to Dartford F.C. in 1924. Ben Bateman died in 1961.

Lieutenant Colonel George Cline returned to Canada in June 1919 and was discharged upon demobilization. The Great War had elevated men like Cline to a new professional and social status. George had been one of the many 'Temporary Officers' and 'Temporary Gentlemen' who were called upon to be leaders of men 'for the duration of the war only'.[40] He had been promoted several times, had worked with senior commanders at Canadian Corps Headquarters and had been mentioned in despatches and awarded numerous decorations. For ex-officers such as George Cline, leaving the army would entail loss of authority as well as rank, and there would be no guarantee that either would be secured on their return to the teaching profession. Nevertheless, Mr Cline returned to his post as Instructor at UTS – and resumed an active role in the Canadian Militia (2nd Battalion Canadian Signal Corps). He was still teaching Physics at UTS after the Second World War, and died in 1960, at the age of seventy-one. George Cline was buried in the family plot in Greenwood Cemetery, Burlington, Ontario. His impressive group of medals, complete with ribbons and presentation cases, were sold at auction in his home town in 2019 for $3,001.

Fred Albrecht also went back to teaching – and then went on to fight another war. He did not immediately return home after his trip to Paris. Instead, he made the most of his paid leave to attend an Arts Course at the University of Edinburgh. Fred finally disembarked at Fremantle at the end of February 1920 and took up his 'held-over' post at Midland Junction near Perth. Over the following two decades he taught in fourteen other schools. In 1938 he applied for a pension on grounds of defective eyesight due to his wartime injury, but was nevertheless considered fit enough to be called up as a Reservist in the Second World War. Fred left his post as headteacher of Eden Hill School and attested for a second time in March 1941. One of his first military duties took place at sea, training Australian troops on board ships making the same journey to the Middle East that he had made over two decades earlier. In February 1942, however, he left Fremantle for a different theatre of war. Two months later, he was reported as missing – a 'battle casualty' – on the island of Java. He had been captured by the Japanese. Fred was released from his POW camp at the end of the war and spent months convalescing in hospital. This remarkable man then resumed his teaching career and taught in Albany, Geraldton and Perth, before finally retiring in 1954. Fred Albrecht died in Perth in 1979.

Whilst some of the teachers-soldiers responded a second time to the call to arms, others spent the rest of their lives fighting against war. Following his return to New Zealand in April 1919, Ormond Burton studied for a Master's Degree at Auckland University College and spent much of his time researching and writing the histories of the New Zealand Division and the Auckland Regiment. Writing specifically for an audience of ex-servicemen, he looked back on 'the many happy days we spent together' in 'rough and dangerous times'.[41] Camaraderie extended across individual units, and home ties were important to Enzeds thousands of miles from home. This was not simply nostalgia on Ormond Burton's part; in 1916, *The Kiwi* noted how the men from ATC maintained their affiliation at Gallipoli:

Wells was the first Training College man to 'go under'. All Old As are as brothers; at the Front they realize more than ever the worth of good fellowship. It is pleasant to know that Wells' fellow-students lined his grave with a shrub resembling our manuka, truly a fitting tribute to one who ever lived up to the motto *Totis Viribus*.[42]

ATC's magazine, the *Manuka*, later published a letter from Ormond Burton in which he reported on a reunion of twenty-four Old As on the Western Front in June 1917.[43] Ormond and his fellow Aucklanders met at a café at Authie, just six miles behind the front line trenches on the Somme. After dining on salmon and salad, tinned fruit and custard, they drank a toast to their fallen comrades.

Private Burton of the NZMC had deliberately left his non-combatant role and, as a front-line infantryman, had chosen to wage war to the full and to kill his fellow man. Despite the losses and privations, Second Lieutenant Burton had done his duty, and now wrote about the many positive aspects of a war in which he had been fully involved. Victory and peace, however, had not ushered in the new world for which he had fought. This son of Methodist Sunday School teachers, and member of both the Young Men's Bible Class movement and Temperance League in his younger days, had genuinely believed that he had been engaged in a just war, a crusade against the evil of Prussian militarism. The harsh treatment of Germany at the Treaty of Versailles left him disillusioned and determined to promote pacifism to all who would listen. He did not return to teaching until 1924, and only then after insisting upon the insertion of conscience clause into a contract which required an oath of allegiance to the British Crown. In the early 1930s he began training as a Methodist minister, and from 1934 led the congregation at Webb Street, a slum area in Wellington markedly different from the affluent settlement of Remuera where he had spent his childhood. Just days after the outbreak of the Second World War in September 1939, this thrice-wounded and decorated officer from the Great War – 'the war to end all wars' – gave vent to his anti-war feelings. Ormond had joined the Christian Pacifist Society of New Zealand in 1936, and he became an outspoken and persistent critic of his country's involvement in the war. This demonstrably brave and committed former soldier was accused in the press of cowardice, and in 1942 his own Methodist Church expelled him for failing to comply with their prohibition on anti-war teaching. Arrested and released on several occasions, Ormond eventually served nineteen months of a thirty-month jail sentence after the Supreme Court found him guilty of publishing subversive literature. Ten years after the war he was readmitted to the Methodist Church. In a new age, when the horrors of second major conflagration had converted many others to pacifism, he spoke out against the war in Vietnam and the stockpiling of nuclear weapons. Ormond Burton, the teacher-turned-soldier and warrior-turned-pacifist, died in Wellington in 1974.

Memorials to The Fallen of the Great War came in many forms. Each of the individual casualties had multiple affiliations: families, schools, home towns, service units and nations. Each community was dislocated by the loss of a son, a former student, a colleague, a neighbour, a comrade and a citizen. Less than a month after his death at Pozières in 1916, the 'sorrowing mother, brothers and sisters' of Sydney Forbes reported his 'duty nobly done' in the 'Family Notices' pages of the *Western Mail*.[44] Two months later, Mary Forbes received tangible reminders of her son's war service when a suitcase and kitbag containing Sydney's 'effects' – wallet, maps, whistle, knife and items of uniform – arrived at the family home in Perth courtesy of AIF Base Records and Thomas Cook & Sons. The family suffered another blow when news came through that Alick Forbes had been seriously wounded at Pozières just days after his brother's death. Alick returned to the family home in August 1917, totally incapacitated by blindness and other injuries, and dependent upon a war pension. Like hundreds of thousands of families across Britain and its Dominions, the Forbes family duly received a Memorial Plaque and the relevant British War and Victory Medals. So too did the Barbers in The Rectory at Picton, the Wilsons in Dublin Street, Ponsonby and the Baswitzes in North End Road, Fulham.

The schools which had taught the fallen servicemen and the colleges which had trained them also began the process of remembrance before the war had even ended. The compilers of the original Rolls of Honour began adding notations against the names of heroes who had been wounded or killed in action; the sheer number of casualties from some institutions led to the collation of separate rolls of The Fallen. The sacrifices made by these alumni demanded appropriate forms of memorialization after the war. Latymer Upper School in London unveiled its war memorial in

1921. Field Marshal Sir John French, the guest of honour, paid tribute to those from the school who fell in the service of their country; amongst the 221 names on the memorial in the School Hall are those of Baswitz, Garland, Handley and Mount.[45] Frank Wilson and Jock MacKenzie are listed with 266 other former pupils on the impressive stone obelisk in the grounds of Auckland Grammar School which was unveiled in 1922 by Lord Jellicoe, the Governor General of New Zealand. Lieutenant Colonel George Cline returned to the University of Toronto Schools in 1920 to officiate with President Falconer and Headmaster Crawford at the ceremony to remember the sixty-three former pupils and staff named on the bronze Memorial Tablet, and 'to contemplate the untimely taking off of these gallant youth'.[46] If Perth Boys' School commissioned a war memorial, it no longer exists. Claremont Teachers College began remembering their fallen as early as 1916. In April that year the college welcomed back several wounded alumni, including Captain Rockliff and Lieutenant Archibald, to an unveiling ceremony. A Roll of Honour, inscribed upon a sheet of hammered copper mounted on oak, contained the names of seventy-two former trainees who had enlisted by then. Plaques for each of the men who had been killed at Gallipoli, including Walter Blair, were also unveiled and the Last Post was sounded. More individual memorials were added – including one for Sydney Forbes – as the later campaigns on the Western Front took their toll. The plaques were covered up temporarily in the 1990s during 'an era of political correctness' and changing attitudes towards war.[47] A stone obelisk was also erected in front of the college after the war and contains the names of most, but not all, of the thirty-eight CTC alumni who lost their lives between 1914 and 1919. CTC has since been subsumed within Edith Cowan University, but the memorial (see plate 21) still stands in front of the original main building of the college on what is now the campus of the University of Western Australia. The first official war memorial at Auckland Training College was dedicated to the founding Principal. Under the headline 'Teacher and Soldier. Late Lieutenant Milnes', the *New Zealand Herald* of 25 September 1918 informed the wider community of the forthcoming ceremony to be held at the school. The Milnes Memorial, a brass tablet, carried a photographic image of the esteemed Principal together with his (and ATC's) motto, *Totus Viribus*. It is still on display today, on the wall of the office of the Dean of the Faculty of Education at Auckland University (see plate 27). In 1926 another memorial to Bert Milnes and thirty-two of his Old As was installed in the Library at ATC's new Epsom Campus. One of the most impressive of all institutional war memorials, however, was built in Toronto. The thirty fallen students from University of Toronto Faculty of Education are remembered along with hundreds of other university alumni in the Soldiers' Tower. The foundation stone of this huge gothic construction was laid as cavalry trumpeters played the Last Post on Armistice Day 1919. The Tower still forms the backdrop for the university's annual Service of Remembrance. Its carillon of fifty-one bronze bells rings out daily, 'for all time an audible reminder of the sacrifices of the university community during the Great War'.[48] In stark contrast, the memorial for Albert Baswitz and his fellow trainees from the London Day Training College is a modest affair, blighted by the fog of war and later demobilizations. Despite Percy Nunn's meticulous record keeping, the small bronze plaque contains spelling errors, omissions and the names of at least two men who survived the war. Having spent many years in storage, it was put back on public display as part of Institute of Education's commemoration of the centenary of the Great War.

Beyond the walls of scholastic institutions, local communities also came together to honour their dead. Remembrance was part of a wider social phenomenon. Villages, towns and cities throughout Britain began to erect war memorials of all shapes and sizes and degrees of sculptural decoration. Their counterparts in the Dominions followed suit. The city of Guelph in Ontario lost 216 of its citizens during the Great War.[49] Gordon Scott's name appears on several memorials in his home town, alongside that of the soldier poet John McCrae, the author of *In Flanders Fields*, who died of pneumonia whilst on active service in January 1918. These include the Collegiate Institute Honour Roll, and the civic war memorial which was erected in Guelph's Trafalgar Square in 1926. The latter was preceded by another memorial erected near the railway station two years earlier by a voluntary organization, the Imperial Order Daughters of the Empire (IODE), whose proudly pro-British motto was, 'One Flag, One Throne, One Empire'. Gordon Scott's mother Margaret was a senior member of the order's Guelph Branch. The IODE's Cross of Sacrifice was unveiled on 24 May 1924, Empire Day. As part of the service of dedication, Gordon's sister Alice presented a sword, forming part of the cross, in memory of the young teacher and RNAS pilot who was shot down over Ypres.

The confluence of civic and familial remembrance is also evident in Perth. The State War Memorial in King's Park is the setting for the Anzac Day dawn service attended by some 40,000 people each year. The nearby Honour Avenues are sites of quiet contemplation, where over 1,700 plaques, originally paid for by the families of fallen servicemen like Adolph Knäble (see plate 17), stand before sugar gums planted by comrades-in-arms who returned from the war. Survivors of the 32nd Battalion's actions at Fromelles held annual reunions in King's Park from 1917 to 1966. The gathering of the '19th of July Men' served as a powerful collective response to one man's plea on a battlefield in Flanders: 'Don't forget me, cobber.' (see plate 17)[50]

Nations remember their dead, too, but remembrance and nationalism are uneasy bedfellows. Commemorating the service and sacrifice of individuals has all too often been subsumed within a collective and highly politicized agenda. Debates about 'Anzac' in Australia, and to a lesser extent about 'Vimy' in Canada, have gone beyond simply paying respect. Instead, wartime actions are depicted as causal factors in the birth of a nation. Australian troops started the war by carrying Union Jacks, before replacing them – in the popular press at least – with standards bearing the Southern Cross (see plate 35). As early as 1915, Perth's *Western Mail* reported, alongside a photograph of King George V with the caption 'One King, One Flag, One Empire', that 'sheer love of England was the strongest of all motives in the hearts of many of the young Australians who sprang to arms at the threat of danger to the old land', but went on to say, 'We are fighting for own (Australian) freedom and independent nationhood.'[51] War transformed 'independent Australian Britons' into Anzac supermen.[52] Despite the failure of the Gallipoli campaign, later engagements led to them being considered, along with the Canadians, as 'crack units ... the spearhead of Allied victory'.[53] Success bred confidence and justifiably reinforced pride in their own ability; failure, as at Fromelles, could be ascribed to 'British bunglers'.[54] Officers promoted from the ranks were depicted as men of proven ability, in stark contrast to the stereotyped portrayal of the high-falutin' and hopeless 'Pommie Jackeroos' leading British units.[55] Lieutenant Sydney Forbes is a tangible example of the former; Albert Baswitz was hardly typical of the latter group, however. Thus was born the legend of the Anzac, the epitome of Australian manhood and potent symbol of a nation's independence and esoteric identity. Like all pervasive legends and shared histories, however, each retelling loses something of the original essence and eventually invites critical reflection. The centenary of the Great War has prompted both considered commemorative ventures, such as the opening in November 2014 of the National Anzac Centre in Albany (WA), and heated public debate. References by 'revisionist' historians to the 'commodification' and 'bellicose claptrap' of Anzac Day, or reminders by journalists of less than glorious episodes such as the infamous Battle of the Wazzir in Egypt in 1915, have been controversial and highly unpopular.[56]

The debate in Canada has run along similar lines. In Toronto, the pages of the *Varsity War Supplement* of July 1915 paid tribute to Great Britain's 'family of nations', in which 'the roots of union were deep beyond all measuring' and based upon 'unconquerable emotion deeper than any reasoning'.[57] Half of the soldiers in the CEF were British-born and many, including Percy Barber, would have shared the sentiment expressed by one of their number: 'I felt I had to go back to England. I was an Englishman, and I thought they might need me.'[58] The military successes of April 1917, however, are for the Canadian public what Gallipoli is to the citizens of Australia. A veteran of the assault on Vimy Ridge claimed later that 'We went up as Albertans and Nova Scotians. We came down as Canadians.'[59] The magnificent memorial (see plate 33) overlooking the Douai Plain is tangible evidence of the confluence of wartime sacrifice and national identity. The recent judgement by one Canadian historian, however, that 'Vimy, like all legends, is a layered skein of stories, myths, wishful thinking, and conflicting narratives' is indicative of a debate in which long-held shared beliefs and detailed historical research collide.[60]

Running parallel to the contested narratives in both countries is a much more positive story, namely a greater public awareness of military events other than Anzac and Vimy. The opening of a new CWGC cemetery in 2010 has highlighted a lost history of Australian involvement on the Western Front. Investigative research by Melbourne schoolteacher Lambis Englezos and British historian Peter Barton, conducted over two decades despite (or because of) official scepticism, has revealed what happened to the missing legions of Fromelles. Bavarian Army archives in Munich, Red Cross records in Geneva, carefully excavated body parts from a field near the village of Fromelles, and DNA samples taken from soldiers' descendants in Western Australia have been used to identify many of those who disappeared in this previously all but forgotten defeat. Corporal Adolph Knäble is one of the many 'missing' men of the 32nd Battalion now known to have been buried in a mass grave within days of the battle in July 1916. Nearby Pheasant Wood has given its name to the new CWGC cemetery in which over 200 young Australian servicemen have since been re-interred with all due ceremony and military honours. Canada now remembers a forgotten victory. In August 2017, exactly 100 years after Arthur Currie's Canucks stormed Hill 70, a new memorial park was officially opened amidst the slag heaps on the outskirts of Lens.

New Zealanders still refer to Gallipoli as the event which 'cemented our identity'.[61] For Ormond Burton and his fellow Enzeds, it was the Battle of the Somme which provided 'the last suffering required to make New Zealand a nation'.[62] By the end of the war

> no longer was the New Zealander English, Irish, or Scotch. No longer was he even an Australasian. He was a New Zealander, proud of his nationality and passionately proud of the deeds which had given his people a place amongst the free nations of the world.[63]

Whilst the authorities in London began planning for the wholesale formal interment and memorialization of fallen subjects under the auspices of the Imperial (later Commonwealth) War Graves Commission (IWGC and CWGC), the Dominions pressed ahead with their own schemes. Distinct memorials were financed and constructed, such as those at Villers-Bretonneux (Australia), Vimy Ridge (Canada), Delville Wood (South Africa) and Beaumont-Hamel (Newfoundland). Elsewhere, cemeteries were particularized, for example by planting maple trees around Canadian graves. Headstones, too, with their emblematic rising suns, silver ferns and maple leaves, reflected membership of 'national' rather than regional or technical associations as was the case for the majority of men recruited in the British Isles. Today, thousands of pilgrims from the former British Dominions visit sites dedicated to people who fought and died 'for them'. They stand on ground declared sacred by the politicians back home, stare at the long lists of the missing from their homeland and try to make connections through time and space with individuals whose life stories were markedly different from their own.

Most of the CWGC cemeteries on the Western Front transcend all national boundaries, their location decided by proximity to the killing fields, the carvings on their headstones determined by the disparate affiliations of combatants who fell there. The hundreds of war cemeteries on the Somme and in the Ypres Salient, and their associated monuments to the missing at Thiepval and the Menin Gate respectively, testify to the common enterprise that resulted in the deaths of millions. Tommies, Diggers, Enzeds and Canucks are buried alongside one another in 'the empires of the dead'.[64] Tyne Cot (see plate 26) is the largest of them all. Overlooking what the German's called the *Englisches Totenfeld* (the English field of death), and with views beyond that to the rebuilt towers of Ypres on the horizon, Tyne Cot contains the mortal remains of nearly 12,000 men, many of whom are still unidentified.[65] Lieutenant Percy Barber is amongst the hundreds of Canadians buried here, just yards from where they fell during the final assaults on Passchendaele Ridge. Percy's grave, one of the first to be dug at Tyne Cot, lies close to the Cross of Sacrifice, which was built on the remains of a pillbox captured by the 3rd Australian Division. Captain Thomas Bone of the division's 44th Battalion, a former trainee at Claremont Teachers College in Perth, is buried nearby. The white headstones of men from the 3rd Auckland Battalion stand row upon row in the meticulously maintained grounds. Second Lieutenant Bert Milnes was originally buried half a mile away, close to where he fell near the pillbox at Otto Farm, but like many of the battlefield dead was moved later to the concentration cemetery at Tyne Cot. More New Zealanders are listed on the Memorial to the Missing. Amongst the 35,000 names are those of Second Lieutenant Kenneth White, a teacher from Auckland who was killed fighting alongside his former college Principal on the same day in October 1917. A nearby panel bears the name of John Preedy, alumnus of LDTC and commissioned officer in the 2nd Londons. All these men were teacher-soldiers, brothers in arms drawn from schools and colleges across the British Empire. Buried just yards apart in a foreign field, these 'kinsfolk of the Old Land' are part of what George V, their King and Emperor, called a 'massed multitude of silent witnesses to the desolation of war'.[66]

Epilogue

Flat Iron Copse

It is hard to believe today that the rough track which locals call the Rue Santin was once a major thoroughfare of war. Modern guidebooks to the battlefields of the Somme warn of the hazards facing vehicles attempting to travel along the narrow, snaking road, especially when heavy downpours of rain have turned parts of it into muddy furrows. The gently sloping farmland through which it runs was once known as Happy Valley, before the Great War changed its name to Death Valley. In the summer and autumn months of 1916 men from all parts of the British Empire assembled here, awaiting their turn to attack an unseen enemy entrenched in fields beyond the horizon. It was from here that the Deccan Horse launched one of the few cavalry charges of the war. Their mechanized successors, tanks, gathered here too, on the night before they began their first lumbering advance across a battlefield. Captain Baswitz and the London Territorials had also slogged their way through here and taken up their positions in the trenches in front of High Wood; so too had thousands of other troops from the British Empire who fought and perished on the Somme battlefields.

A century later, and High Wood is as green and leafy as it had been before the war, but it now displays signs stating *Propriété Privée* and is closed to visitors. Thousands of men, both British and German, were killed during the fighting in the wood. The remains of many lie where they fell, disarticulated bones and remnants of uniforms entangled in the masses of concrete and barbed wire, tree roots and live ammunition. Some of the casualties whose bodies were recovered at the time were buried in the CWGC London Cemetery, just across the road from the wood. Others joined the wounded on a journey back to the Advanced Dressing Stations (ADS) and makeshift graveyards.

Albert Baswitz was killed in action to the east of High Wood on 16 September 1916. Admired by his men and senior officers alike for his unfailing cheerfulness and inspirational leadership, he fell in front of his company, leading them in an attack on the Switch Line. It would have taken the RAMC stretcher-bearers as much as six hours to carry his dead body back across the battlefield, navigating a shattered terrain of mud and shell holes. They followed, albeit in the opposite direction, the same route taken earlier by the attacking force, back through what had once been the village of Bazentin Le Grand, past Crucifix Corner and on to Death Valley. They left the wounded at the ADS in Flat Iron Copse, and deposited the dead in a little graveyard that bore the same name. Albert was buried there, under a simple wooden marker inscribed with his name and details, in a ceremony conducted by an army chaplain. And then the world moved on. Albert's fellow Londoners in the 22nd Battalion and the 47th Division finished their stint on the Somme and moved north to fight alongside other British and Dominion troops at Ypres in 1917. In the final weeks of the Great War they finally drove the German defenders off Aubers Ridge, liberated Fromelles and led the victory parade through Lille on 28 October 1918.

Most battlefield tourists today pass by CWGC Flat Iron Copse (see plate 40) without stopping; just a few hundred yards further along Rue Santin stands the magnificent Red Dragon Memorial which commemorates the attack by the 38th (Welsh) Division at nearby Mametz Wood. Albert's final resting place is no longer the small collection of graves it once was. Flat Iron Copse became a concentration cemetery, in which men originally buried near the villages of Contalmaison, Montauban, Mametz and the Bazentins were re-interred. It later became an official war cemetery established – and still maintained – by the CWGC. The original wooden crosses are long gone, replaced by the all-too-familiar headstones standing in their serried ranks. Each stone, though seemingly uniform, begins the narrative of an individual whose life was cut short by war. Not far from the entrance to Flat Iron Copse is the headstone (see plate 40) marking the earthly remains of Albert Baswitz. The inscription proclaims his name, rank, unit and military honours, and his age on the day he died. A carefully carved Star of David tells us something about his origins and religious affiliation. Unlike many such markers, it has no carved epitaph. Nearby headstones variously depict other BEF battalion badges, or Rising Suns, Fern Leaves, Maple Leaves and the occasional

Springbok, testament to the 1,572 soldiers from Britain, Australia, New Zealand, Canada and South Africa buried there. In the surrounding fields there are other formal reminders of their collective actions and sacrifices during the Battle of the Somme in 1916: the 47th (London) Divisional Memorial on the edge of High Wood, the Australian Memorial on the site of the windmill at Pozières, the New Zealand Division Memorial overlooking the village of Flers and the Canadian Memorial at Courcelette. Further afield, there are hundreds of other memorials, thousands of other cemeteries and millions of other headstones which mark the passing of those who fought in the Great War of 1914 to 1919.

The lives of individual soldiers are all too easily forgotten, subsumed within the endless lists of the names of The Fallen and the passage of time. Families mourned their lost loved ones at the time and for many years afterwards, but memories fade over passing generations. Institutions, too, have their own histories – complete with foundation myths and tales of heroic alumni – but need suitable forms and opportunities for remembrance. One hundred years after their deaths we remember them once more. The Centenary Commemorations of the Great War, in particular, have encouraged schools and colleges – and communities of all kinds – to look again at the names on their Rolls of Honour, to revisit their archive collections and to tell the story of their former students to new audiences. In 2014, the 'gallant fair-haired officer' Captain Baswitz was once more remembered in the pages of his old school's magazine, the *Latymerian*. Albert and the thousands of other teacher-soldiers who fought and died in the Great War have not been forgotten.

As they made in common an offering of their lives, they each received praise that will not grow old and the noblest of tombs, not in the place where they lie, but rather where, on every occasion calling for word or deed, their fame is left behind them in everlasting remembrance.[1]

Notes

Prologue: The Assembly
1. *Latymerian*, May 1919.
2. A phrase used by Australian war correspondent Charles Bean, in Pedersen, P. (2007) *The ANZACS. Gallipoli to the Western Front*, Scoresby: Viking Books, p.4.

Chapter 1: To Be a Teacher
1. Blades, B.A. (2015) *Roll of Honour: Schooling and the Great War, 1914–1919*, Barnsley: Pen & Sword Military.
2. See Kadish, S. (1995) 'A Good Jew and a Good Englishman'. *The Jewish Lads' and Girls' Brigade 1895–1995*, London: Valentine Mitchell.
3. Mayhew, H. (1861; 2002) *London Labour and the London Poor*, Oxford: Oxford University Press, p.5.
4. Booth, C. (1886–1903) *Inquiry into the Life and Labour of the People of London* www.booth.lse.ac.uk
5. Féret, C. J. (1900) *Fulham Old and New. Being an Exhaustive History of the Ancient Parish of Fulham*, London: The Leadenhall Press.
6. See Blades, B.A. (2003) 'Deacon's School, Peterborough, 1902-1920: a Study of the Social and Economic Function of Secondary Schooling', University of London PhD thesis, p.56.
7. Aldrich, R. (2002) *The Institute of Education 1902–2002: A Centenary History*, London: Institute of Education, University of London, p.115.
8. Booth op. cit.
9. *West London Observer* 21 December 1911.
10. Watson, N. (1995) *Latymer Upper School. A History of the School and its Foundation*, London: James & James (Publishers) Ltd, p.43.
11. Aldrich op. cit. p.5.
12. See Harte, N. (1986) *The University of London 1836–1986. An Illustrated History*, London: The Athlone Press, pp.63–4.
13. Kenyon Jones, C. (2008) *The People's University. 150 Years of the University of London and its External Students*, London: University of London External System.
14. *London Daily News* 4 November 1907.
15. Aldrich op. cit. p.15.

16. Data extrapolated from IE/STU/A5/1-3 Admissions Registers (1900 to 1920).
17. *Londinian* Lent Term 1912, p.22.
18. Ibid. Summer Term 1914, p.17.

Chapter 2: To Be a Soldier Too
 1. Dymond, D. (1955) (ed.) *The Forge. The History of Goldsmiths' College 1905–1955*, London: Methuen & Co. Ltd, p.110.
 2. Ibid.
 3. Firth, A.E. (1991) *Goldsmiths' College: A Centenary Account*, London: The Athlone Press Ltd, p.54.
 4. Dymond op. cit. p.147.
 5. Beckett, I.F.W. (1991; 2011) *Britain's Part-Time Soldiers. The Amateur Military Tradition 1558–1945*, Barnsley: Pen & Sword Military, p.198.
 6. See Blades (2015) for biographical details for John Paulson and Archibald Buckle.
 7. University of London (1921) *University of London Officer Training Corps Roll of Service 1914–1919*, London: Military Education Committee of the University of London.
 8. Ibid.
 9. Tozer, M. (2015) *The Idea of Manliness. The Legacy of Thring's Uppingham*, Truro: Sunnyrest Books, pp.295–6.
10. Haig-Brown, A.R. (1915) *The OTC in the Great War*, London: Country Life, p.82.
11. IE/STU/A5/1-3; University of London (1921) op. cit.
12. IE/STU/A5/1-3. Of the forty-one trainees commissioned in 1914, thirty-three had been members of the ULOTC.
13. Ibid.
14. Goldsmiths' College Archive LOR/3/1/10; *The Goldsmithian*, December 1914.

Chapter 3: Tommies
 1. Maude, A.H. (1922; 2016) (ed.) *The 47th (London) Division 1914–1919* (Kindle), London: Amalgamated Press Ltd, loc 362.
 2. Holmes, R. (2004; 2005) *Tommy. The British Soldier on the Western Front 1914–1918*, London: Harper Perennial, pp.129–34.
 3. IE/STU/A5/1-3.
 4. Bostridge, M. (2014) *The Fateful Year. England 1914*, London: Penguin Books, pp.299–314.
 5. UWD TNA WO 95/2743/1-2.
 6. Maude op. cit. loc 522.
 7. Gilbert, M. (1994; 2004) *The First World War: A Complete History*, New York: Henry Holt and Company, p.160.

8. UWD TNA WO 95/2743/1-2.
9. Ibid.
10. Lloyd, N. (2006; 2013) *Loos 1915* (Kindle), Stroud: The History Press, loc 1669.
11. Maude op. cit. loc 778.
12. Ibid. loc 764.
13. Doyle, P. and Foster, C. (2013) *Remembering Tommy. The British Soldier in the First World War*, Stroud: Spellmount, p.63.
14. Maude op. cit. loc 798.
15. Rawson, A. (2002) *Battleground Europe. French Flanders. Loos – Hill 70*, Barnsley: Leo Cooper, p.88.
16. Maude op. cit. loc 942.
17. Lloyd (2006; 2013) loc 3504.
18. Maude op. cit. loc 556; Doyle and Foster op. cit. pp.137–40.
19. Maude op. cit. loc 1146.
20. UWD TNA WO 95/2743/1-2.
21. Ibid.
22. Ibid.
23. Maude op. cit. loc 1234.
24. Ibid. loc 1065.
25. Ibid. loc 1510.
26. Terraine, J. (1965; 1997) *The Great War*, Ware: Wordsworth Editions Ltd, p.119.
27. Maude op. cit. loc 1617.
28. Masefield (1917; 1918) *The Old Front Line*, New York: The Macmillan Company, p.22.
29. Ibid. p.23.
30. Burton, O.E. (1935) *The Silent Division: New Zealanders at the Front, 1914–1919*, Sydney: Angus and Robertson Limited, p.82.
31. Corporal H.F. Hooton in Norman, T. (1984; 2009) *The Hell They Called High Wood. The Somme 1916* (Kindle), Barnsley: Pen & Sword Books Ltd, loc 1310.
32. Graves, R. (1929; 2000) *Goodbye to All That*, London: Penguin Classics, p.179.
33. Maude op. cit. loc 1510.
34. Private D. Sweeney (1st Lincolnshire Battalion), in Emden, R. van (2008; 2010) *The Soldier's War. The Great War Through Veterans' Eyes* (Kindle), London: Bloomsbury, loc 2886.
35. Graves op. cit. p.180.
36. Liddell Hart, B. (1934) *A History of the World War 1914–1918*, London: Faber & Faber Limited, pp.326–7.
37. Gilbert op. cit. pp.264–80.
38. Masefield op. cit. p.23.

39. UWD TNA WO 95/2743/1-2.
40. Burton op. cit. pp.162–7.
41. Ibid.
42. Corporal T. Ball 'The Cockneys in High Wood', in *The War Illustrated Album De Luxe* (1917) 'Volume VII. The Autumn Campaigns – 1916', London: The Amalgamated Press Ltd, p.2258.
43. Burton op. cit. pp.162–7.
44. *The War Illustrated Album De Luxe* op. cit. p.2258.
45. Ibid.
46. Ibid.
47. Corporal M.J. Guiton, in Youel, D. and Edgell, D. (2006) *The Somme Ninety Years on – a Visual History*, London: Dorling Kindersley, p.107.
48. Sheldon, J. (2005) *The German Army on the Somme 1914–1916* (Kindle), Barnsley: Pen & Sword Military, loc 6588.
49. Terraine (1982) p.238.
50. Second Lieutenant G. Foley (Somerset Light Infantry), in Emden op. cit. loc 2968.
51. Burton op. cit. p.166.
52. Maude op. cit. loc 1594.
53. UWD TNA WO 95/2743/1-2.
54. Terraine (1965; 1967) p.119.
55. Ibid. p.117.
56. Churchill's verdict on the first deployment of tanks, in Gilbert op. cit. p.286.
57. Sheffield, G. (2001; 2002) *Forgotten Victory. The First World War: Myths and Realities*, London: Headline Review, p.175.
58. HMSO (1919; 1988) *Officers Died in the Great War 1914–1919*, Polstead: J.B. Hayward & Son.
59. UWD TNA WO 95/2743/1-2.
60. Maude op. cit. loc 1617.

Chapter 4: Anzacs

1. Edwin Greenslade Murphy (1866–1939), known as 'Dryblower', was a popular poet regularly featured in the Perth *Sunday Times* during the Great War.
2. *Western Mail* 6 April 1907.
3. Battye, J.S. (1924; 2005) *Western Australia: A History from its Discovery to the Inauguration of the Commonwealth*, Oxford: The Clarendon Press, Chapter 7 www.gutenberg.net.au (accessed 28.06.2020).
4. Ibid. Chapter 16.
5. Ibid.
6. Ewers, J.K. (1947) *Perth Boys' School 1847–1947*, Perth (published by the school), p.32.
7. Education Committee *Blue Book* of 1848.

8. Ewers op. cit. pp.61–2.

9. Ibid. p.97.

10. Ibid. p.110.

11. Thomas Sten interview SLAW B1893.

12. Ibid. For women trainees at CTC see Trotman, J. (2008) *Girls Becoming Teachers. An Historical Analysis of Western Australian Woman Teachers, 1911–1940*, New York: Cambria Press, p.23.

13. The *West Australian* 19 November 1913.

14. Bolton, G. and Byrne, G. (2001) *The Campus That Never Stood Still. Edith Cowan University 1902–2002*, Churchlands (Perth): Edith Cowan University, p.13.

15. Rourke, W.H. (1980) *My Way. W.H. (Bill) Rourke's 50 Years Adventure in Education*, Perth: Carroll's Pty Ltd, p.45.

16. *The West Australian* 6 August 1914, p.6.

17. Ibid.

18. Ibid.

19. Data extrapolated from Green, N. (2009) *Western Australian Teacher Soldiers of World War I 1914–1918*, Cottesloe: Focus Education Services.

20. Gammage, B. (1974) *The Broken Years. The Australian Soldiers in the Great War*, Canberra: Australian National University Press, p.7; see also Hurst, J. (2018) *The Landing in the Dawn. Dissecting the Legend – the Landing at Anzac, Gallipoli, 25 April 1915*, Solihull: Helion & Company Ltd, pp.34–7.

21. The *Concise Oxford Dictionary*'s definition is 'hooligan'.

22. NAA B2455 Forbes, S.T.

23. The Thomas Steane Louch Memoirs www.11btn.wags.org.au

24. www.11btn.wags.org.au

25. *Western Mail* (1915) p.14.

26. www.11btn.wags.org.au

27. Ibid.

28. Schuler, P.F.E. (1916) *Australia in Arms. A Narrative of the Australasian Imperial Force and Their Achievement at Anzac*, Melbourne (Victoria), p.37.

29. Ibid.

30. Ibid. p.42.

31. www.11btn.wags.org.au

32. *Gallipoli* (1981), directed by Peter Weir.

33. Bean, C.E.W. (1916) (ed.) *The Anzac Book*, London: Cassell and Company Ltd, p.127.

34. See Hart, P. (2011; 2013) *Gallipoli*, London: Profile Books Ltd, p.49.

35. Facey, A.B. (1981; 2014) *A Fortunate Life*, Melbourne: Penguin Group (Australia), p.390, uses the term 'Gyppos'; Bean op. cit. p.138 refers to the widespread use of the term 'Gyppies'.

36. Burton, O.E. (1922) *The Auckland Regiment*, Auckland: Whitcombe and Tombs Limited, p.22.

37. In Hurst op. cit. p.70.
38. www.11btn.wags.org.au
39. Schuler op. cit. p.149.
40. Ibid.
41. *Sunday Times* (Perth) 11 July 1915.
42. In Pedersen op. cit. pp.37–8.
43. Hurst op. cit. p.44.
44. Bean (1916) p.1: 'The Landing. By a Man of the Tenth.'
45. Anon (1916; 2013) *On the Anzac Trail; Being Extracts from the Diary of a New Zealand Sapper, by "Anzac"* (Kindle), Pickle Partners Publishing, loc 993.
46. *Sunday Times* (Perth) 11 July 1915.
47. Ibid.
48. Ibid.
49. See Map 6 (Anzac Gallipoli). Lieutenant Colonel Arthur Plugge, a former science master from Auckland, was commanding officer of the NZEF Auckland Battalion.
50. Macleod, J. (2015) *Gallipoli*, Oxford: Oxford University Press, p.31.
51. *Sunday Times* (Perth) 11 July 1915.
52. Ibid.
53. Ibid.
54. Ibid.
55. Bean (1916) p.72.
56. Ibid. pp.71–95.
57. UWD AWM 4-23/11/28/2.
58. Ibid.
59. Extract from 'Captain Everett's Lecture the Landing on Gallipoli' in the *Northam Advertiser* 11 December 1915.
60. UWD AWM 4-23/11/28/4.
61. Bean, C.E.W. (1946; 2014) *Anzac to Amiens*, Melbourne: Penguin Group, p.190.
62. Pedersen op.cit. p.116.
63. Belford, W.C. (1940; 2010) *'Legs-Eleven'. Being the Story of the Eleventh Battalion AIF in the Great War*, Uckfield: The Naval & Military Press and The Imperial War Museum, p.221.
64. Ibid. p.234.
65. The *West Australian* 20 July 1917.
66. NAA B2455 Knable, A.T.
67. *The West Australian* 24 September 1915.
68. *The Advertiser* (Adelaide) 19 August 1915.
69. Bean (1946) op. cit. p.199.
70. Barton, P. (2014) *The Lost Legions of Fromelles. The Mysteries Behind One of the Most Devastating Battles of the Great War*, London: Constable, p.174
71. Pedersen op. cit. p.128.

72. Pedersen, P. (2002; 2015) *Battleground Europe. French Flanders. Fromelles*, Barnsley: Pen & Sword Military, p.51.
73. Barton (2014) p.xii.
74. Gammage op. cit. pp.158–61.
75. Pedersen (2002) op. cit. p.106.
76. Cobb, P. (2007; 2010) *Fromelles 1916*, Stroud: The History Press, p.113.
77. Bennett, S. (2011; 2012) *Pozières. The Anzac Story*, Melbourne: Scribe Publications Pty Ltd, p.10.
78. Manning, F.E. (1930; 2014) *The Middle Parts of Fortune*, Melbourne: Penguin Group (Australia), p.19.
79. Pedersen (2007) op. cit. p.147.
80. Gary Sheffield, in Hampton, M. (2016a) *Attack on the Somme. 1st Anzac Corps and the Battle of Pozières Ridge, 1916*, Solihull: Helion & Company Limited, p.xiii.
81. Hampton op.cit. p.29.
82. Belford op.cit. p.280.
83. Terraine op. cit.
84. Keech, G. (1997; 2015) *Battleground Europe. Somme. Pozières*, Barnsley: Pen & Sword Military p.47.
85. *Sunday Times* (Perth) 20 August 1916.
86. *Daily News* (Perth) 4 October 1916.
87. *Sunday Times* (Perth) 8 October 1916.
88. Bennett op. cit. p.xii.

Chapter 5: Enzeds
1. Moorehead, A. (1915; 2016) *Gallipoli*, London: Aurum Press, p.340.
2. Burton (1922) op. cit.
3. Pugsley, C. (1984; 2014) *Gallipoli: The New Zealand Story*, Auckland: Libro International, p.342.
4. Burton (1922) p.79.
5. Waite, F. (1921; 2016) *The New Zealanders at Gallipoli*, Auckland: Whitcombe and Tombs Limited, p.240.
6. Burton (1922) p.79.
7. Harper, G. (2015) *Johnny Enzed. The New Zealand Soldier in the First World War 1914–1918* (Kindle), Auckland: Exisle Publishing Limited, loc 5086.
8. Burton (1922) op. cit. pp.80–1.
9. Ibid. p.81.
10. Harper op.cit. loc 3678.
11. Burton (1922) op. cit. pp.84–5.
12. Pugsley op. cit. p.345.
13. *Auckland Star* 5 August 1914.
14. Recollections of Joe Gasparich, in Pugsley op. cit. p.67.
15. Harper op. cit. loc 969.

16. Burton (1922) op. cit. p.25.
17. McGibbon, I. (2014) *Gallipoli: A Guide to New Zealand Battlefields and Memorials* (Kindle), New Zealand ePenguin, loc 534.
18. Waite op. cit. p.215.
19. Ibid. p.219.
20. Burton (1922) op. cit. p.66.
21. Ormond Burton's description of his close friend.
22. Burton (1922) op cit. p.79.
23. Auckland Grammar School *Chronicle* (1916 Third Term) p.13.
24. Figures from 'New Zealand in the 19th Century: 1870–1900' www.nzhistory.govt.nz.
25. Barr, J. (1922) *The City of Auckland New Zealand, 1840–1920*, Auckland: Whitcombe & Tombs Limited, p.239.
26. Auckland Grammar School *Chronicle* (1916 Third Term) p.13.
27. ATC Register Vol. 1, 1906–1913 www.specialcollectionsauckland.ac.nz
28. Auckland Grammar School *Chronicle* (1916 Third Term) p.13.
29. Barr op. cit. p.219.
30. ANZ R107881170 Wilson, F.R.
31. Burton (1922) op. cit. p.70.
32. Ibid. pp.101–2.
33. Ibid. p.102.
34. Ibid. p.104; ANZ R107881170 Wilson, F.R.
35. Burton (1935) op. cit. p.175.
36. Burton (1935) op. cit. pp.179–80.
37. Harper op. cit. loc 6264.
38. 1871 National Census.
39. An alumnus of Borough Road College.
40. Burrell, A. (1922) *Bert Milnes. A Brief Memoir* (published by the author); Shaw, L. (2006) *Making a Difference: A History of Auckland College of Education 1881–2004*, Auckland: Auckland University Press, p.43.
41. *Auckland Star* 1 November 1905.
42. The 'Northern Union' version was the forerunner of modern rugby league.
43. Auckland Star 5 February 1905.
44. Shaw op. cit. p.35.
45. Ibid. p.21.
46. See Mangan, J.A and Hickey, C. (2000) 'A Pioneer of the Proletariat: Herbert Milnes and the Games Cult in New Zealand', *International Journal of the History of Sport*, 17(2–3), 31–48.
47. Shaw op. cit. p.44.
48. Ball, T. (2011) 'Rubbing off the Corners: The Rite of Passage of the Teacher Trainee in 20th Century New Zealand', *Australian Journal of Teacher Education*, 36, 11, 79–105.
49. *New Zealand Herald* 25 September 1918.

50. Ibid. 3 October 1912.
51. Ibid. 29 June 1911.
52. Ibid. 1 September 1913.
53. *The Kiwi*, Vol. 13 August 1918.
54. ANZ R21375900 Milnes, H.A.E.
55. Harper op. cit. loc 1412.
56. *The Great War* Vol. X. Part 182. February 1918, p.513.
57. Barton, P. (2007) *Passchendaele. Unseen Panoramas of the Third Battle of Ypres*, London: Constable & Robinson Ltd, p.231.
58. Lloyd, N. (2017) *Passchendaele. A New History*, London: Viking p.198.
59. *The Great War* op. cit. p.513.
60. Burton (1922) op. cit. p.67.
61. Holt, T. and V. (1996; 2008) *Major & Mrs Holt's Battlefield Guide to the Ypres Salient & Passchendaele*, Barnsley: Pen & Sword Military, pp.78–9.
62. Macdonald, L. (1978; 1979) *They Called it Passchendaele. The Story of the Third Battle of Ypres and of the Men Who Fought it*, London: Michael Joseph, p.190.
63. Burton (1922) op. cit. p.167.
64. *The Great War* op. cit. p.514.
65. Stewart, H. (1921; 2013) *New Zealand Division 1916–1919. A Popular History Based on Official Records* (Kindle), Pickle Partners Publishing, loc 5180.
66. Burton (1922) op. cit. p.168.
67. From the official history of 4th Guard Infantry Division published in 1920, in Lloyd (2017) op. cit. p.212.
68. Barton (2007) op. cit. p.194.
69. *The Great War* op. cit. p.514.
70. Sheldon op. cit. p.206.
71. Palmer, A. (2007; 2016) *The Salient. Ypres, 1914–18*, London: Constable, p.167.
72. www.nzhistory.govt.nz
73. Harper op. cit. loc 72.

Chapter 6: Canucks
1. Butts, E. (2017a) *Wartime: The First World War in a Canadian Town*, Toronto: James Lorimer & Company, p.73.
2. www.fleetairarmoa.org
3. 'The Navy's Air War 1914–18' www.fleetairarm.com
4. Hellwig, A. (2006) *Australian Hawk over the Western Front. A Biography of Major R. S. Dallas DSO, DSC, C de G Avec Palme*, London: Grub Street, p.128.
5. RNAS pilot Guy Leather, quoted in Smith, M. (2014) *Voices in Flight: The Royal Naval Air Service in the Great War* (Kindle), Barnsley: Pen & Sword Aviation, loc 2511.

6. Ellis Barker, J. (1918) 'The Red Battle Flyer', *The War Times Journal* www.wtj.com
7. Ibid.
8. TNA ADM 273/10/293 Scott, G.B.G.
9. Wood, B.A. (1994) 'Constructing Nova Scotia's "Scotchness": The Centenary Celebrations of Pictou Academy in 1916', *Historical Studies in Education*, 6, 2, 281–302.
10. *Guelph, Berlin, Waterloo, Galt, Preston and Hespeler Industrial Edition 1903* (Directory).
11. *Inspector's Annual Report(s) of the Guelph Public Schools and Report of the Guelph Collegiate Institute for the Year 1901, 1904.*
12. Briggs, W. (1915) *Ontario Normal School Manuals. History of Education*, Toronto: Ontario Ministry of Education.
13. Press, M. (2011) *Education and Ontario Family History. A Guide to Resources for Genealogists and Historians*, Toronto: Dundurn Press, p.95.
14. Briggs op. cit. p.224.
15. Kitchen, J. and Petrarca, D. (2014) 'Teacher Preparation in Ontario: A History', *Teaching & Learning* 8 (1), 56–71, p.59.
16. Legislative Assembly of Ontario (1912) *Report of the Minister of Education, Province of Ontario*, Toronto.
17. *City of Toronto Municipal Handbook 1911.*
18. Ibid.
19. Ibid.
20. Ontario Institute for Studies in Education (2006) *Inspiring Education. A Legacy of Learning 1907–2007. Celebrating 100 Years of Studies in Education at the University of Education*, Toronto: OISE/UT, p.14.
21. *University of Toronto President's Report 1915*, p.45.
22. Ibid. (1915 to 1918).
23. Ontario Institute for Studies in Education op. cit. p.27.
24. Ontario Board of Education (1871) *The Normal School for Ontario: Its Design and Functions. Chiefly Taken from the Report of the Chief Superintendent of Education for Ontario, for the Year 1869*, Toronto: Hunter, Rose & Co., p.5.
25. *The Varsity Magazine Supplement 1917*, p.108.
26. Taken from the stated aims of Henry Job Crawford, first UTS Principal, in *University of Toronto President's Report 1915*, p.17.
27. *University of Toronto President's Report 1915*, p.34.
28. Cook, T. (2014) 'The Eager Doomed: The Story of Canada's Original WWI Recruits', Toronto: *The Globe and Mail* 1 August 2014.
29. Annis, J. (2009) 'The Royal City Goes to War: How the Guelph Evening Mercury Covered the First World War' in *Historic Guelph*, Volume 48. See also Butts, E. (2017b) 'Guelph in the First World War' www.thecanadianencyclopaedia.ca
30. www.theglobeandmail.com

31. Friedland, M.L (2002) *The University of Toronto. A History*, Toronto: University of Toronto Press, pp.219, 253.
32. *The Varsity* 30 September 1914.
33. Ibid.
34. Ibid.
35. Ibid.
36. *The Varsity* 2 October 1914.
37. *University of Toronto President's Report 1915*, p.8.
38. *The Varsity Illustrated War Supplement 1915*, p.31.
39. *University of Toronto President's Report 1916*, p.7.
40. *The Varsity Illustrated War Supplement 1915*, p.32.
41. *Torontonensis* 1915, p.10.
42. *The Varsity Illustrated War Supplement 1915*, p.10.
43. Census of Canada 1911.
44. *The Illustrated War News* 9 September 1914.
45. Reed, P. (1998; 2016) *Battleground Europe. Somme. Courcelette*, Barnsley: Pen & Sword Military p.15; Cook (2014) op. cit.
46. Reed op. cit. p.15.
47. Cook (2014) op. cit.
48. Cook, T. (2017) *Vimy: The Battle and the Legend*, Canada: Allen Lane, p.10.
49. Cook (2014) op. cit.; Cook (2017) op. cit. p.15.
50. Cook (2017) op. cit. p.16; Reed op.cit. p.17.
51. Reed op. cit. p.17.
52. LAC UWD 21st Battalion CEF.
53. 'Varsity in Flanders' by R.A. Uttley in *The Varsity Magazine Supplement 1917*, p.125.
54. LAC UWD 21st Battalion CEF.
55. Cook (2017) op. cit. pp.21–2.
56. www.canada.yodelout.com
57. Quotation from the 21st Battalion's UWD for the later action at Hill 70.
58. LAC UWD 21st Battalion CEF for 9 April 1917.
59. Cook (2017) op. cit. p.74.
60. Vimy War Diary Project www.cefresearch.com
61. Cook (2017) op. cit. p.1.
62. LAC UWD 21st Battalion CEF.
63. Ibid.
64. Ibid.
65. Audette, A. (1919) *A Few Verses and a Brief History of the Canadians on the Somme and Vimy Ridge in the World War 1914–1918*, Montreal (self-published). Audette was a corporal in 22nd Battalion CEF.
66. LAC UWD 21st Battalion CEF.
67. Ibid.
68. Ibid.

69. Ibid.
70. Ibid.
71. Sheldon, J. (2007; 2014) *The German Army at Passchendaele*, Barnsley: Pen & Sword Military p.288.
72. LAC Barber, P.L.
73. LAC UWD 21st Battalion CEF.
74. www.warmuseum.ca

Chapter 7: Victory … and a New World
 1. Waite op. cit. p.77.
 2. Lloyd, N. (2013; 2014) *Hundred Days. The End of the Great War*, London: Penguin Books p.31.
 3. Bean (1946) op. cit. p.363. Both Australian and New Zealand troops often referred to themselves as 'Diggers'.
 4. See Messenger, C. (2008) *The Day We Won the War. Turning Point at Amiens, 8 August 1918*, London: Weidenfeld & Nicolson. General Ludendorff referred to 8 August 1918 as the 'Black Day'.
 5. Currie's motto in Lloyd (2013) op. cit. pp.31–2.
 6. *Toronto Star*, 2 January 1918.
 7. Stewart op. cit. loc 8492.
 8. *Sunday Times* (Perth) 5 March 1916. The *All-British Journal* had included Adolph Albrecht in its list of school teachers with German names.
 9. The full title of the battalion was the 2nd (City of London) Battalion, The London Regiment (Royal Fusiliers).
10. TNA WO329-126.
11. John Masefield, in Crane, D. (2013) *Empires of the Dead. How One Man's Vision Led to the Creation of WW1's War Graves*, London: William Collins, p.95.
12. Crystal Palace F.C. records refer to Ben Bateman being 'noted at one time as recovering from wounds and would be returning soon to the trenches'. www.cpfc.co.uk
13. *University of Toronto President's Report 1918*; University of Toronto (1921) *University of Toronto Roll of Service*, Toronto: Toronto University Press.
14. *University of Toronto President's Report 1916*, pp.7–9.
15. University of Toronto (1921) op. cit. Seven were promoted from the ranks.
16. Friedland op. cit. p.259.
17. *University of Toronto President's Report(s) 1915 to 1918*.
18. *Torontonensis* 1916, pp.7–9.
19. *The Varsity Magazine Supplement 1918*, p.10.
20. University of Toronto (1921) op. cit.
21. Canadian War Museum figures state that 61,000 were killed and 172,000 were wounded. www.warmuseum.ca

22. *University of Auckland Roll of Honour* www.specialcollections.auckland.ac.nz
23. Data extrapolated from *University of Auckland Roll of Honour.*
24. The New Zealand Department of Education *1914–18 Snapshots of Education* states that over 1,000 teachers served and nearly 200 were killed or died from their wounds.
25. *University of Auckland Roll of Honour.*
26. *The Kiwi,* Vol. 13, August 1918 www.specialcollections.auckland.ac.nz
27. Data extrapolated from Green op. cit.
28. In Green op. cit. p.62.
29. Data extrapolated from IE/STU/A5/1-3 Admissions Registers (1900 to 1920), IE/PUB/12/3/5-13 *The Londinian* (1909 to 1920), University of London (1918) *University of London War List*, London: The University of London Press, Ltd, and University of London (1921) *University of London Officer Training Corps Roll of Service 1914–1919*, London: Military Education Committee of the University of London.
30. Aldrich op. cit. pp.57–8.
31. Borough Road College War Memorial Records www.brunel.ac.uk
32. Dean, A.E. (1955) 'Fifty Years of Growth' in D. Dymond (1955) (ed.) *The Forge. The History of Goldsmiths' College 1905–1955*, London: Methuen & Co. Ltd p.17.
33. Graveson, C. (1955) 'Daily Life in College' in Dymond op. cit. p.98.
34. Goldsmiths' College War Memorial Records www.gold.ac.uk
35. Title of a poem by A.E. Housman (1922).
36. IE/STU/A5/1-3.
37. Aldrich op. cit. p.60.
38. Ibid. Also attending were three men from the USA and five from New Zealand; *Londinian* Easter 1919.
39. IE/STU/A5/1-3.
40. See Blades (2003) op. cit. pp.149–68.
41. Burton (1922) op. cit. author's foreword paragraph 1.
42. *The Kiwi* (1918).
43. *The Manuka*, 1919, pp.13–14, in Shaw op. cit. p.56.
44. *The Western Mail* 18 August 1916.
45. www.latymer-upper.org
46. The words of head master H.J. Crawford in *The Annals*, 1914–1916 www.utschools.ca
47. Green op. cit. p.7.
48. www.alumni.utoronto.ca
49. Butts, E. (2017a) op. cit.
50. www.bgpa.wa.gov.au
51. *Western Mail* (1915) p.ix.
52. Gammage op. cit. p.3.

53. Terraine, J. (1982) *White Heat. The New Warfare 1914–1918*, London: Sidgwick & Jackson p.137.
54. Lindsay, P. (2007) *Fromelles*, Victoria: Hardie Grant Books p.5.
55. Facey op. cit. p.389; Gammage op. cit. pp.239–40; Harper op. cit. loc 5165 notes that disdain for pompous 'Toff Johnies' was also evident amongst Enzeds.
56. See www.honesthistory.net.au/wp/gallipoli-club-peter-stanley 30 November 2015 12:17; www.theconversation.com 29.04.2015; www.theage.com.au/comment/political-rhetoric-makes-a-parody-of-remembrance-20150421-1mqdc2
57. 'Canada's Part in the War' by Professor G.M. Wrong, *The Varsity War Supplement July 1915*, p.37.
58. In Cook (2014) op. cit.
59. Quoted by Canadian Prime Minister Justin Trudeau in his official statement of 9 April 2017 marking the centenary of the Battle of Vimy Ridge www.pm.gc.ca
60. Cook (2017) op. cit. p.6.
61. Pugsley op. cit. p.352.
62. Burton (1935) op. cit. pp.179-180.
63. Burton (1922) op. cit. p.168.
64. Crane op. cit.
65. Holt (1996; 2008) op. cit. pp.77–81.
66. Waite op. cit. p.222; Lloyd (2017) op. cit. p.283.

Epilogue: Flat Iron Copse
1. Pericles' Oration, Thucydides II. 43.

Abbreviations

AGS	Auckland Grammar School
AIF	Australian Imperial Force
AK	Auckland
ANZ	Archives New Zealand
ANZAC	Australian and New Zealand Army Corps
ATC	Auckland Training College
AUC	Auckland University College
AWM	Australian War Museum
BEF	British Expeditionary Force
BRC	Borough Road College
BRID	Bavarian Reserve Infantry Division
BRIR	Bavarian Reserve Infantry Regiment
CDSC	Canadian Divisional Signal Company
CEF	Canadian Expeditionary Force
CFA	Canadian Field Artillery
COTC	Canadian Officers' Training Corps
CTC	Claremont Teachers College
CWGC	Commonwealth War Graves Commission
DSC	Distinguished Service Cross
DSO	Distinguished Service Order
GCI	Guelph Collegiate Institute
GMS	Guelph Model School
HIJMS	His Imperial Japanese Majesty's Ship
HMAS	His Majesty's Australian Ship
HMAT	His Majesty's Australian Transport
HMHS	His Majesty's Hospital Ship
HMNZT	His Majesty's New Zealand Transport
HMS	His Majesty's Ship
HMSO	His Majesty's Stationery Office

HQ	Headquarters
IOE	Institute of Education
KCL	King's College London
LAC	Library and Archives Canada
LCC	London County Council
LDTC	London Day Training College
LEA	Local Education Authority
LUS	Latymer Upper School
MC	Military Cross
MEF	Mediterranean Expeditionary Force
MM	Military Medal
NAA	National Archives Australia
NCO	Non-Commissioned Officer
NZ	New Zealand
NZAD	New Zealand & Australian Division
NZD	New Zealand Division
NZEF	New Zealand Expeditionary Force
NZIB	New Zealand Infantry Brigade
NZMC	New Zealand Medical Corps
NZRB	New Zealand Rifle Brigade
OG	Old German (Line)
OISE	Ontario Institute for Studies in Education
Ont.	Ontario
OTC	Officer Training Corps
PBS	Perth Boys' School
POR	Post Office Rifles
POW	Prisoner of War
RAF	Royal Air Force
RE	Royal Engineers
RFC	Royal Flying Corps
RNAS	Royal Naval Air Service
SA	South Australia
SLNSW	State Library of New South Wales
SLWA	State Library of Western Australia
SMLE	Short Magazine Lee Enfield
SS	Steam Ship

ST	Student Teacher
TA	Territorial Army
TF	Territorial Force
TNA	The National Archives
TNS	Toronto Normal School
UCL	University College London
ULOTC	University of London Officer Training Corps
UTFE	University of Toronto Faculty of Education
UTRA	University of Toronto Rifle Association
UTS	University of Toronto Schools
UWD	Unit War Diary
VC	Victoria Cross
WA	Western Australia
WAGS	Western Australian Genealogical Society
WFA	Western Front Association
YMCA	Young Men's Christian Association

Acknowledgements

Teachers at the Front, 1914-1919 builds upon the research conducted initially for *Roll of Honour: Schooling & the Great War, 1914-1919*, which was published by Pen & Sword Books Ltd in 2015. I would like to thank, once again, those institutions (especially Deacon's School, Peterborough, and University College London Institute of Education) and individuals (most notably Sir Anthony Seldon and the late Professor Richard Aldrich) who inspired, encouraged and supported me during the initial research and subsequent publication process.

For both books, the team of archivists at the Institute of Education, led by Sarah Aitchison, has been a constant source of support, and the material relating to the London Day Training College (LDTC), the Institute's predecessor institution, became my chief source of biographical material for British teacher-soldiers. Dr Percy Nunn's meticulous record keeping at the time prompted a whole series of further questions about individuals, like Albert Baswitz, who had chosen teaching as a career but subsequently became combatants in the Great War. Data extracted from the LDTC Attendance Registers were used to construct a detailed database. This revealed the large number of stories that might be told, each worthy of merit and detailed further research, and collectively offering numerous permutations regarding coverage of wartime service and experience. Ultimately, the selection of individuals was based upon the availability of additional material (school archives, census data, military records, physical remains et al.) and the potential for making biographical connections over both time and space.

The choice of individuals was conditioned by the availability of institutional records. In this respect, I am particularly grateful to Malcolm Smith, Hon. Archivist at Latymer Upper School (LUS). Malcolm provided material and guidance on the history of LUS generally, responded with great interest to specific questions about

Albert Baswitz and his fellow scholarship winners, read draft chapters and suggested valuable amendments. I am also grateful to Lianne Smith who, by forwarding copies of photographic images from King's College London's War Memorials archive, made it possible to put faces to names.

The Special Collections and Archives Department at Goldsmiths, University of London, was also most helpful. David Loring, the grandson of Captain William Loring, has recently deposited a trove of personal letters and a photograph album relating to the founding Warden of Goldsmiths' College, stating 'I know in my heart that they are where they belong; safe and sound and available for anyone to see'. My thanks to David, and to Lesley Ruthven, for permission to use this material.

My initial research focused squarely upon British teacher-soldiers and teacher training institutions. A chance encounter with similar research undertaken in Australia, however, transformed the book. Dr Neville Green graciously invited me to his home on the outskirts of Perth in Western Australia (I was there on holiday at the time) and handed over another treasure trove of material relating to the young trainees from Claremont Teachers College (CTC) whose stories he had told in 2009 in his book *Western Australian Teacher Soldiers of World War 1 1914-1918*. This material underpinned another database, scrutiny of which led to the selection for further biographical research of teachers who had become 'Anzacs'. The records of Auckland Training College (ATC) and the University of Toronto Faculty of Education (UTFE), many of them now freely available on the internet, identified more teacher-soldiers, namely 'Enzeds' from New Zealand and 'Canucks' from Canada, respectively.

My thanks extend to those who provided additional material relating to the teachers who served in the forces of the three British Dominions during the Great War. Lois Collins at Edith Cowan University in Perth provided the photograph of the 1913 CTC Cricket Team. My niece Sally Jones took the photographs of the CTC War Memorial and the Honour Avenues plaques in the city's King's Park. Ian Loftus provided useful comments on, and necessary corrections to, the chapter outlining the history of the 11th Battalion AIF. Similar contributions came from New Zealand. Professor Graeme Aitken and Maree Ferrens at the University of Auckland Faculty of Education provided additional material on Herbert Milnes, the founding Principal of ATC. They also forwarded the image taken on 4 October 2017, exactly 100 years to the day since 'Bert' had fallen at Broodseinde. My thanks are also due to Phaedra Cassidy at Brunel University in England for material relating to Herbert Milnes' earlier career at Borough Road College, and to Dr Stephen Clarke for reading the 'Enzeds' chapter and responding to it with valuable observations and manifest enthusiasm. Library and Archives Canada provided much of the material used to construct the narratives relating to the early lives, education and military careers of the Canadian teacher-soldiers. Additional material was also gratefully received from Marika Pirie and Anne-Mae Archer. Acknowledgement of photographic images supplied by third parties is attached to the plates themselves.

Many other individuals, institutions and organisations have contributed to the material in this book. I am particularly indebted to those who, having served at the front themselves, went on to write the 'official' histories of their own battalions and divisions. Individual Service Records and Unit War Diaries held by The National Archives in London and its counterparts in Australia, Canada and New Zealand, have added vital information on the location of key individuals at key points in their military service. The Commonwealth War Graves Commission deserves enormous credit for the way in which it takes care of The Fallen. Secondary works written by historians on the battles of Gallipoli, Loos, Fromelles, Pozières, High Wood and Passchendaele have been enormously helpful, adding much-needed additional detail and wider context to my biographical approach. To all who have contributed in this way, I give my sincere thanks, and trust that I have represented your findings faithfully and cited them accurately in the notes and bibliography.

I would like to thank Pen & Sword Books Ltd for commissioning and producing *Teachers at the Front, 1914–1919*. Heather Williams has been extremely efficient in getting the book through the submission, editorial and production processes, George Chamier has edited the work with skill and enthusiasm, and Dominic Allen has once again designed a book jacket which reflects the spirit of the Schooling and the Great War research project.

Finally, I would like to thank my wife Heather for accompanying me on two separate field trips to the battlefields and cemeteries of the Western Front, and for helping to find Albert Baswitz in a foreign field far from home.

Bibliography

ARCHIVAL SOURCES

Australia
Australian War Memorial (AWM)
(www.awm.gov.au)
Unit War Diaries:
   AWM 23/11/1-29 11th Battalion AIF
   AWM 23/49/1-44 32nd Battalion AIF
   AWM 23/61/1-31 44th Battalion AIF
   AWM 23/68/1-39 51st Battalion AIF
   AWM 133 Australian Imperial Force Nominal Roll 1914–1918

National Archives Australia (NAA)
(www.naa.gov.au)
Personnel Service Records:
   NAA B883, WX11049 Albrecht, F.
   NAA B2455 Archibald, J.A.
   NAA B2445 Blair, W.B.
   NAA B2455 Crossing, W.L.
   NAA B2445 Forbes, A.
   NAA B2455 Forbes, S.T.
   NAA B2445 Hardwick, R.P.
   NAA B2455 Knable, A.T.
   NAA B2455 Sten, T.
   NAA AI, 1914/3586 Naturalization: Knäble, A.M.

State Library of Western Australia (SLWA)
(www.slwa.wa.gov.au)
SLWA B1789198 Interview: John Peatfield Tuke
SLWA B1831672 Interview: Thomas Sten
Perth Boys' School Magazine (1914–15)

The Western Australian Genealogical Society (WAGS)
(www.11btn.wags.org.au)
Cheops Pyramid Image
The Thomas Steane Louch Memoirs

Canada
Guelph Museums, Ontario
(www.guelphmuseums.ca)
Guelph, Berlin, Waterloo, Galt, Preston and Hespeler Industrial Edition (Directory, 1903)
Guelph Model School (Year Group Photographs, 1911, 1912, 1913)
Guelph Social Register (1912)
Historic Guelph (Journal of the Guelph Historical Society)
Inspector's Annual Report of the Guelph Public Schools and Report of the Guelph Collegiate Institute (1901, 1904)
Knox Presbyterian Church 100ᵗʰ Anniversary Services (1944)
The Torch Year Book (1948)

Library and Archives Canada (LAC)
(www.central.bac-lac.gc.ca)
Personnel Records of the First World War:
   LAC Archer, M.H.
   LAC Barber, P.L.
   LAC Buchanan, W.P.
   LAC Cline, G.A.
   LAC Durant, W.E.
   LAC Forsyth, G.
   LAC Goodyear, H.
   LAC Scott, G.B.G.
Unit War Diaries:
   LAC UWD 21ˢᵗ Battalion CEF

Ontario Institute for Studies in Education, University of Toronto
(www.oise.library.utoronto.ca)

Ontario Department of Education:
(Public and Separate) Schools and Teachers in the Province of Ontario (1911 to 1920)

University of Toronto Archives & Records Management Service
(www.utarms.library.utoronto.ca)
Faculty of Education Calendar (1908 to 1917)
The Calendar of the University of Toronto (1915–1916)
The University of Toronto Song Book (1887, 1918)
The Varsity (1914 to 1920)
The Varsity Illustrated War Supplement (1915)
The Varsity Magazine Supplement (1916 to 1918)
Torontonensis (1914 to 1918)
University of Toronto President's Report (1908, 1915 to 1919)

Veterans Affairs Canada: The Canadian Virtual War Memorial
(www.veterans.gc.ca)
Canada, Virtual War Memorial Index, 1900–2014
First World War Book of Remembrance

Great Britain
The National Archives (TNA), London
(www.nationalarchives.gov.uk)
Unit War Diaries:
    TNA AIR 1/40/15/9/7-9 1st (Navy) Squadron
    TNA WO 95/2740/4 142nd Infantry Brigade: Headquarters
    TNA WO 95/2743/1-2 1/22nd Battalion London Regiment (The Queen's)
    TNA WO 95/1612/3 1/2nd Battalion London Regiment (Royal Fusiliers)
    TNA WO 95/2960/1-5 1/2nd Battalion London Regiment (Royal Fusiliers)
    TNA WO329 Service Medal and Award Rolls
Other:
    TNA HO 144/60/9356 Gottheil

Brunel University
(www.brunel.ac.uk)
Borough Road College:
HAE Milnes records
War Memorial Records

Goldsmiths' University of London
(www.gold.ac.uk)
Goldsmiths' College:
LOR1-6 Loring Papers
The Goldsmithian
War Memorial Records

King's College, London
(www.kcl.ac.uk)
King's College Review
War Memorial Records

Latymer Upper School, London
(www.latymer-upper.org)
A Commemoration of the Former Latymerians and Staff Members Who Gave their Lives in the First World War of 1914-1918, whose Names are Honoured on the Memorial Tablets in the School Hall.
Latymerian
University College London Institute of Education (UCL/IOE) Library and Archives
(www.ucl.ac.uk)

London Day Training College*:*
  IE/PHO/2-3 Photographs
  IE/PUB/12/3/5-13 *The Londinian* (1909 to 1920)
  IE/STU/A5/1-3 Admissions Registers (1900 to 1920)
University College Roll of Honour

University of London Archives (Senate House)
Student Records, 1836 to 1945

New Zealand
Archives New Zealand (ANZ)
(www.archway.archives.govt.nz)
New Zealand Defence Force Service Files:
  ANZ R121890454 Burton, O.E.
  ANZ R116785164 Gasparich, J.G.
  ANZ R110921876 MacKenzie, J.
  ANZ R19788057 Milnes, H.A.E.
  ANZ R107881170 Wilson, F.R.

Auckland Grammar School
(www.ags.recollect.co.nz)
Chronicle (1916 Third Term)

Auckland Museum
(www.aucklandmuseum.com)
Roll of Honour – Auckland Province
War Memorial Online Cenotaph

The University of Auckland Libraries and Learning Services
(www.specialcollections.auckland.ac.nz)
First World War Centenary 2014–18
The Kiwi
University of Auckland Roll of Honour

PUBLISHED SOURCES (CONTEMPORARY)

Almanacs and directories
City of Toronto Municipal Handbook, 1911
Kelly's Directory for Essex, 1898
London City Street Directory, 1885
The Western Australian Directory (Wise's), 1914
Toronto Might Directory, 1914
White's Directory, 1875

Newspapers, magazines and periodicals

Auckland Weekly News
Bunbury Herald (WA)
Daily News (WA)
Daily Sketch
Evening Post
Jewish Chronicle
Kalgoorlie Miner (WA)
London Daily News
New Zealand Herald
Observer (NZ)
Southern Times (WA)
Sunday Times (WA)
Pall Mall Gazette
The Advertiser (SA)
The Auckland Star
The Australian
The Bradford Daily Telegraph

The Burlington Gazette (C)
The Canadian Champion
The Collie Miner (WA)
The Great War
The Illustrated London News
The Illustrated War News
The London Gazette
The Times History and Encyclopaedia of the War
The Times History of the War
The Toronto Star
The Northam Advertiser (WA)
The War Illustrated
The West Australian
The Western Mail (WA)
West London Observer
Westralian Worker

Books

21st Canadian Infantry Battalion (1919) *Historical Calendar,* Aldershot: Gale & Polden Ltd

Adler, M. (1922) (ed.) *British Jewry Book of Honour,* London: Caxton Publishing Company, Limited

Anon (1916; 2013) *On the Anzac Trail; Being Extracts from the Diary of a New Zealand Sapper, by 'Anzac',* Pickle Partners Publishing

Audette, A. (1919) *A Few Verses and a Brief History of the Canadians on the Somme and Vimy Ridge in the World War 1914–1918,* Montreal (self-published)

Barr, J. (1922) *The City of Auckland New Zealand, 1840–1920,* Auckland: Whitcombe & Tombs Limited

Battye, J.S. (1924; 2005) *Western Australia: A History from its Discovery to the Inauguration of the Commonwealth,* Oxford: The Clarendon Press www.gutenberg.net.au (accessed 28.06.2020)

Bean, C.E.W. (1916) (ed.) *The Anzac Book,* London: Cassell and Company Ltd

Birchenough, C. (1914) *History of Elementary Education in England and Wales from 1800 to the Present Day,* London: University Tutorial Press

Blunden, E. (1928; 2000) *Undertones of War,* London: Penguin Classics

Board of Education (1903) *Regulations for the Instruction and Training of Pupil-Teachers and Students in Training Colleges* (CD 1666), London: HMSO

Board of Education (1907) *Regulations for the Preliminary Education of Elementary School Teachers* (Cd 3444), London: HMSO

Board of Education (1911) *Regulations for the Training of Teachers for Elementary Schools,* London: HMSO

Board of Education (1919) *Annual Report 1917–1918*, London: HMSO

Booth, C. (1886–1903) *Inquiry into the Life and Labour of the People of London*, www.booth.lse.ac.uk

Briggs, W. (1915) *Ontario Normal School Manuals. History of Education*, Toronto: Ontario Ministry of Education

Burrell, A. (1922) *Bert Milnes. A Brief Memoir* (published by the author)

Burton, O.E. (1922) *The Auckland Regiment*, Auckland: Whitcombe and Tombs Limited

Burton, O.E. (1935) *The Silent Division: New Zealanders at the Front, 1914–1919*, Sydney: Angus and Robertson Limited

Department of Education (1922) *The Roll of Honour of the Ontario Teachers who Served in the Great War 1914–1918*, Toronto: Ryerson Press

Dudley Ward, C.H. (1921; 2018) *The Fifty-Sixth Division 1914–1918. The Story of the 1st London Division*, London: John Murray

Ellis Barker, J. (1918) 'The Red Battle Flyer', *The War Times Journal*, www.wtj.com

Feret, C.J. (1900) *Fulham Old and New. Being an Exhaustive History of the Ancient Parish of Fulham*, London: The Leadenhall Press

Graves, R. (1929; 2000) *Goodbye to All That*, London: Penguin Classics

Haig-Brown, A.R. (1915) *The OTC in the Great War*, London: Country Life

HMSO (1919; 1988) *Officers Died in the Great War 1914-1919*, Polstead: J.B. Hayward & Son

HMSO (1922) *Statistics of the Military Effort of the British Empire During the Great War. 1914–1920*, London: HMSO

Hodgkins, J.G. (1910) *The Establishment of Schools and Colleges in Ontario*, Toronto: L.K. Cameron

Legislative Assembly of Ontario (1912) *Report of the Minister of Education, Province of Ontario*, Toronto: L.K. Cameron

Lewis, C. (1936; 1999) *Sagittarius Rising*, London: The Folio Society

Manning, F.E. (1930; 2014) *The Middle Parts of Fortune* (Kindle), Melbourne: Penguin Group (Australia)

Masefield, J. (1917; 1918) *The Old Front Line*, New York: The Macmillan Company

Maude, A.H. (1922; 2016) (ed.) *The 47th (London) Division 1914–1919* (Kindle), London: Amalgamated Press Ltd

Mayhew, H. (1861; 2012) *London Labour and the London Poor*, Oxford: Oxford University Press

McCrae, J. (1919) *In Flanders Fields and Other Poems* (Kindle)

Moorehead, A. (1915; 2016) *Gallipoli* (Kindle), London: Aurum Press

Norton, H.T. (1916) 'From a New Zealand Soldier Fighting on the Western Front' in M. Tanner (2016) (ed.) *War Letters 1914–1918*. Volume 5 (Kindle)

Ontario Board of Education (1871) *The Normal School for Ontario: Its Design and Functions. Chiefly Taken from the Report of the Chief Superintendent of Education for Ontario, for the Year 1869*, Toronto: Hunter, Rose & Co.

Richards, F. (1933; 2015) *Old Soldiers Never Die*, Parthian
Schuler, P.F.E. (1916) *Australia in Arms. A Narrative of the Australasian Imperial Force and Their Achievement at Anzac*, Melbourne (Victoria)
Stewart, H. (1921; 2013) *New Zealand Division 1916–1919. A Popular History Based on Official Records* (Kindle), Pickle Partners Publishing
The War Illustrated Album De Luxe (1916) 'Anzac Supermen' in 'Volume IV. The Summer Campaign – 1915' (1916) London: The Amalgamated Press Ltd
The War Illustrated Album De Luxe (1917) 'The Cockneys in High Wood' in 'Volume VII. The Autumn Campaigns - 1916', London: The Amalgamated Press Ltd
Toronto Department of Education (1922) *The Roll of Honour of Ontario Teachers Who Served in the Great War, 1914–1918*, Toronto: Ryerson Press
Toronto Normal School (1914) *Yearbook* (published by the school)
University of London (1918) *University of London War List*, London: The University of London Press, Ltd
University of London (1921) *University of London Officer Training Corps Roll of Service 1914–1919*, London: Military Education Committee of the University of London
University of Toronto (1921) *University of Toronto Roll of Service 1914–1918*, Toronto: Toronto University Press
Waite, F. (1921; 2016) *The New Zealanders at Gallipoli*, Auckland: Whitcombe and Tombs Limited
Walford, E. (1878) 'Fulham: Walham Green and North End' in *Old and New London. Volume 16*, London: Cassell, Petter & Galpin

PUBLISHED SOURCES (SECONDARY)

Books and articles
Albany Advertiser (2014) *Convoy Centenary 100. Albany Remembers 1914–2014*
Aldrich, R. (2002) *The Institute of Education 1902–2002: A Centenary History*, London: Institute of Education, University of London
Aldrich, R. (2013) 'The British and Foreign School Society, Past and Present', *History of Education Researcher*, 91, 5–12
Annis, J. (2009) 'The Royal City Goes to War: How the Guelph *Evening Mercury* Covered the First World War', *Historic Guelph*, 48
Arthur, M. (2006) *Lost Voices of the Edwardians*, London: Harper Press
Ash, D.L. (1984) *Memories of a London Childhood*, London: Fulham and Hammersmith Historical Society
Ball, T. (2011) 'Rubbing Off the Corners: The Rite of Passage of the Teacher Trainee in 20th Century New Zealand', *Australian Journal of Teacher Education* 36, 11, 79–105
Barber, M. (2010) *Royal Naval Air Service Pilot 1914–18*, Oxford: Osprey Publishing

Barcan, A. (1980) *A History of Australian Education*, Melbourne: Oxford University Press

Barton, P. (2007) *Passchendaele. Unseen Panoramas of the Third Battle of Ypres*, London: Constable & Robinson Ltd

Barton, P. (2014) *The Lost Legions of Fromelles. The Mysteries Behind One of the Most Devastating Battles of the Great War*, London: Constable

Batten, S. (2018) *Futile Exercise? The British Army's Preparation for War 1902–1914*, Warwick: Helion & Company Limited

Bean, C.E.W. (1946; 2014) *Anzac to Amiens*, Melbourne: Penguin Group

Beckett, I.F.W. (1991; 2011) *Britain's Part-Time Soldiers. The Amateur Military Tradition 1558-1945*, Barnsley: Pen & Sword Military

Belford, W.C. (1940; 2010) *'Legs-Eleven'. Being the Story of the Eleventh Battalion AIF in the Great War*, Uckfield: The Naval & Military Press and The Imperial War Museum

Bennett, S. (2011; 2012) *Pozières. The Anzac Story*, Melbourne: Scribe Publications Pty Ltd

Black, G. (1998) *J.F.S. The History of the Jews' Free School, London Since 1732*, London: Tymsder Publishing

Black, G. (2003) *Jewish London. An Illustrated History*, Derby: The Breedon Books Publishing Company Limited

Blades, B.A. (2003) 'Deacon's School, Peterborough, 1902–1920: a Study of the Social and Economic Function of Secondary Schooling', University of London PhD thesis.

Blades, B.A. (2015) *Roll of Honour: Schooling and the Great War, 1914–1919*, Barnsley: Pen & Sword Military

Bolton, G. and Byrne, G. (2001) *The Campus That Never Stood Still: Edith Cowan University, 1902–2002*, Churchlands: Edith Cowan University

Bostridge, M. (2014) *The Fateful Year. England 1914*, London: Penguin Books

Brimmell, H. (1997) 'The IODE in Guelph 1909–1997', *Historic Guelph*, 36

Bruce, J. and Kelly, K. (1997; 2003) 'The Royal Flying Corps and the Struggle for Supremacy in the Air over the Salient' in P.H. Liddle (ed.) *Passchendaele in Perspective. The Third Battle of Ypres*, Barnsley: Pen & Sword Military

Butts, E. (2017a) *Wartime: The First World War in a Canadian Town*, Toronto: James Lorimer & Company

Butts, E. (2017b) 'Guelph in the First World War' http://www.thecanadian encyclopaedia.ca

Cave, N. (1996; 2013) *Battleground Europe. Arras. Vimy Ridge*, Barnsley: Pen & Sword Military

Cave, N. (1997; 2016) *Battleground Europe. Ypres. Passchendaele. The Fight for the Village*, Barnsley: Pen & Sword Military

Chambers, S. (2008) *Battleground Gallipoli. Anzac. The Landing* (Kindle), Barnsley: Pen & Sword Military

Chapman, P. (2016) *Tyne Cot Cemetery & Memorial: In Memory and Mourning*, Barnsley: Pen & Sword Military

Cobb, P. (2007; 2010) *Fromelles 1916*, Stroud: The History Press

Commonwealth War Graves Commission (2016) *Somme Battlefield Companion*, Maidenhead: CWGC

Cook, T. (2014) 'The Eager Doomed: The Story of Canada's Original WWI Recruits', Toronto: *The Globe and Mail* 1 August 2014

Cook, T. (2017) *Vimy: The Battle and the Legend*, Canada: Allen Lane

Crane, D. (2013) *Empires of the Dead. How One Man's Vision Led to the Creation of WWI's War Graves*, London: William Collins

Crane, E. (1986) *I Can Do No Other: A Biography of Ormond Burton*, Auckland: Hodder & Stoughton

Dean, A.E. (1955) 'Fifty Years of Growth' in D. Dymond (ed.) *The Forge. The History of Goldsmiths' College 1905–1955*, London: Methuen & Co. Ltd

Dent, H.C. (1977) *The Training of Teachers in England and Wales 1800–1975*, London: Hodder & Stoughton

Doyle, P. (2011) *Battle Story: Gallipoli 1915*, Stroud: The History Press

Doyle, P. (2012) *Battle Story: Loos 1915* (Kindle), Stroud: The History Press

Doyle, P. and Foster, C. (2013) *Remembering Tommy. The British Soldier in the First World War*, Stroud: Spellmount

Dymond, D. (1955) (ed.) *The Forge. The History of Goldsmiths' College 1905–1955*, London: Methuen & Co. Ltd

Emden, R. van (2008; 2010) *The Soldier's War. The Great War Through Veterans' Eyes* (Kindle), London: Bloomsbury

Endelman, T.M. (2002) *The Jews of Britain, 1656 to 2000*, Berkeley and Los Angeles: University of California Press

Ewers, J.K. (1947) *Perth Boys' School 1847–1947*, Perth (published by the school)

Facey, A.B. (1981; 2014) *A Fortunate Life*, Melbourne: Penguin Group (Australia)

Franks, N. (2003; 2015) *Dog-Fight: Aerial Tactics of the Aces of World War 1*, Barnsley: Pen & Sword Books Ltd

Freeman, R. (2006) *Second to None – A Memorial History of the 32nd Battalion A.I.F. 1915 – 1919*, Norwood SA: Peacock Publications

Friedland, M.L (2002) *The University of Toronto. A History*, Toronto: University of Toronto Press

Gammage, B. (1974) *The Broken Years. The Australian Soldiers in the Great War*, Canberra: Australian National University Press

Gelman, S. (1990) 'The 'Feminization' of the High Schools? Women Secondary School Teachers in Toronto: 1871–1931', *Historical Studies in Education*, 2, 1, 119–48

Gilbert, M. (1994; 2004) *The First World War: A Complete History*, New York: Henry Holt and Company

Gliddon, G. (1987; 1996) *The Battle of the Somme. A Topographical History*, Stroud: Sutton Publishing

Graveson, C. (1955) 'Daily Life in College' in D. Dymond (ed.) *The Forge. The History of Goldsmiths' College 1905–1955*, London: Methuen & Co. Ltd

Green, N. (2009) *Western Australian Teacher Soldiers of World War 1 1914–1918*, Cottesloe: Focus Education Services

Green, N. (2015) *Not Just a Name: 1914–1918 Service Men and Women Honoured by Cottesloe, Mosmon Park and Peppermint Grove Districts*, Clarkson: Focus Education Services

Halstead, T. (2017) 'The Junior OTC; Playing at Soldiers or Nation in Arms?', *British Journal for Military History*, 3, 2, 62–81

Hampton, M. (2016a) *Attack on the Somme. 1st Anzac Corps and the Battle of Pozières Ridge, 1916*, Solihull: Helion & Company Limited

Hampton, M. (2016b) 'Hubert Gough, the Anzacs and the Somme: A Descent into Pointlessness', *British Journal for Military History*, 2, 3, 47–61

Harper, G. (2007; 2015) *Dark Journey. Passchendaele, the Somme and the New Zealand Experience on the Western Front*, Auckland: Harper Collins Publishers

Harper, G. (2015) *Johnny Enzed. The New Zealand Soldier in the First World War 1914–1918* (Kindle), Auckland: Exisle Publishing Limited

Harrison, M. (2017) *High Wood*, Barnsley: Pen & Sword Military

Hart, P. (2011; 2013) *Gallipoli*, London: Profile Books Ltd

Harte, N. (1986) *The University of London 1836–1986. An Illustrated History*, London: The Athlone Press

Harvey, T. (2017) 'In Search of a "Forgotten Victory"', *Bulletin* (The Western Front Association), 108, 48–50

Hattersley, R. (2004; 2005) *The Edwardians*, London: Little, Brown

Hellwig, A. (2006) *Australian Hawk over the Western Front. A Biography of Major R.S. Dallas DSO, DSC, C de G avec Palme*, London: Grubb Street

Holmes, R. (2004; 2005) *Tommy. The British Soldier on the Western Front 1914–1918*, London: Harper Perennial

Holmes, R. (2011) *Soldiers. Army Lives and Loyalties from Redcoats to Dusty Warriors*, London: Harper Press

Holt, T. and V. (1996; 2000) *Major & Mrs Holt's Battlefield Guide to the Somme*, Barnsley: Leo Cooper

Holt, T. and V. (1996; 2008) *Major & Mrs Holt's Battlefield Guide to the Ypres Salient & Passchendaele*, Barnsley: Pen & Sword Military

Hurst, J. (2005; 2011) *Game to the Last. The 11th Australian Infantry Battalion at Gallipoli* (Kindle), Newport (NSW): Big Sky Publishing Pty Ltd

Hurst, J. (2018) *The Landing in the Dawn. Dissecting the Legend – the Landing at Anzac, Gallipoli, 25 April 1915*, Solihull: Helion & Company Ltd

Keech, G. (1997; 2015) *Battleground Europe. Somme. Pozières*, Barnsley: Pen & Sword Military

Kenyon Jones, C. (2008) *The People's University. 150 Years of the University of London and its External Students*, London: University of London External System

Kitchen, J. and Petrarca, D. (2014) 'Teacher Preparation in Ontario: A History', *Teaching & Learning*, 8 (1), 56–71

Lewis, P. (1959) *Squadron Histories. RFC, RNAS & RAF 1912–59*, London: Putnam

Liddell Hart, B. (1934) *A History of the World War 1914–1918*, London: Faber & Faber Limited

Liddle, P.H. (1997; 2013) (ed.) *Passchendaele in Perspective. The Third Battle of Ypres* (Kindle), London: Leo Cooper

Lindsay, P. (2007) *Fromelles*, Victoria: Hardie Grant Books

Lloyd, N. (2006; 2013) *Loos 1915* (Kindle), Stroud: The History Press

Lloyd, N. (2013; 2014) *Hundred Days. The End of the Great War*, London: Penguin Books

Lloyd, N. (2017) *Passchendaele. A New History*, London: Viking

Macdonald, L. (1978; 1979) *They Called it Passchendaele. The Story of the Third Battle of Ypres and of the Men Who Fought it*, London: Michael Joseph

Macleod, J. (2015) *Gallipoli*, Oxford: Oxford University Press

Mangan, J.A. and Hickey, C. (2000) 'A Pioneer of the Proletariat: Herbert Milnes and the Games Cult in New Zealand', *International Journal of the History of Sport*, 17(2-3), 31–48

McGibbon, I. (2014) *Gallipoli: A Guide to New Zealand Battlefields and Memorials* (Kindle), New Zealand ePenguin

McGibbon, I. (2016) *New Zealand's Western Front Campaign*, Auckland: Bateman

McWilliams, J. and Steel, R.J. (2007; 2016) *Amiens 1918. The Last Great Battle* (Kindle), Stroud: The History Press

Messenger, C. (2005) *Call-to-Arms. The British Army 1914–18*, London: Cassell

Nash-Chambers, D. (2015) 'Guelph in 1915: Patriotism and Public Service in Lt.-Col John McCrae's Birthplace', *Historic Guelph*, 53

Messenger, C. (2008) *The Day We Won the War. Turning Point at Amiens, 8 August 1918*, London: Weidenfeld & Nicolson

Norman, T. (1984; 2009) *The Hell They Called High Wood. The Somme 1916* (Kindle), Barnsley: Pen & Sword Books Ltd

O'Connor, M. (2001; 2004) *Battleground Europe. Airfields and Airmen. Ypres*, Barnsley: Leo Cooper

Olson, W. (2006) *Gallipoli: The Western Australian Story*, Perth: University of Western Australia Press

Ontario Institute for Studies in Education (2006) *Inspiring Education. A Legacy of Learning 1907–2007. Celebrating 100 Years of Studies in Education at the University of Education*, Toronto: OISE/UT

Openshaw, R., Lee, G. and Lee, H. (1993) *Challenging the Myths. Rethinking New Zealand's Educational History*, Palmerston North: The Dunmore Press Ltd

Palmer, A. (2007; 2016) *The Salient. Ypres, 1914–18*, London: Constable

Pedersen, P. (2002; 2015) *Battleground Europe. French Flanders. Fromelles*, Barnsley: Pen & Sword Military

Pedersen, P. (2007) *The ANZACS. Gallipoli to the Western Front*, Scoresby: Viking Books

Pidgeon, T. (2002) *Battleground Europe. Somme. Flers & Gueudecourt*, Barnsley: Leo Cooper

Press, M. (2011) *Education and Ontario Family History. A Guide to Resources for Genealogists and Historians*, Toronto: Dundurn Press

Pugsley, C. (1997; 2003) 'The New Zealand Division at Passchendaele' in P.H. Liddle (ed.) *Passchendaele in Perspective. The Third Battle of Ypres*, Barnsley: Pen & Sword Military

Pugsley, C. (1984; 2014) *Gallipoli : The New Zealand Story*, Auckland: Libro International

Rawson, A. (2002) *Battleground Europe. French Flanders. Loos – Hill 70*, Barnsley: Leo Cooper

Rawson, A. (2006) *The British Army Handbook 1914–1918*, Stroud: Sutton Publishing Limited

Reed, P. (1998; 2016) *Battleground Europe. Somme. Courcelette*, Barnsley: Pen & Sword Military

Reed, P. (2011) *Battleground Somme. Walking the Somme. A Walker's Guide to the 1916 Somme Battlefields* (Kindle), Barnsley: Pen & Sword Military

Roach, J. (1991) *Secondary Education in England, 1870–1902: Public Activity and Private Enterprise*, London: Routledge

Robertshaw, A. (2014) *Battle Story: Somme 1916* (Kindle), Stroud: The History Press

Rogan, E. (2015; 2016) *The Fall of the Ottomans. The Great War in the Middle East, 1914–1920*, London: Penguin Books

Rourke, W.H. (1980) *My Way. W.H. (Bill) Rourke's 50 Years Adventure in Education*, Perth: Carroll's Pty Ltd

Shaw, L. (2006) *Making a Difference: A History of Auckland College of Education 1881–2004*, Auckland: Auckland University Press

Sheehan, N.M. (1990) 'Philosophy, Pedagogy and Practice: the IODE and the Schools in Canada, 1900–1945', *Historical Studies in Education*, 2, 2, 307–21

Sheffield, G. (2001; 2002) *Forgotten Victory. The First World War: Myths and Realities*, London: Headline Review

Sheffield, G. (2016) 'John Terraine's "The True Texture of the Somme" Revisited', The Western Front Association *Bulletin*,106, 36-37

Sheffield, G. (2017) 'Shaping British and Anzac Soldiers' Experience of Gallipoli: Environmental and Medical Factors, and the Development of Trench Warfare', *British Journal for Military History*, 4, I, 23–43

Sheldon, J. (2005) *The German Army on the Somme 1914–1916* (Kindle), Barnsley: Pen & Sword Military

Sheldon, J. (2007; 2014) *The German Army at Passchendaele*, Barnsley: Pen & Sword Military

Sheldon, J. (2016) 'The True Texture of the Somme: Thoughts from the German Perspective', The Western Front Association *Bulletin*, 106, 37–38

Shutt, G.M. (1961) *The High Schools of Guelph*, Guelph: Board of Education for the City of Guelph

Smith, M. (2014) *Voices in Flight: The Royal Naval Air Service in the Great War* (Kindle) Barnsley: Pen & Sword Aviation

Spiers, E.M. (2015) *University Officers' Training Corps and the First World War*, COMEC Occasional Paper No. 4

Stevenson, R. (2007) 'The Forgotten First. The 1st Australian Division in the Great War and its Legacy', *Australian Army Journal*, 4, 1, 185–99

Strachan, H. (1976) *History of the Cambridge University Officer Training Corps*, Tunbridge Wells: Midas Books

Taylor, W. (1990) 'Education' in F.M.L. Thompson (ed.) *The University of London and the World of Learning. 1836–1986*, London: The Hambledon Press

Terraine, J. (1965; 1997) *The Great War*, Ware: Wordsworth Editions Ltd

Terraine, J. (1982) *White Heat. The New Warfare 1914–1918*, London: Sidgwick & Jackson

Terraine, J. (1991; 2016) 'The True Texture of the Somme', The Western Front Association *Bulletin*, 106, 27–35

Thompson, F.M.L. (1990) (ed.) *The University of London and the World of Learning. 1836–1986*, London: The Hambledon Press

Thompson, J., Pedersen, P. and Oral, H. (2015) *Gallipoli*, London: Andre Deutsch

Tibble, J.W. (1961) 'Sir Percy Nunn: 1870–1944', *British Journal of Educational Studies*, 10, 1, 58–75

Tozer, M. (2015) *The Idea of Manliness. The Legacy of Thring's Uppingham*, Truro: Sunnyrest Books

Triolo, R. (2009) *Shell-Shocked: Australian Teachers, Their Schools and Families after Armistice*, Canberra: Paper presented to the National Archives of Australia on 18 March 2009

Trotman, J. (2008) *Girls Becoming Teachers. An Historical Analysis of Western Australian Woman Teachers, 1911–1940*, New York: Cambria Press

Tully, K. & Whitehead, C. (2003) 'Staking out the Territory: The University of Western Australia, the Diploma in Education and Teacher Training 1914–1956', *Australian Journal of Teacher Education, 28*, 1

Watson, N. (1995) *Latymer Upper School. A History of the School and its Foundation*, London: James & James (Publishers) Ltd

Westlake, R. (1994; 2004) *British Battalions on the Somme* (Kindle), Barnsley: Pen & Sword Select

Wood, B.A. (1994) 'Constructing Nova Scotia's "Scotchness": The Centenary Celebrations of Pictou Academy in 1916', *Historical Studies in Education*, 6, 2, 281–302

Wright, M. (2005; 2015) *Western Front. The New Zealand Division 1916–18* (Kindle), Wellington: Intruder Books (New Zealand)

Youel, D. and Edgell, D. (2006) *The Somme Ninety Years On – a Visual History*, London: Dorling Kindersley

FAMILY HISTORY AND GENEALOGY COLLECTIONS

www.ancestry.com
www.findmypast.co.uk
Australia Electoral Rolls 1903–1980
Australian Imperial Force Embarkation Roll 1914–1918
Australian Imperial Force Nominal Roll 1914–1918
Australia Marriages 1788–1935
Canadian Passenger Lists 1865–1935
Census of Canada 1861–1911
Civil Registration Birth Index, England & Wales 1837–1915
Deaths and Burials, England 1815–1985
National Census, England & Wales 1841–1911
Outward Passengers Lists (Great Britain) 1890–1960
Ontario, Canada Births 1858–1913
Perth, Western Australia, Rate Books 1880–1946
Unassisted Immigrant Passenger Lists (Australia) 1826–1922
Victoria Births
Victoria Coastal Passenger Lists 1852–1924
Victoria Inward Passenger Lists 1839–1923
Victoria Marriages 1836–1942
Victoria Outward Passenger Lists 1852–1915
Western Australia Birth Index
Western Australia Death Index

WEBSITES

www.11thbattalionaif.com
www.21stbattalion.ca
www.ags.school.nz
www.aif.adfa.edu.au
www.alumni.utoronto.ca
www.anzacsigthsound.org
www.archive.org
www.aristoteliansociety.org.uk
www.aucklandcity.govt.nz
www.aucklandlibraries.govt.nz
www.bac-lac.gc.ca
www.bgpa.wa.gov.aus
www.billiongraves.com
www.booth.lse.ac.uk
www.canada.yodelout.com
www.canadiangreatwarproject.com
www.carnamah.co.au

www.cefresearch.ca
www.cefresearch.com
www.cottesloersl.org.au
www.cpfc.co.uk
www.cwgc.org
www.dnbnz.govt.nz
www.digitalnz.org
www.education.auckland.ac.nz
www.education.govt.nz
www.englandfootballonline.com
www.fleetairarm.com
www.globeandmail.com
www.gommecourt.co.uk
www.guelph.ca
www.guelphhistoricalsociety.ca
www.guelph.pastperfectonline.com
www.gutenberg.net.au

www.heritage.utoronto.ca
www.honesthistory.net.au
www.nationalanzaccentre.com.au
www.newsamnews.ioe.ac.uk
www.news.google.ca
www.ngatapuwae.govt.nz
www.nzhistory.govt.nz
www.nzhistory.net.nz
www.nzwargraves.org.nz
www.oise.library.utoronto.ca
www.ourroots.ca
www.ozrnas.org.au
www.paperspast.natlib.govt.nz
www.pm.gc.ca
www.pubshistory.com
www.rcsigs.ca
www.roll-of-honour-com
www.rugbymuseum.co.nz

www.somme-roll-of-honour.com
www.theage.com.au
www.thecanadianencyclopaedia.ca
www.theconversation.com
www.thestar.com
www.toronto1914.wordpress.com
www.torontofamilyhistory.org
www.trent.ca
www.trove.nla.gov.au
www.utschools.ca
www.veterans.gc.ca
www.warmuseum.ca
www.wartimememoriesproject.com
www.westernfrontassociation.com
www.worldrugbymuseum.com
www.wtj.com
www.ww1cemeteries.com
www.wwi.utschools.ca

Index